Student's Vegetarian Cookbook

FOR

DUMMIES®

by Connie Sarros

WILEY

Wiley Publishing, Inc.

Student's Vegetarian Cookbook For Dummies®

Published by
Wiley Publishing, Inc.
111 River St.
Hoboken, NJ 07030-5774
www.wiley.com

Copyright © 2011 by Wiley Publishing, Inc., Indianapolis, Indiana

Published simultaneously in Canada

For general information on our other products and services, please contact our Customer Care Department within the U.S. at 877-762-2974, outside the U.S. at 317-572-3993, or fax 317-572-4002.

For technical support, please visit www.wiley.com/techsupport.

Wiley also publishes its books in a variety of electronic formats. Some content that appears in print may not be available in electronic books.

Library of Congress Control Number: 2011926322

ISBN: 978-0-470-94291-8

Manufactured in the United States of America

10 9 8 7 6 5 4 3 2 1

WILEY

About the Author

Connie Sarros has been creating recipes for people on special or limited diets since 1991. She is the author of six cookbooks and a DVD: *Gluten-Free Cooking For Dummies* (Wiley); *Wheat-Free, Gluten-Free Cookbook for Kids and Busy Adults* (McGraw-Hill); *Wheat-Free, Gluten-Free Dessert Cookbook* (McGraw-Hill); *Wheat-Free, Gluten-Free Reduced Calorie Cookbook* (McGraw-Hill); *Recipes for Special Diets* (self-published); *The Newly Diagnosed Survival Kit* (self-published); and *All You Wanted to Know about Gluten-Free Cooking* (a DVD created by Munson Hospital in Traverse City, Michigan). She also has ten-day menus with recipes for people who are on special diets, including a special menu for diabetics and a menu that's low-fat and low-carb.

Her recipes have been featured in *First Magazine, Living Without,* and *Cooking Light Magazine.* Connie has been a featured speaker at national health conferences and conventions, and she travels throughout the United States speaking to support groups. She has an *Ask the Cook* column, is a featured writer for *The Journal of Gluten Sensitivity,* and is a contributing author to many health magazines and newsletters. She also puts out two monthly newsletters.

Connie has been interviewed by newspapers across the country. The *Washington Post* and *Cleveland Plain Dealer* are just two newspapers that have done a complete front-page spread in their health sections about Connie's contributions.

She has a website that's filled with helpful information: www. gfbooks.homestead.com.

Dedication

This book is dedicated to my husband, Ted. He definitely has earned the badge of courage. While working on this book, I would create new experiments in the kitchen every night, and he would obligingly taste each and every one and offer his opinion. Many of the meals were absolutely delicious, but some definitely needed tweaking. Never once did he complain. Instead, he considered it an adventure as he tasted each concoction and added his input. I thank him for his patience and his support.

Author's Acknowledgments

No one works in a vacuum. This book could never have been written without the help of so many other people.

I sincerely thank Mike Lewis, acquisitions editor at Wiley Publishing, for asking me to write this book. Little did I know at that time what a great adventure this would become and how much fun I was going to have in the kitchen creating all these new recipes. If you've never written a book, it's hard to explain all the editing steps that a book goes through. Georgette Beatty, senior project editor, and Todd Lothery, copy editor, were so patient with me and helped me through every step. I owe them my sincere gratitude.

Ginny Messina, the technical reviewer, gave me so many wonderful suggestions on making recipes vegan-friendly. Patty Santelli, the nutritional analyst, patiently supplied all the nutritional information for the recipes. A special thanks goes to Emily Nolan, who tested every recipe; her suggestions and comments were not only helpful but often hilarious! She kept me smiling throughout this project.

The staff at Wiley Publishing are special. They guided, advised, encouraged, and helped me through every phase of this book, and I thank them all.

Thank you, too, to all the wonderful people who shared their ideas with me, the types of foods they prefer, the reasons they became vegetarians, and some of the health conditions that complicated their diet. This helped me focus on the impact a vegetarian diet has on a person's everyday life.

Publisher's Acknowledgments

We're proud of this book; please send us your comments at http://dummies.custhelp.com. For other comments, please contact our Customer Care Department within the U.S. at 877-762-2974, outside the U.S. at 317-572-3993, or fax 317-572-4002.

Some of the people who helped bring this book to market include the following:

Acquisitions, Editorial, and Media Development

Senior Project Editor: Georgette Beatty

Acquisitions Editor: Michael Lewis

Copy Editor: Todd Lothery

Assistant Editor: David Lutton

Technical Editor: Virginia Messina, MPH, RD

Recipe Tester: Emily Nolan

Nutritional Analyst: Patty Santelli

Editorial Manager: Michelle Hacker

Editorial Assistant: Jennette ElNaggar

Art Coordinator: Alicia B. South

Cover Photo: © iStockphoto.com/ Ryan Klos/Arthur Kwiatkowski

Cartoons: Rich Tennant (www.the5thwave.com)

Composition Services

Project Coordinator: Nikki Gee

Layout and Graphics: Brent Savage, Corrie Socolovitch, Christin Swinford

Proofreader: The Well-Chosen Word

Indexer: Steve Rath

Illustrator: Elizabeth Kurtzman

Publishing and Editorial for Consumer Dummies

 Diane Graves Steele, Vice President and Publisher, Consumer Dummies

 Kristin Ferguson-Wagstaffe, Product Development Director, Consumer Dummies

 Ensley Eikenburg, Associate Publisher, Travel

 Kelly Regan, Editorial Director, Travel

Publishing for Technology Dummies

 Andy Cummings, Vice President and Publisher, Dummies Technology/General User

Composition Services

 Debbie Stailey, Director of Composition Services

Contents at a Glance

Recipes at a Glance

Lunches

Dinners

Snacks, Appetizers, and Baked Goods

Desserts

Table of Contents

Introduction

*W*riter Gerald Lieberman once defined a vegetarian as *a person who eats only side dishes*. That's funny, but it's also a major misstatement. You have so many fantastic ways to prepare all the foods that grow from the ground that your options are limitless.

The purpose of this book is to present those options to you while making sure that you don't spend a fortune on fancy-shmancy ingredients (I realize that college students don't have a ton of cash to throw around!). All of the recipes in this book also adhere to one more requirement — they're super simple to make and take very little time to prepare.

More and more people are giving up eating meat, and more companies are offering more wholesome, vegetarian food options. Restaurants are doing the same thing by adding vegetarian choices to their menus. And now, with this book, you have more choices of what to make for breakfast, lunch, and dinner at home. The pages that follow put the vegetarian lifestyle into perspective, showing that meals can be inexpensive, quick to prepare, healthy, and tasty — all at the same time.

About This Book

This book is perfect for browsing when you're looking for new and different vegetarian dishes to create. In addition, Part I is loaded with insight and information about the vegetarian lifestyle (so it makes good reading when you want to curl up in the evening with a good book).

This isn't a novel, so you don't have to start on page 1 and read through the book in order to make sense of the story line. (It's also not a mystery novel, so you don't have to quickly check out the last page to see *who done it*.) Take a look at the table of contents and read the parts of the book first that interest you the most; you can always go back and read the rest of the book later if you want.

Conventions Used in This Book

This book has a number of conventions that you should know before you dig in. For instance, when I use the term *vegetarian,* I use it to describe all the various types of vegetarianism, such as *lacto, ovo, lacto ovo, vegan,* and the like. When I want you to know something specific to a particular type of vegetarianism, I mention the type by name. Also, because lacto ovo vegetarianism is the most common type in the Western world, many of this book's recipes feature eggs and dairy products, but I provide suggestions for vegan substitutions whenever possible.

At the beginning of each recipe in Parts II and III you find some important information — the recipe's preparation and cooking time and how many people the recipe serves. The ingredients are pretty self-explanatory, but here are a few helpful tips:

✔ I use butter instead of margarine because it's natural — margarine isn't. If you want to use a butter spread instead, use Earth Balance because it, too, is all natural.

✔ When I list an egg as an ingredient, use a large egg.

✔ All onions are yellow unless stated otherwise.

✔ I use baking mix instead of flour whenever appropriate. Baking mixes have the baking powder already included, so it's one less thing you have to worry about storing.

All oven temperatures are Fahrenheit (check out the appendix to convert temperatures to Celsius). Unless the directions instruct you to do otherwise, preheat the oven for 10 minutes or longer before putting a pan in to bake.

Here are a few other standard conventions to help you navigate this book:

✔ I use **bold** text to highlight key words in bulleted lists and actions to take in numbered lists.

✔ *Italics* spotlight new terms and add emphasis.

✔ All Web addresses appear in `monofont`.

When this book was printed, some Web addresses may have needed to break across two lines of text. If that happened, rest assured that I haven't put in any extra characters (such as a hyphen) to indicate the break. So when using one of these Web addresses, just type in exactly what you see in this book, pretending as though the line break doesn't exist.

What You're Not to Read

Ideally, you'll read this book cover to cover, but that's not always the way things work. People buy a cookbook and immediately open it up to the recipes. Go figure!

Here are a few items that you can skim over or skip altogether, because they're meant to supplement the recipes and information but they're not absolutely vital:

- **Technical Stuff icon:** Anything that follows this icon is, well, technical stuff. When you read it, you get a deeper understanding of the issue, but you don't *need* to read it to understand the topic at hand.

- **Sidebars:** The great thing about sidebars (the shaded gray boxes throughout the book) is that they give you a little more information about a topic, but again, they're not priority reading.

- **Vary It!:** The information that follows this term in a recipe gives you ideas for alternative ingredients you can use and how to use up foods that are already in your refrigerator, but these suggestions aren't absolutely crucial to making the recipe in its original form.

- **Copyright page:** Though these pages are necessary to include in any book, they don't exactly hold your attention unless you're into Library of Congress statistics.

Foolish Assumptions

I assume that you're reading this book for one of the following reasons:

- You're a college-age vegetarian, and you're either tired of cooking the same foods all the time or interested in discovering how to cook in the first place. You're looking for more variety in your diet, but you don't want to sacrifice time, money, and taste.

- You're a college student who's thinking of becoming vegetarian and want to find out more about the lifestyle and diet.

- You're not a vegetarian but you want to start eating less meat and more fruits, vegetables, and grains for health reasons.

If you have a huge kitchen filled with glitzy, fancy gadgets — great! (How did you score a college apartment like that?) But in writing this book, I assume that your kitchen is slightly larger than your backpack and that you have only a few appliances.

How This Book Is Organized

This book is a blend of vegetarian recipes and lifestyle information; it consists of the following four parts.

Part 1: Living the Vegetarian Lifestyle

You've seen mazes. They have a *Start Here* arrow to get you going. Part I is the part that gets you started through the maze of living the vegetarian lifestyle. It describes reasons for becoming a vegetarian and the different types of vegetarianism. It also discusses how to stick to a vegetarian diet when you have special health considerations and how to make sure you're getting the right nutrition. The last few chapters of Part I are filled with practical information about handling tough social situations regarding your vegetarianism, setting up your kitchen, and shopping smart for vegetarian ingredients.

Part 11: Vegetarian Vittles

Ah, here's where the long-awaited recipes begin. Part II starts out with quick breakfasts (taking roughly 5 minutes to prepare) and then stretches into breakfasts that take 20 minutes or less to get ready. Lunches and dinners follow; some take only a few minutes to cook, while others take around 20 to 30 minutes, but they're all delicious!

Part 111: Beyond Three Squares

After you've eaten your three square meals a day, there's all the other stuff you love to eat: snacks, appetizers, and those oh-so-delicious desserts. Part III has recipes for all these foods. It also has a fun chapter on how to change recipes and use up everything that's been sitting in your refrigerator — everything can be recycled into a new meal!

Part IV: The Part of Tens

For Dummies books are famous for having a Part of Tens filled with quick bits of useful information, and the Part of Tens in this book won't disappoint you. Chapter 16 lists handy hints for creating special vegetarian feasts. Chapter 17 lists tips for converting any recipe into a dish that's vegetarian-friendly.

The appendix is helpful, too; it features charts to help you convert measurements and oven temperatures to the metric system.

Icons Used in This Book

When you take notes in class, you may use a star or a big dot or a yellow marker to highlight important points. In *For Dummies* books, icons are used to point out special things. Here's what the icons in this book mean:

 I use this icon to point out information that's so important that you should remember it long after you close the book.

 This icon points out statistics, scientific facts, or other forms of specific and detailed information that are interesting but not crucial to understanding vegetarian cooking.

 You see this icon whenever I mention a helpful hint — an idea that helps make cooking easier or a suggestion on how to save time and/or money.

 Pay attention to this icon. It precedes information you need to know to avoid pitfalls and danger.

Where to Go from Here

The real beauty of any *For Dummies* book is that you can start reading it anywhere you like. If you're not a committed vegetarian yet, start with Part I to get a better understanding of what's involved with the vegetarian lifestyle. If you're going to be moving into your dorm room or apartment soon, start with Chapters 5 and 6 to find out what equipment you need and how to stock your kitchen with vegetarian ingredients. For those who already know how to move around comfortably in the kitchen, open the book directly to Parts II and III and start cooking!

Part I
Living the Vegetarian Lifestyle

The 5th Wave   By Rich Tennant

"When you're finished shredding carrots, I'd like my electric pencil sharpener back."

In this part . . .

*T*he first part of this book takes a look at everything you need to know before you actually start cooking vegetarian recipes. After examining different types of (and reasons for) vegetarianism, you discover how that choice influences many of the things you do. I include nutritional guidelines to help you plan vegetarian meals so you get all the vitamins and minerals your body needs. I discuss awkward dining situations you may find yourself in and provide a detailed list of where you can turn when you need support. And I include all kinds of hints to help you navigate the aisles of a grocery store and efficiently set up your kitchen.

Chapter 1

Vegetarian Cooking 101

● ●

In This Chapter

▶ Discovering different types of (and reasons for) vegetarianism

▶ Getting essential nutrients and dealing with health issues

▶ Handling social situations and dining out diplomatically

▶ Shopping for food and setting the stage for cooking at home

▶ Finding support

● ●

If you're of college age, can find your way to the kitchen, and are a vegetarian or thinking of becoming a vegetarian, then this book is definitely for you. In this chapter, I introduce the basics you need to start cooking vegetarian meals at home.

Checking Out Different Categories of Vegetarians

Vegetarianism has been described as *eating nothing that has a face.* But few things in life are that simple. There's no single *right way* to be a vegetarian; you have to settle on a diet that works for you. Will you eat all eggs, no eggs, or just eggs from free-range chickens? What about dairy products — yea or nay? Or perhaps you are or want to become a *vegan* — someone who avoids all animal products in food, clothing, and beyond?

Several basic categories of vegetarianism exist, but you may not fit neatly into one of the preset divisions, and that's okay. Don't make a vegetarian diet so involved that it's overwhelming; stick with foods that you're comfortable eating. Flip to Chapter 2 for more information on different types of vegetarianism.

Recognizing Why People Become Vegetarians

You are what you eat, but you're also what you *don't* eat. Most people who switch to a vegetarian lifestyle do so because they feel compassion for animals, hope to fight pollution and conserve the planet's natural resources, and/or want to improve their health.

There are almost as many reasons for becoming a vegetarian as there are vegetarians. You have to decide *why* you want to give up meat and then really commit to it. See Chapter 2 for full details on reasons why people become vegetarians.

Getting a Handle on Vegetarian Nutrition Know-How

Most vegetarians will tell you that they eat healthier than most people. Actually, this isn't necessarily the case. When you give up an entire food group, you have to give some attention to getting good nutrition from other foods. Vegetarians probably eat far more fresh veggies and fruits than most nonvegetarians, and that's good. But they may eat more junk food as well because a lot of junk food is technically vegetarian (potato chips, anyone?).

Being a vegetarian and eating healthy go together very well *if* you're aware of the balance of carbohydrates, protein, and fat you need to eat at each meal. The key is to eat a variety of foods. To help you out, the Mayo Clinic has developed a food pyramid for vegetarians (see it online at www.mayoclinic.com/health/vegetarian-diet/HQ01596; a more detailed version is at www.mayoclinic.com/health/medical/IM02769).

What if you're dealing with a health condition such as an allergy, diabetes, or a weight problem? Yes, sticking to a vegetarian diet is still possible with a little planning. Head to Chapter 3 for the full scoop on getting necessary nutrients and handling health issues on a vegetarian diet.

Dealing Gracefully with Social Situations and Dining Out

Here's the hard truth: Some people will feel awkward about your vegetarian diet, and maybe you're afraid that people will judge you. Some people may even feel like *you're* judging *them* if they eat meat. What to do? Try to look at the situation through their eyes. Reassure them that you're still the person you've always been and that you won't judge them if they don't judge you.

You may also have some trouble when you dine out rather than cook in the comfort of your home. If you're going to a friend's house, for example, make sure he or she knows in advance that you don't eat meat (or eggs, dairy, or any other foods that aren't in your diet). Before you go to a restaurant, look up the menu online and call the restaurant if you have questions. If you'll be traveling, take a backpack filled with snacks just in case you have trouble finding foods you can eat on the road. Sure, it may take a little extra effort to eat out, but don't let that keep you from enjoying life away from home.

Keep things in perspective. Lots of vegetarians face these kinds of challenges every day, and somehow they manage to deal with them while actually having a good time. You can too; just flip to Chapter 4 for some handy pointers.

Shopping Smart for Vegetarian Food

To start cooking at home, you need to shop for vegetarian ingredients. Before you venture out, though, you should make a list of vegetarian staples, such as veggies, fruit, beans, nuts, and grains. You also need to figure out how to decipher nutrition labels while you shop. These little bits of information tell you whether a food is filled with hidden animal ingredients and help you determine just how nutritious the food is.

Chapter 5 is filled with pointers on which vegetarian staples to stock in your kitchen. It also provides guidelines on interpreting food labels so that you always buy vegetarian-friendly, nutritious goodies.

Preparing to Cook on Your Own

You're almost ready to start cooking, but wait — do you have all the gear you need? Be sure you have essential tools and gadgets such as a mixing bowl, a sharp knife, a cutting board, a whisk, and a baking pan on hand. (You're probably also going to need some potholders; you don't want to burn yourself!)

Keep in mind that cooking is much easier when your kitchen is organized, too. Are your counters cleared so you have room to cook? Are spices and seasonings handy? If similar products are neatly grouped together in your pantry, seeing what you have on hand at a glance is much easier — having a lot of one particular item may help you decide what to cook so you can use up excess ingredients. And before you begin mixing ingredients for a recipe, set out all the utensils, pans, and foods that you're going to need.

Suppose you're in the middle of trying a recipe, but you don't understand some of the terms you're reading. Do you know the difference between *simmer* and *boil?* Between *sauté* and *brown?* Understanding the terms used in a cookbook or on package directions can often make the difference between making something that tastes delicious and something that's burnt.

Chapter 6 is filled with helpful hints on getting basic kitchen gear, organizing your kitchen, and understanding a variety of cooking terms.

Getting Support

Whether you're new to vegetarianism or a veteran vegetarian, you have a lot of resources to help you. Give the ones in the following sections a whirl.

Dietary resources

Even if you have health issues to deal with, a dietitian can help you squeeze everything you need into your vegetarian diet.

- ✔ *Vegetarian Journal* explains why you need a dietitian: www.vrg.org/journal/dietitian.htm
- ✔ Get a list of dietitians in your area from the American Dietetic Association site: www.eatright.org/programs/rdfinder

✔ At the *Ask the Dietitian* forum, you can type in a question and a registered dietitian will answer you: www.vegfamily.com/dietician/index.htm

✔ You can find basic food guides at The Vegan RD: www.theveganrd.com

Local vegetarian groups

Joining a local vegetarian group is fun and reassuring because everyone there has similar interests and experiences. Most colleges and universities have vegetarian clubs; here are some additional sites where local groups are listed by state:

✔ Soy Stache Vegetarian Organizations: www.soystache.com/vegorg.htm

✔ Vegan & Vegetarian Societies and Vegetarian Organizations: www.veganfood.com

✔ Vegetarian Resource Group: www.vrg.org/links/local.htm

✔ Vegetarians in Paradise: www.vegparadise.com/directory.html

National vegetarian societies

National organizations offer helpful links, diet suggestions, ways to get involved in your community, and more:

✔ American Vegan Society; phone 856-694-2887; www.americanvegan.org/index.htm

✔ Christian Vegetarian Association; phone 216-283-6702; www.christianveg.com

✔ FARM (Farm Animal Reform Movement); phone 888-327-6872; www.farmusa.org

✔ In Defense of Animals; phone 415-388-9641; www.idausa.org

✔ Jewish Vegetarians of North America; phone 410-754-5550; www.jewishveg.com

✔ Last Chance for Animals; phone 310-271-6096; www.lcanimal.org

✔ North American Vegetarian Society; phone 518-568-7970; www.navs-online.org

- ✔ PETA (People for the Ethical Treatment of Animals); phone 757-622-7382; www.peta.org
- ✔ Vegan Action; phone 804-502-8736; www.vegan.org
- ✔ Vegan Outreach; www.veganoutreach.org
- ✔ Vegetarian Awareness Network (VEGANET); phone 800-834-5463; http://library.thinkquest.org/20922/index.shtml

Vegetarian magazines

The following magazines have free information on their Web sites. Topics include book reviews, food articles, recipes, frequently asked questions, vegetarian- and vegan-specific health issues, vegetarian-friendly restaurants, and much more.

- ✔ *VegNews:* www.vegnews.com/web/home.do
- ✔ *Vegetarian Journal:* www.vrg.org/journal
- ✔ *Vegetarian Times:* www.vegetariantimes.com
- ✔ *Veggie Life:* www.veggielife.com

Online blogs, chat rooms, and forums

Online blogs, chat rooms, and forums are perfect when you want to ask a question or share what's happening in your life.

Online blogs to check out include the following:

- ✔ The Garden Diet: www.thegardendiet.com
- ✔ Vegan Peace: www.veganpeace.blogspot.com/2007/11/vegan-forums.html
- ✔ VegWeb: www.vegweb.com

Chat rooms include the following:

- ✔ Happy Cow: www.happycow.net/chat.html
- ✔ VegWeb: www.vegweb.com/index.php?action=chat
- ✔ Vegan Freak: www.veganfreak.com/chat
- ✔ Vegan Passions: www.veganpassions.com/defun/chat.html
- ✔ Vegetarian Passions: www.vegetarianpassions.com/defun/chat.html

Forums include the following:

- ✔ Minoesj: The Vegetarian Voice: `http://members.for tunecity.com/ricardo005/Ricardo4you/id9.html`
- ✔ Vegan Discussion Forums: `www.veganclub.org/forums`
- ✔ Vegan Forum: `www.vegtalk.org`

Vegetarian restaurant locators

You're in luck. Aside from actual vegetarian restaurants, Asian and Indian restaurants have lots of veggie options. And don't totally ignore steakhouses and seafood joints; even they're beginning to offer vegetarian choices. Here are some links to sites that will do the searching for you. Now how easy is that!

- ✔ Happy Cow (the site automatically displays vegetarian restaurants in your city): `www.happycow.net`
- ✔ VegDining: `www.vegdining.com/Home.cfm`
- ✔ VegGuide (the site also has info for area vegetarian and vegan grocery stores): `www.vegguide.org/region/2`
- ✔ Vegetarian, Vegan, and Raw Restaurants: `www.vegetarian-restaurants.net`
- ✔ Veggie Life: `www.veggielife.com`

Chapter 2

Understanding Types of (and Reasons for) Vegetarianism

In This Chapter

▶ Scoping out the varieties of vegetarians

▶ Understanding why people make the vegetarian commitment

*B*efore you embark on all the enlightening topics covered in the rest of this book, you first need a good understanding of the definition of a vegetarian. A vegetarian . . .

    a. Eats no meat

    b. Eats no meat, poultry, or fish

    c. Eats no meat, poultry, fish, or dairy

    d. Eats no meat, poultry, fish, dairy, or eggs

Guess what? A vegetarian can be any one of the above. Confused? Don't worry; this chapter is here to help. I take a closer look at what it really means to be a vegetarian by describing different categories and the reasons why people choose to become vegetarians.

Categorizing Different Kinds of Vegetarians

When you're a vegetarian, you get to choose a subtitle, kind of like assuming a middle name, to further describe who you are. Basically, you have three choices, but within those three choices are even more options, as you find out in the following sections.

Semi-vegetarian

Semi indicates "partial." In this case, it means someone who usually gives up meat, poultry, and/or fish but not necessarily all three. (They usually eat eggs and dairy products, though.) If you choose this category, you get to select what *kind* of semi-vegetarian you want to be:

- ✔ **Flexitarian:** One who avoids meat, poultry, fish, and shellfish most of the time but eats these foods under certain circumstances or situations.

- ✔ **Pollotarian:** One who doesn't eat any meat, fish, or shellfish but does eat poultry.

- ✔ **Pescetarian:** One who doesn't eat any meat or poultry but eats fish and shellfish.

Semi-vegetarians take pride in their diet, but other vegetarians generally don't accept their diet as legitimate. If someone avoids meat, fish, shellfish, and/or poultry *most* of the time, doesn't that count? Or does a true vegetarian have to stick to the diet consistently and refrain from eating *all* animal life *all* the time? The answers to these questions depend on who you ask and your own personal opinion.

Traditional vegetarian

People in the traditional vegetarian category give up all meat, poultry, fish, and shellfish under all circumstances. They eat no products that are derived from slaughtering another living creature (including products such as gelatin, which is made from bone marrow, and Worcestershire sauce, which contains anchovies). However, some do eat animal products that aren't the result of slaughter, such as dairy products and eggs. This sounds simple enough to understand, but even here you have choices:

- ✔ **Lacto ovo vegetarianism:** This diet includes both dairy products and eggs.

  In the United States and most Western countries, lacto ovo vegetarianism is the most prevalent form of vegetarianism. For this reason, many of the recipes in this book contain dairy products and eggs, but quite a few recipes don't.

- ✔ **Ovo vegetarianism:** This diet includes eggs but no dairy products. (*Note:* Some vegetarians who eat eggs only eat free-range eggs. The term *free range* applies to meat, eggs, and dairy farming; it means that livestock are permitted to roam without being fenced in or contained in any manner.)

✔ **Lacto vegetarianism:** This diet includes dairy products but no eggs.

✔ **Sattvic diet:** The sattvic diet, also referred to as the *yoga diet,* is meant to clear the mind and bring tranquility, both of which are beneficial to the body. The sattvic diet includes the consumption of water, fruit, cereal, bread, vegetables, beans, nuts, grains, honey, and milk and dairy products (cheese, butter, ghee, cream, yogurt, and so on). People on this diet avoid all canned food, all frozen food, all food with preservatives added, and anything packaged; only fresh, organic products are consumed. Meat, alcohol, tobacco, onions, garlic, and fermented foods (such as vinegar) are also forbidden on this diet.

Vegan

Vegans eat no meat, poultry, fish, seafood, foods derived from slaughtering another living creature, or foods that are products from animals (dairy, eggs). Many vegans don't eat honey, and some vegans don't eat food that's processed with animal products, even though the food itself contains no animal products (like sugar and some wines). A lot of vegans also avoid *any* animal-derived product, such as leather shoes and wool clothing.

Animal products can be hidden in a variety of foods. For example, sugar is sometimes processed with animal bone char, and many wineries use casein and gelatin. A can of vegetable soup may contain chicken or beef broth. Omega-3 enriched bread may contain fish oil, and refried beans often contain lard. That shiny red coating on apples is frequently made from beetles, and hard candies may contain gelatin. And the list goes on! If you're thinking about becoming a vegan (or you already are one), you need to become a wise consumer.

It's time to make choices again:

✔ **Dietary veganism:** This diet is vegan but doesn't exclude all nonfood uses of animals.

✔ **Raw veganism:** This diet consists of unprocessed vegan foods that haven't been heated above 115 degrees Fahrenheit. "Raw foodists" believe that foods cooked above this temperature lose significant nutritional value and can be harmful to the body. The primary foods that people on this diet eat are whole grains, fruits, vegetables, greens, beans soaked in water, nuts, seeds, and sprouts. Some raw vegetarians eat raw dairy and eggs.

If you opt to be vegan, you may not realize that a lot of foods are processed with meat products. You can access some very reliable and updated lists online to help you find out more about processed foods:

✔ **CyberParent:** This Web site promotes sustainable lifestyles with articles on all kinds of everyday topics. You can find an extensive list of hidden animal products in foods here: www. cyberparent.com/eat/hiddenanimalsinfood.htm.

✔ **Suite101:** This freelance writing site has articles on subjects from A to Z, including a list of hidden nonvegetarian ingredients grouped by category: http://vegetarian-issues.suite101.com/ article.cfm/hidden_nonvegetarian_ingredients.

Unsure of what kind of vegetarian you want to be? Quiz yourself!

If you're thinking about becoming a vegetarian but still haven't decided what type of vegetarianism matches your personal style and reflects the real you, here's a pop quiz that can help. No previous studying is required, and because you're grading your own answers, give yourself an *A:*

1. Are you inner body–conscious? Do you want to eat healthier, eliminate saturated fats, lower cholesterol levels, and increase the amount of fiber you consume?

2. Is vegetarianism a frugality issue for you? Meat is expensive; by eliminating it from your grocery bill, do you hope to save money?

3. Is vegetarianism about making a statement for a social cause, like animal cruelty and environmental issues? On a related note, perhaps you want to become a vegetarian because the thought of possibly consuming diseased meat is gross to you now?

4. Are you motivated to become a vegetarian because you're in a my-friends-are-vegetarians-so-I-want-to-be-one-too frame of mind?

5. Do you want to become a vegetarian because of religious beliefs and the desire to lead as spiritual a life as possible, being kind to and having respect for all God's living creatures?

After you decide the "why" of becoming a vegetarian, think about the "how." Which kind of diet can you honestly commit to for the long term, based on your reasons for becoming a vegetarian? (Check out the earlier section "Categorizing Different Kinds of Vegetarians" for help.) Think about the foods you will and won't be able to eat. For example, if you're a lacto vegetarian, you won't be able to get a flu shot or eat most cakes because they contain eggs. If you're an ovo vegetarian, that means no cheese; nondairy cheese alternatives exist, but the taste isn't the same as the real thing. If you're a vegan, you won't be able to eat the buttered vegetables at a family gathering. Are you okay with that?

Examining Reasons Why People Become Vegetarians

You have to be pretty motivated and committed to voluntarily give up an entire food group. People choose to give up meat (and sometimes meat byproducts; see the earlier section "Categorizing Different Kinds of Vegetarians" for details) for lots of reasons, but usually the reasons can be whittled down to a few basic categories: They feel compassion for animals, they want to make a stand against pollution, or they want to stay as healthy as possible.

They feel compassion for animals

Compassion for animals is the most common reason people become vegetarians (perhaps it's the reason you became one or are thinking of becoming one?). Many people can't bear to think of animals that are raised for food being mistreated. Without going into a lot of gory detail, suffice it to say that animals are not being raised in a natural environment. For instance:

- Baby cows, pigs, and chickens are taken from their mothers and fed hormones so they grow quicker and fatter (even though their limbs and organs can't grow fast enough to handle the extra weight).

- Their living conditions are crowded, and sanitary conditions are nonexistent.

- Certain parts of their anatomy are removed (without anesthetic) to prevent them from injuring other animals.

Fish suffer a different fate. They, too, live in unbelievably overcrowded conditions, and their water tanks are so polluted that many fish die before harvesting.

By becoming a vegetarian, you're consciously making a commitment to do your part to lessen the demand for mistreated animals. Think about it this way: If millions of Americans went out tonight and ordered steak for dinner at restaurants, you better believe that the food industry would notice the increase in the sales of beef. Now reverse that thinking; millions of American vegetarians *won't* be ordering steak tonight, and this, too, makes an equally profound, noticeable statement. (The current estimate is that 3 percent of all Americans are vegetarians.) You may not be able to change the whole world, but you have complete control over the choices you make in your own world.

They want to fight pollution

Maybe you became a vegetarian because you feel that it's just not right that animals pollute people's surroundings. They certainly don't do it on purpose, but that doesn't negate the fact that they do it anyway. How? Part of the problem is their sheer numbers. When people consume massive amounts of meat, massive numbers of livestock must be raised, which means that massive amounts of land, food, energy, and water are needed to raise these animals. In fact, farmers need the majority of all U.S. farmland to raise the animals and grow the crops to feed them.

When farmers need more land for their animals and crops because of increased demand for meat, they clear more land (yup, they cut down more trees). Trees have roots that help hold the ground together and absorb tremendous amounts of water quickly during a big rainfall. This keeps the soil from washing away. Fewer trees means fewer roots to hold down the soil, which means large amounts of soil — and the vital nutrients necessary to grow crops — are washed away. Eventually, with enough rain, the soil can't support crops.

Trees also clean the air, and, of course, air is a pretty important natural resource. Did you know that the air people need to breathe has ammonia in it and that most of that ammonia comes from (hmm, how can I word this delicately?) animal emissions? The trees can't help clean up the air like they used to because so many of them have been cut down, so the air is getting more polluted. This isn't good; polluted air has been shown to cause arsenic poisoning; nerve damage; *hyperkeratosis* (severe skin rash); pigment changes; cancer of the lung, bladder, kidney, and liver; circulatory problems; and lead poisoning that can lead to mental retardation, coma, convulsions, and death.

If Americans consume less meat, the demand for meat will be reduced; this means that farmers will need less land to raise crops needed to feed the farm animals. Trees can then be planted once again on the unused crop land, and there will be less air pollution.

The process of raising animals for food also affects water. Water is used several different ways, but the major use is to clean up after the animals. After animals are loaded on a truck to go to the slaughterhouses, their living quarters have to be washed out with water. When the animal quarters are washed out, some of the water drains into the water tables and streams. I'm not talking about *clean* water here. Well water near big farms has been found to contain E. coli.

One last thing about water: Fish swim in it. If the water's polluted, the fish become polluted, and then people eat that fish. Fish absorb the heavy metals, phosphorus, and nitrogen from manure that's in the water, which, in turn, is ingested by people who eat fish. It's believed that, because of the beef feces in the water, fish can be carriers of Creutzfeldt-Jakob disease (a variant of which is better known as mad cow disease — an untreatable, fatal disease). Even though the fish don't die from it, they can pass it on to humans. Studies are being done now to confirm this.

 Becoming a vegetarian doesn't guarantee that you're never going to get sick, but your chances of getting sick from an animal-borne disease will be nearly eliminated. That leaves the concern of water pollution. Your body needs water, so that's one product you just can't eliminate from your diet. If you want to check your home water for bacteria and E. coli, you can get the inexpensive Water Works EZ Coliform Test Kit at `www.filtersfast.com/P-EZ-Coliform-Cult-Bacteria-Check-Test-Kit.asp`. Another option is to drink bottled water and use bottled water for cooking.

They want to improve their health

Maybe you decided to give up meat for health reasons. Perhaps your family has a history of heart disease and you want to avoid as much fat as possible. Here's some great news for all of you watching your fat intake for one reason or another — things that grow from the ground have no cholesterol. How great is that? Your body needs good fats, but the saturated stuff typically found in meat just clogs up your arteries, much like solid shortening does when you pour it down the kitchen sink. (Don't try that at home.)

 Different meats have different amounts of saturated fat, but so do the *same* meats. For example, if you're a semi-vegetarian who eats poultry, eat free-range chicken. A chicken that's been pasture-fed can have as much as 20 times less saturated fat than a factory-farmed chicken. That's impressive! (For more about semi-vegetarians and other types, check out the earlier section "Categorizing Different Kinds of Vegetarians.")

 You can't avoid fats entirely; the right kinds (namely mono-unsaturated fat, found in olive or peanut oil, avocados, and nuts) are part of a healthy diet. But here's a good fact to know: Fiber is good for your body because it slows down the fat absorption from the foods you eat and helps clean the intestines. Plants have fiber, but meats don't. Your best bets for fiber are whole grains (especially bran), brown rice, nuts, seeds (especially flaxseed), beans, lentils, fruits, and vegetables.

Chapter 3

Jumping Over Health Hurdles

· ·

In This Chapter

▶ Considering the nutrition of a vegetarian diet

▶ Coping with allergies when you're a vegetarian

▶ Combining vegetarianism with the treatment of health issues

· ·

Suddenly deciding to stop eating one or more food groups can deprive your body of some of the nutrients it needs. Fortunately, you can find most of these nutrients in plants, but you need to eat a variety of vegetarian-friendly foods to maintain good health and strong muscles and bones.

Becoming a vegetarian may also present difficulties if you have an allergy, such as a dairy allergy, or a health condition, such as diabetes.

The most important step you can take when you become a vegetarian is to educate yourself about health. In this chapter, I describe the nutrients you need for good health and the ways you can get those nutrients on a vegetarian diet. I also explain how you can stick to a vegetarian lifestyle even if you have food allergies and/or health issues.

Knowing (and Getting) the Nutrition You Need

Meat and other animal products have nutrients that are sometimes hard to replace with nonmeat sources. But getting the nutrients you need for good health is still possible when you're any kind of vegetarian — really! As I explain in the following sections, you should make sure to get enough of these nutrients:

✔ Protein

✔ Calcium

✔ Vitamins and minerals such as vitamin B12, vitamin D, iron, and zinc

✔ Omega-3 fatty acids

✔ Iodine

To get the nutrients they need and provide both balance and variety in their diets, vegetarians should eat the following foods:

✔ Beans, nuts, and seeds

✔ Dairy (if you're an ovo vegetarian or a vegan, you should include more calcium-rich foods like leafy greens, broccoli, pinto beans, almonds, and tofu in your diet in place of dairy products; some foods, like some orange juice, breads, and cereals, are fortified with calcium)

✔ Grains

✔ Produce (fruits and vegetables)

It's wise to have your doctor run a blood test once or twice a year to keep a check on your vitamin and mineral levels.

Procuring protein

Protein is part of every cell, tissue, muscle, and organ in the human body. It plays a vital role for practically every internal process (metabolism, digestion, and moving nutrients and oxygen in the blood). You also need protein to produce antibodies to fight infection and illness and to keep your bones strong and healthy.

The body constantly breaks down and replaces proteins. The protein in the foods you eat is digested into amino acids that are later used to replace the proteins in your body. There are 14 *nonessential amino acids;* the body manufactures these so you don't have to get them from the foods you eat. But your body can't produce 8 other amino acids and you must get them through your diet; these are the *essential amino acids.*

All foods that provide protein contain all 8 of the essential amino acids. But protein from grains, beans, nuts, seeds, and vegetables falls a little short of one or more of the amino acids. It's still easy to get all of the amino acids from plant foods, though. As long as you eat a variety of foods and include some higher-protein foods like legumes, you'll get enough of the amino acids even if you don't eat any animal proteins.

Nutritionists recommend that 10 to 15 percent of your daily calorie intake should be made up of protein. Eating too much protein can be as bad for your health as eating too little. According to the American Heart Association, "People who can't use excess protein effectively may be at a higher risk of kidney and liver disorders, and osteoporosis."

On the other hand, protein foods are a good source of iron and other vitamins and minerals, so if you don't get enough protein, your body can feel weak and tired from lack of iron. Your cells need a new supply of protein each day to repair themselves and create new cells; a lack of protein can prevent this natural repair and replacement process.

On average, women between the ages of 19 and 70 need 46 grams of protein per day; men in the same age category need 56 grams of protein per day. Here's an easy way to figure just how much protein your body needs: Take your weight, divide it in half, and then subtract 10. The total is the number of grams of protein you should consume each day. For example, if you weigh 140 pounds, divide that in half and you get 70, and then subtract 10 and you get 60, so you should eat 60 grams of protein daily.

Lacto ovo vegetarians get most of their protein from cheese, eggs, and/or yogurt. Vegans don't eat any of these foods but can get plenty of protein by eating a variety of grains, legumes, nuts, seeds, and vegetables. It's important for vegans to include a few servings — beans or soy foods — in their diet everyday. Consider the following:

- Most cooked beans (black, pinto, lentils, kidney, and so on) have 7 to 10 grams of protein per ½ cup.
- ½ cup cooked soybeans have 12 grams of protein.
- ¼ cup dry-roasted peanuts have 6 grams of protein.
- 2 tablespoons of flaxseeds have 4 grams of protein.
- 2 tablespoons of peanut butter have 8 grams of protein.
- ½ cup of soymilk has 5 grams of protein.
- ¾ cup tofu yogurt has 7 grams of protein.
- ½ cup firm tofu has 10 grams of protein.
- 1 medium-sized baked potato has 5 grams of protein.

Lacto ovo vegetarians have these high-protein options:

- ½ cup low-fat cottage cheese has 14 grams of protein.
- 1 large egg has 6 grams of protein.

✔ 1 cup low-fat plain yogurt has 13 grams of protein.

✔ ½ cup low-fat milk (1% milk fat) has 4 grams of protein.

✔ ¼ cup diced cheddar cheese has 8 grams of protein.

Checking out calcium

Calcium is the most abundant mineral in the human body. It's vital for good bone health, strong teeth, and a healthy heart. It's also important for maintaining muscles and the circulatory system and initiating blood clotting. To maintain healthy bodies, humans need the following amounts of calcium:

✔ 19 to 50 years old: 1000 milligrams daily

✔ 51+ years old: 1200 milligrams daily

If you don't get enough calcium in your diet, it can lead to osteoporosis, bone deformities, muscle cramps, and high blood pressure. Fortunately, calcium is in a lot of the foods you probably already eat.

Dairy foods such as milk and yogurt are loaded with calcium, and that's good news for most vegetarians. Ovo vegetarians and vegans (who don't eat dairy products) can get a fair amount of calcium from the following foods:

✔ Blackstrap molasses (2 tablespoons have 82 mg calcium)

✔ Collards and turnip greens (1 cup chopped and boiled collards has 266 mg; 1 cup turnip greens has 249 mg)

✔ Broccoli (1 cup chopped has 43 mg)

✔ Some legumes (garbanzo beans, great northern beans, navy beans, black-eyed peas, and soybeans) have 40 to 65 mg of calcium per ½ cup; ½ cup firm tofu prepared with calcium sulfate can have between 250 and 350 mg

✔ Almonds (¼ cup whole almonds have 94 mg), Brazil nuts (¼ cup whole nuts have 53 mg), chia seeds (2 tablespoons have 143 mg), and sesame seed butter or tahini (2 tablespoons have 128 mg)

✔ Dried figs (5 figs have 68 mg)

✔ Fortified orange juice (1 cup has 500 mg)

✔ Calcium-fortified soymilk (1 cup has 300 mg), rice milk (1 cup has 150 mg), hemp milk (1 cup has 300 mg), and almond milk (1 cup has 300 mg)

Most vegetarians can consume two servings of dairy products per day, plus 200 milligrams of calcium from vitamins. Ovo vegetarians and vegans should consume calcium-fortified juices, soymilk, and calcium-rich foods daily and also take a daily supplement.

It's nearly impossible to list a specific number of servings per day that you should have of these calcium-rich foods because the number of servings totally depends on what foods you decide to eat. One cup of baked beans has 86 milligrams of calcium, and one cup of fortified orange juice has 500 milligrams, so all sources are not created equal.

But you don't really think getting enough calcium is as easy as that, do you? You have to not only consume calcium but also absorb it and hold onto it. A number of factors help or hinder the absorption of calcium into the body.

Some nutrients help your body to absorb calcium, whereas others interfere with the absorption. Here are some guidelines:

- ✔ Vitamin D and potassium help in absorbing more calcium. Ten to twenty minutes of sunshine every day is the best source for vitamin D, but the vitamin is also present in irradiated button mushrooms, eggs, and fortified soymilk and bran cereals. Foods high in potassium include yams, baked potatoes, lima beans, lentils, kidney beans, soybeans, spinach, tomatoes, Swiss chard, romaine lettuce, collard greens, Brussels sprouts, beets, winter squash, bananas, cantaloupe, papaya, and oranges.

- ✔ High intake of sodium or caffeine decreases the amount of calcium your body will absorb.

- ✔ Phytic acid (found in whole grains, nuts, and legumes) and oxalic acid (found in spinach, beets, celery, rhubarb, pecans, peanuts, tea, and cocoa) can decrease the amount of calcium that's absorbed.

Digging into vitamins and minerals

Your body is a complex machine that functions off the foods you feed it. You need a minimum amount of vitamins and minerals to keep the machine working properly. As a vegetarian, be aware of how to get this proper nutrition — especially vitamins B12 and D, iron, and zinc — from foods that grow in the ground.

Vitamin B12

As you can imagine, there are lots of vitamins in the world. So what's the big deal with *vitamin B12?* You need B12 because it plays an important role in forming red blood cells and because it works with your brain to maintain a healthy nervous system. Your body also needs B12 for DNA during cell division. (Are you totally confused yet? Don't sweat the details; just know that B12 is really important in maintaining good health!) Signs and symptoms of a B12 deficiency can include diarrhea, unusual fatigue, muscle weakness, anemia, nausea, loss of appetite, dementia, hallucinations, nervousness, infertility, and striking behavioral changes.

The recommended amount of vitamin B12 per adult per day is 2.4 micrograms from food sources. If you don't eat dairy or eggs or are vegan, then a 5 microgram (mcg) supplement is essential. B12 is found only in animal foods. Plants can't provide B12. Lacto ovo vegetarians can get their recommended amount of B12 by eating ample amounts of eggs and dairy. An 8-ounce container of yogurt has 1.5 mcg of B12. A whole egg has .45 mcg. One ounce of Swiss cheese has .95 mcg.

Lacto vegetarians who eat no eggs need to make sure they get their B12 from dairy alone. Ovo vegetarians who consume no dairy may find it very difficult to get enough micrograms of B12 through eggs alone, so a vitamin supplement may be needed.

The best way for a vegan to get this vitamin is to take a chewable or sublingual (dissolves beneath the tongue) B12 supplement and eat fortified foods. Fortified foods like cereals, soy products, energy bars, nondairy milks, meat substitutes, and Red Star Nutritional Yeast Vegetarian Support Formula or Twinlab SuperRich Yeast Plus have B12 added. Consuming a little less than 1 tablespoon of nutritional yeast daily supplies 2.4 mcg of vitamin B12 (the recommended daily allowance for adults). Approximately half a cup of fortified cereal also provides 2.4 mcg of B12.

Look at the nutrition facts listed on the back of the packaging. Any food with 20 percent or more of the daily value for B12 is considered a good source. (If you're curious about nutritional yeast, check out the nearby sidebar "Noshing on nutritional yeast.")

There have been claims that B12 can be found naturally in seaweed, barley grass, tempeh, and miso, but these foods contain an inactive form of the vitamin that actually prevents your body from absorbing B12.

Vitamin D

The human body needs *vitamin D* to absorb calcium, which promotes bone growth. Too little vitamin D can result in soft and fragile bones. It may also play a role in preventing asthma, depression, heart disease, diabetes, weight gain, and even cancer.

Noshing on nutritional yeast

Nutritional yeast is a nonactive form of yeast that is rich in a variety of nutrients. It may or may not contain vitamin B12, so be sure to check the label. It has a cheese flavor so you can sprinkle it over popcorn, salads, cereal, and casseroles, or stir it into smoothies, gravies, soups, dips, and juice. The only caution with nutritional yeast is that if you continually use too much of it, you may get an upset stomach.

Buy nutritional yeast that comes wrapped in a package. You can find it in bins at health food stores. Vitamin B12 is extremely sensitive to light; if it's exposed to too much light, it becomes inactive. Transfer the yeast to an airtight glass container or a freezer bag and refrigerate it for up to six months or freeze the yeast for up to two years to prolong its shelf life and to keep it out of the light.

Your body can make its own vitamin D when you're exposed to sunlight, without sunscreen, for 15 minutes (for fair-skinned people) to 30 minutes (for darker-skinned people) at least two to three times a week. If you live in an area that gets a lot of fog or smog, getting ample sunlight may be difficult. If you live in the North, you may not be able to get enough sun during the winter months. Fortunately, you can also get vitamin D from fortified foods like milk, nondairy milks, yogurt, cheese, egg yolks, orange juice, and breakfast cereals.

 People with more body fat need more vitamin D than people who are lean. The recommended daily amounts for anyone between the ages of 10 to 70 are 600 IU (international units) to 2000 IU, depending on the amount of body fat. This dosage amount may increase up to 4000 IU if a person gets no natural sunlight exposure.

Too much vitamin D can cause nausea, constipation, confusion, abnormal heart rhythm, and kidney stones. But getting too much vitamin D from sunlight or from foods is impossible; most overdoses of this vitamin are from vitamin supplements.

 Vitamin D supplements come in two forms: D2 and D3. Both forms are effective. D3 is made from the fat in lamb's wool and is not vegetarian. D2 (or *ergocalciferol*) is what most vegetarians take.

Iron

Iron helps move oxygen within the body and helps regulate metabolism.

An iron deficiency can weaken your resistance to infection, affect your ability to think clearly, drain your energy, cause headaches, and cause anemia (the lack of enough healthy red blood cells).

The percentage of iron you absorb depends on the type of food you eat and what other foods you're eating at the same time. Tea, coffee, cocoa, spinach, oregano, and calcium prevent iron from being absorbed. Ascorbic acid or vitamin C (found in fruits, vegetables, and fortified cereals) improves iron absorption.

The recommended daily amount of iron for men between the ages of 19 to 50 is 8 milligrams per day. For women in that age group, it's 18 milligrams per day. The best amounts/sources of iron include:

- ✔ 1⅓ cup whole-grain Total cereal (18 mg iron)
- ✔ 1 packet instant plain oatmeal (8.2 mg)
- ✔ ½ cup boiled soybeans (4.4 mg)
- ✔ ½ cup cooked lentils (3.3 mg)
- ✔ ½ cup cooked kidney beans (2.6 mg)
- ✔ ⅓ cup whole almonds (1.6 mg)
- ✔ 2 large scrambled eggs (1.6 mg)
- ✔ ¼ cup dried prunes (1.2 mg)

Iron comes in two forms: *heme iron* and *non-heme iron*. Meat contains both types, but plants contain only non-heme. The human body easily absorbs the iron from meat sources, but vegetarians need to eat a good source of vitamin C at every meal with foods high in non-heme iron. Why? Vitamin C boosts absorption of iron from plant foods.

Foods high in vitamin C include

- ✔ 1 cup sliced fresh strawberries (97.6 mg vitamin C)
- ✔ 1 cup chopped broccoli (81.2 mg)
- ✔ 1 kiwi (64 mg)
- ✔ 1 medium orange (52 mg)
- ✔ 1 cup chopped cauliflower (51.6 mg)
- ✔ ½ grapefruit (43.7 mg)
- ✔ 1 small papaya (33 mg)

Other foods high in vitamin C include cabbage, cantaloupe, celery, mustard greens, pineapple, raspberries, and tomatoes.

A few other tips:

- ✔ Eat plenty of fruits and vegetables because they contain organic acids that boost absorption of both zinc and iron.

- ✔ Eat more fermented foods (like tempeh) because iron and zinc are better absorbed from fermented foods.

- ✔ Eat bread made with yeast instead of crackers and flat breads because iron and zinc are better absorbed from foods leavened with yeast.

- ✔ Drink coffee and tea between meals instead of with meals because they inhibit iron absorption.

- ✔ Take calcium supplements between meals because they inhibit iron absorption.

- ✔ Don't overdo it with dairy; milk and other dairy foods don't contain iron, and they reduce its absorption from other foods.

Zinc

Zinc is in almost every cell in the human body, and yet your body can't produce zinc; you have to get it from the foods you eat. Zinc helps wounds to heal and helps maintain a healthy immune system; it helps increase your sense of smell and taste; it's needed in DNA synthesis; it helps the pancreas produce insulin; and it eases skin conditions like rosacea, eczema, and acne. Many people take zinc to prevent or shorten the duration of a cold.

The RDA for people 19 years and older is 8 milligrams of zinc per day. Too much zinc can be just as harmful as too little zinc. Too much zinc in your system can induce severe nausea and vomiting and eventually affect your immune system. Too little zinc can cause hair loss, diarrhea, impotence, loss of appetite, and skin lesions.

Good food sources for zinc are beans, nuts, whole grains including brown rice, dairy, fortified breakfast cereals, potatoes, and especially pumpkin seeds. Your body, however, has a harder time absorbing zinc from nonanimal sources, so many vegetarians take a multivitamin that includes zinc to make sure they get the daily recommended amount.

Focusing on fatty acids

The term *fatty acids* doesn't sound like it would be good for you, but it is. Fatty acids provide energy to your muscles, heart, and other organs. They store energy for your body. What your body doesn't use up as energy, it stores as fat (and that's not so good). Essential acids are *polyunsaturated* fatty acids (vegetable oils, corn, sunflower, and soy) that your body needs but can't produce, so you get these acids from the food you eat.

Omega-3 fatty acids are a class of polyunsaturated fatty acids that vegetarians can get from walnuts, wheat germ, rice bran, flaxseed oil, rapeseed (canola) oil, tofu, Brussels sprouts, green leafy vegetables, and eggs (which contain a small amount). Omega-3 fatty acids help control blood clotting, help build membranes in the brain, can help prevent the risk of sudden cardiac death, and can reduce the risk of coronary heart disease.

If you don't get enough omega-3 fatty acids in your diet, you can experience vision and nerve problems, poor memory, dry skin, poor circulation, heart problems, and mood swings.

The FDA hasn't set guidelines yet for how much omega-3 is needed in the diet. The European Food Safety Agency recommends a daily dose of 250 milligrams daily.

When using flaxseed oil, don't heat it; heat breaks down the molecules. For cooking purposes, use olive oil or rapeseed (canola) oil, both of which are rich in omega-6 fatty acids and can withstand higher cooking temperatures.

Omega-6 is another fatty acid that your body needs, but it's important to have the right balance between omega-6 and omega-3 fatty acids. Food sources for omega-6 include nuts, seeds, soybean oil, olives, and whole grains.

Investigating iodine

Your body needs iodine to convert food into energy and to keep your thyroid functioning properly. Without enough iodine, your body can't synthesize the hormones in the thyroid that regulate your entire body's metabolism.

People 14 years of age and older should get 150 micrograms of iodine daily. Most get this amount from iodized salt (¼ teaspoon of salt has 95 micrograms), but iodine is also found in kelp, yogurt, cow's milk, strawberries, mozzarella cheese, and vegetables grown in iodine-rich soil.

If you don't get enough iodine in your diet, over a period of time your thyroid will become enlarged and you could have chronic fatigue and weight gain. Because iodized salt is so readily available in the United States and the United Kingdom, iodine deficiency in these two countries is extremely rare. If iodine deficiency does occur, it's usually not due to a lack of iodine but to the thyroid not being able to process it.

Addressing Annoying Food Allergies on a Vegetarian Diet

It's a bummer when you can't eat certain foods because they cause you physical problems. You need to take some allergies, like peanut and tree nut allergies, very seriously, because even inhaling little particles of the offensive food can send you into anaphylactic shock.

The only way to really avoid food reactions is to avoid the particular foods that cause those reactions. There are as many types of food allergies and intolerances as there are foods, but 90 percent of the reactions are caused by eight foods:

- ✔ Eggs
- ✔ Fish
- ✔ Milk
- ✔ Peanuts (which are actually legumes)
- ✔ Shellfish
- ✔ Soy
- ✔ Tree nuts
- ✔ Wheat

As a vegetarian, you don't have to worry about fish and shellfish allergies because those foods aren't included in your diet anyway. But what can you do about the other allergens on this list? If you have special health considerations in addition to trying to stick to a vegetarian diet, don't despair — it's just a minor glitch. With a little planning, the added limitations shouldn't prevent you from successfully following a nutritious vegetarian diet. Just follow the tips and tricks in the following sections.

If you haven't done so already, check with your doctor to confirm your allergies and, if necessary, consult with a dietitian to help you choose the right kinds of food for your specific health issues.

Excluding eggs

One whole egg is a mini warehouse jam-packed full of vitamins, proteins, iron, and all the essential amino acids (which build the proteins that your body needs). If you're allergic to eggs, you can get this good stuff from other food sources, but the nutrients don't come packaged all in one food like they do in an egg. When you have an egg allergy, variety in your diet is key because different beans and vegetables have different amino acids.

If your heart is set on cooking recipes that feature eggs, you're in luck; *egg replacer,* which is primarily potato starch, is available. Don't confuse egg replacer with egg substitutes, which contain egg whites. Egg replacer is available at most health food stores and online. It comes packaged in a 16-ounce box and has a shelf life of almost a year. Egg replacer is great to use in a cake or cookie recipe, or when making pancakes or muffins, but you can't use it to make scrambled eggs. When a recipe calls for 1 whole egg, use 1½ teaspoons of egg replacer mixed with 2 tablespoons of warm water; stir the mixture into the other liquid ingredients. It's as simple as that.

If you can't eat eggs, don't let that stop you from baking. When whipping up a batch of muffins, cookies, cakes, or breads, substitute one of the following combinations for each egg called for in a recipe:

- ✔ For breads, dissolve 1 tablespoon of golden flaxseed meal in 2 tablespoons of warm water.

- ✔ For muffins, quick breads, and cookies, substitute ¼ cup yogurt or ¼ cup puréed silken tofu.

- ✔ Eggs add moisture to a mix, but they also make the baked goods lighter in texture. To get the same results without eggs, increase the amount of baking powder and/or baking soda by ¼ teaspoon per cup of flour.

Moving away from milk

Cow's milk has three components: casein (protein), whey (protein), and lactose (sugar). Casein and whey can cause allergies, and many people have an intolerance to lactose. An allergy creates an immediate reaction to a food. An intolerance has a slower reaction because the digestive system can't process the food.

Because the FDA has revised labeling laws, if dairy products (or any of the top eight allergens) are in foods, the label must now indicate the offending ingredient. If casein or whey is in the mixture, the label will state that milk is included. Read labels carefully because you'll find casein in very unlikely places.

Luckily, cow's milk is one of the easier ingredients to substitute in vegetarian cooking; just use equal amounts of any of these other choices:

- Soymilk
- Rice milk
- Coconut milk
- Hemp milk
- Almond milk
- Water
- Fruit juice (apple, pineapple, pear, orange, or part lemon juice or lemonade; apricot nectar also works well)
- Brewed coffee

Of course, dairy products include more than just milk. Here's how you can substitute for other dairy products when cooking:

- When a recipe calls for yogurt, you can substitute soft or silken tofu; stir it a bit so it has the same consistency as yogurt. For recipes that call for vanilla yogurt, just stir a little vanilla into the tofu. Nondairy coconut yogurt is available at health food stores. You can find nondairy yogurt-style cultured soy and probiotics soy yogurt.

- Tofutti Sour Supreme and Better Than Sour Cream, Vegan Gourmet Sour Cream Alternative, and canned coconut cream are all good to use in place of dairy sour cream.

- Vegan cheese substitutes are getting tastier every day. They now look, taste, and melt like real cheese. Nondairy cheese options now include blue, feta, cream, Parmesan, and tex-mex pseudo cheeses. You can find soy cheese spreads, cheese blocks, cheese slices, and shredded cheeses that are all nondairy.

- Although a lot of butter alternatives are available, one of the best is Earth Balance margarine. In many recipes, you can use oil in place of butter (¾ cup of oil for every 1 cup of butter in the recipe).

✔ This list wouldn't be complete if I didn't include ice cream alternatives. Although you can find ice cream made from a rice base, it tends to taste a little like paper and, depending on the brand, may leave an aftertaste. Better options are Luna & Larry's ice cream (made from a coconut base) or Turtle Mountain ice cream (made from either a coconut or soy base). Both brands taste delicious.

Saying no to peanuts and tree nuts

Eating peanuts (a type of legume) and tree nuts (such as walnuts, pecans, and almonds) is encouraged for vegetarians (actually, for everyone) because of their health benefits. Both peanuts and tree nuts are packed full of protein, vitamins, antioxidants, and minerals and are a good source for healthy fats. Oh, and they taste good, too. Of course, none of this is beneficial to you if you're allergic to them.

Some people have a peanut allergy yet seem to tolerate tree nuts, and others are allergic to both peanuts and tree nuts. If you do have a nut allergy, about the only thing that may console you is that you won't be consuming all the calories in nuts. (Yes, they do pack a caloric punch — 219 calories in ¼ cup of dry-roasted peanuts, 206 calories in ¼ cup of whole almonds, and 191 calories in ¼ cup of chopped walnuts.)

An allergy to peanuts and/or tree nuts can be very serious. *Read labels!* Peanuts and tree nuts are occasionally used in products where you'd never suspect them, like spaghetti sauce, barbecue sauce, flavorings, crackers, and more. You can find artificial nuts on the market, but they're usually flavored with a peanut base to make them taste like other nuts. And watch out: *Arachis oil* is simply another name for peanut oil.

Even when a food's label doesn't list peanuts and tree nuts, exercise caution, because the product may be made on production lines and equipment that have processed nuts. Chocolate candies and baked goods are famous for this. Asian foods may not contain pieces of nuts, but they may have been cooked in peanut oil. Sunflower seeds are often manufactured on the same equipment used to produce peanuts. And alternative nut butters (almond butter, cashew butter, hazelnut butter, and so on) are frequently made on the same lines used to make peanut butter. Fortunately, many companies list on their labels if a product has been made in a facility that also processes nuts.

Need some vegetarian substitutions for peanuts and tree nuts? Try the following:

✔ In place of nuts for snacking, enjoy some seasoned soy nuts or edamame. (Edamame are green soybeans that are picked before they've matured.) You can chop up these nuts to use in or on breads, muffins, and desserts.

✔ Shredded coconut is a good nut alternative on salads and in baked goods and candies.

✔ And don't forget the ever-popular chocolate chip pieces. Dark chocolate usually contains no milk (but read the label to make sure, if you need to avoid milk) and can be melted, shaved, chopped, and otherwise made to conform to most any dessert recipe in place of the use of nuts.

As for replacing the nutritional value you'd get from nuts, you can still get good fats by cooking with olive oil. You can get your protein from dairy products and/or eggs or legumes, and you can get most of the vitamins and minerals in nuts from vegetables and fruits.

Severing from soy

So many products made for vegetarians use soy to mimic foods that contain meat. You can find soy burgers, soy sausages, soy vegetable broths and bouillon cubes, soy this and soy that. Tofu is made from soy as well. If you're allergic to soy, though, the vegetarian challenge is a bit more challenging.

Soy is packed with protein, but don't despair. You can get your protein from other vegetarian sources like nuts, seeds, legumes, and grains.

✔ If you can tolerate gluten, enjoy *seitan*. It's made from wheat and absorbs flavors, so you can use it in place of tofu.

✔ Instead of adding tofu to a stir-fry, serve the sautéed veggies over hot quinoa for added protein.

✔ You can often replace soft tofu in dessert recipes with coconut cream.

✔ In place of soy pastas, get pasta made from whole wheat or quinoa.

✔ Daiya brand has a line of cheeses that are vegan and soy-free. Their products are made primarily from tapioca and arrowroot flours, canola or sunflower oil, nutritional yeast, and flavorings.

✔ Quorn products from Great Britain (made from fungi similar to mushrooms) are becoming more readily available in the United States. The company makes meat-free soy-free burgers, chicken-like nuggets, and more.

✔ Most health food stores carry rice protein powder and hemp protein powder. Stir this powder into smoothies, shakes, and yogurt. You can also replace about 20 percent of the flour called for in a recipe with protein powder.

✔ In place of soymilk, use rice milk (for cereal); for baking, use vanilla rice milk, coconut milk, hemp milk, or almond milk.

Craving a veggie burger but can't eat soy? Some brands of veggie burgers contain no soy (they're made from walnuts and other neat stuff).

✔ If you live in Wisconsin, Nature's Bakery makes burgers primarily from brown rice, millet, and veggies. The company also has a burger made of Brazil meal, brown rice flour, and carrots. If you don't live in Wisconsin, contact a health food store in your area and request that it carry products from Nature's Bakery.

✔ You can go to www.walnutburger.com and order burgers made primarily from walnuts, mozzarella cheese, eggs, and breadcrumbs.

✔ Trader Joe's carries the Vegetable Masala Burger, which is made from potatoes.

✔ Amy's Kitchen makes vegan products that are sold in most grocery store freezers. Amy's makes several different kinds of burgers that are soy-free.

✔ Sunshine Burgers are made mostly from brown rice and sunflower seeds and can be found in most grocery freezers.

✔ If you want to create your own soy-free burgers, make them from lentils, chickpeas, black beans, walnuts, or oatmeal.

Giving up wheat and gluten

Wheat is the most popular grain in the United States, and it's found in *so* many products. Wheat allergies are fairly common. A little rarer are intolerances to gluten (found in wheat, rye, barley, malt, spelt, bulgur, graham flour, and semolina, among other grains). People with *celiac disease* (an autoimmune disease in which the small intestine can't absorb nutrients into the body when even minute amounts of gluten are consumed) must maintain a

100 percent lifelong abstinence from all gluten. Because 1 in 100 people in the United States have celiac disease, some colleges are beginning to respond by offering gluten-free foods . . . but many don't yet.

Sometimes a product is gluten-free, but the facility where it's processed isn't, so there's a real risk of cross-contamination. Read labels very carefully to find out whether a product contains hidden gluten. Many medications, soaps, shampoos, and brands of makeup contain gluten, too.

Fortunately, a lot of companies have developed and are continuing to develop gluten-free mainstream products.

- ✔ Betty Crocker was the first company to come out with gluten-free cake and cookie mixes.

- ✔ Kraft Foods was the first to start putting a label on the front of its packaging to indicate that a product is gluten-free.

- ✔ Amy's Kitchen was the first to offer gluten-free meals in your grocer's frozen food section.

- ✔ Bob's Red Mill is a brand that's sold in most grocery stores throughout the country, and the company has packages of just about every combination of gluten-free flours imaginable. So baking without wheat flour is possible, and the finished products can be every bit as good as their wheat counterparts.

- ✔ Many pizza chains now offer gluten-free pizza, and many restaurants are starting to offer gluten-free menus.

Gluten-free products tend to be low in vitamins B and D, calcium, iron, zinc, magnesium, and fiber. Earlier in the chapter I discuss how to get ample amounts of vitamins B and D, calcium, iron, and zinc in your diet, so here's some advice on magnesium and fiber for those who have an intolerance to gluten.

Magnesium is a necessary electrolyte that's a part of all your cells. Foods that are high in magnesium include grapefruit, oranges, figs, corn, coconut, milk, eggs, cooked spinach, black beans, pumpkin and squash seeds, okra, and nuts. Adult females should get 310 milligrams of magnesium per day; adult males should get 400 milligrams.

Fiber is roughage. There's soluble fiber, which dissolves in water and helps control your blood sugar levels, and there's insoluble fiber, which doesn't dissolve and helps prevent constipation. Both types of fiber absorb water, and your body needs both kinds to function properly. You can add fiber to your diet by eating vegetables and fruits, whole grains, legumes, and oats, to name a few sources. The recommended amount of fiber for adults per day is 20 to 30 grams.

One of the easiest ways to get more fiber into your diet is to add golden flaxseed meal to foods. Start slowly so that your body can adjust, and then slowly increase the amount until you're adding 2 to 3 tablespoons of meal per day to foods. Golden flaxseed meal is tasteless and dissolves instantly, so you can sprinkle it on cereal or add it to scrambled eggs, salad dressing, soup, breading, peanut butter, pudding . . . just about anything.

Handling Health Conditions When You're a Vegetarian

Health conditions can complicate matters for college students, but any special diet requirements can usually be incorporated into a vegetarian diet with a little planning. Dealing with diabetes or weight problems are no exceptions. Taking difficult courses and trying to fit in the extracurricular activities at school can cause you enough stress — you don't need to stress about your diet, too. Figure out what you need to eat, plan your meals, and then enjoy your new life. Surround yourself with people you trust and who will be supportive of your diet choices and needs.

Dealing with diabetes

Legumes, slow-digesting whole grains, and a low-fat, plant-based diet improve blood glucose control and are recommended for diabetics. This sounds like a vegetarian diet to me! The two diets are very compatible.

Here are a few important points to keep in mind:

✔ Eat about the same amount of food each day.

✔ Eat your meals and snacks at about the same time each day.

✔ Don't skip meals or snacks.

✔ Take any medicines needed at the same time each day.

Type 1 diabetes

With type 1 diabetes, the body produces no insulin at all to regulate blood sugar levels. People with type 1 diabetes have to supply the insulin through shots. They have to time these shots so that the insulin reaches the bloodstream at the same time that the glucose from the digested food is being absorbed from the gut (usually one to two hours after eating). This is why it's so important to consider not only *what* you eat, but *how much* you eat and *when*. If you have type 1 diabetes (which has no cure), talk with your doctor about how to tailor your insulin injections to match your lifestyle.

If you faithfully watch the kinds and amounts of carbs you consume and don't skip meals, you should be able to adhere to a vegetarian diet without problems. Here are some basic guidelines:

- ✔ Because carbohydrates aren't created equal, different carbs react differently inside the body. For example, bran cereal takes longer to break down in the bloodstream than frosted, sugary cereal. Similarly, whole-wheat bread takes longer to break down than a cinnamon roll. (You may assume that sugary cereal and cinnamon rolls break down more quickly because of the cane sugar, but that's not the case. It's because sugary cereal is made with high fructose corn syrup, and cinnamon rolls are made with white, bleached flour. Healthier items like bran and whole wheat, which contain fiber, break down more slowly in the body.)

  Fat slows down the rate at which the stomach empties, which, in turn, slows down the rate that the glucose (sugar) is absorbed. Cooking with healthy fats like olive oil instead of butters and margarines helps slow down the absorption rate of carbs.

- ✔ To use round figures, each serving of starch, fruit, or milk has about 15 grams of carbohydrates. Three servings of vegetables have 15 grams of carbs. Each carbohydrate gram provides 4 calories. A type 1 diabetic on a 1,600-calorie diet should aim to have no more than 30 to 45 grams of carbo-hydrates per meal, depending on his or her doctor's recommendation.

- ✔ Eat foods that have a low *glycemic index* (GI), which measures how quickly foods you eat convert to sugar in your system. Foods with a high glycemic level cause a quick rise; foods with a low glycemic level are absorbed more slowly into your bloodstream and help you maintain a more stable blood sugar level. In addition, foods with a low glycemic index are usually higher in fiber. You can find lists of foods with a low GI (55 or below) online, but some include pearl barley, instant or regular brown rice, yogurt, milk, soymilk, most fruit juices, whole-grain and multi-grain breads, all-bran cereal, cherries, grapefruit, dried apricots, apples, pears, plums, peaches, oranges, grapes, protein-enriched spaghetti, peanuts, low-sugar jams and marmalades, tomato soup, lentil soup, and most fresh vegetables. And yes, M&M peanut candies have a low glycemic index. (For more info, check out *The Glycemic Index Diet For Dummies,* by Meri Raffetto, RD, LDN, published by Wiley.)

✔ One of the biggest hurdles for college-age vegetarians who are type 1 diabetics is to never skip meals. Skipping meals plays havoc with your sugar levels. If you think you won't have access to food for quite a few hours, stuff something yummy and vegetarian into your pocket or book bag (peanuts, cheese, crackers, fruit, anything!). And be sure to have a healthy vegetarian snack before you go to bed to ensure that your blood glucose doesn't fall too low during the night. Do the same if you're going to expend a large amount of energy (exercising or running to class because you're late).

Here are some additional recommendations for type 1 diabetics who are vegetarians:

✔ Less than 30 percent of your daily calories should be from fat, and try to eliminate almost all saturated and trans fats.

✔ Switch to low-fat or fat-free dairy products, and limit the number of egg yolks you eat each week to keep your cholesterol intake below 200 milligrams per day. This task is important because adults with diabetes are at high risk for cardiovascular diseases leading to heart attacks and strokes. Lowering cholesterol helps keep the blood vessels clear of fat deposits that slow the flow of blood. Cholesterol intake should be no more than 100 milligrams for every 1000 calories eaten. Some diabetics need to lower their cholesterol intake to 100 milligrams per day no matter how many calories they consume.

Check nutrition labels. Just because something is fat-free (or sugar-free) doesn't mean that other ingredients haven't been added to replace the fat (or sugar), and those ingredients may be just as bad for you or worse.

✔ The majority of diabetics have elevated blood pressure readings, which can lead to heart problems and stroke. Lowering salt intake can lower blood pressure in many cases. Remove the salt shaker from the table. Cook with a little salt, but don't add more salt after the food is cooked. This goes for foods you don't cook, too: Instead of potato chips for a snack, grab a handful of unsalted nuts.

✔ Instead of using chemically-altered sweeteners, try natural sugar substitutes (like agave nectar, honey, date sugar, and Just Like Sugar). Stevia is a viable natural substitute for sweetening foods and drinks that you don't cook (when exposed to high temperatures, Stevia can break down and leave a metallic taste). If you're a diabetic, you have to severely limit your sugar consumption, but choosing an artificial sweetener isn't in your best interest. Aspartame breaks down into formaldehyde, formic acid, and diketopiperazine (a chemical that can cause brain tumors). Splenda is sugar that's processed with a chlorocarbon (an atomic element found in bleach, disinfectants, insecticides, and poison gas). Chlorocarbons have been proven to cause cancer, birth defects, and immune system destruction, among other dangers. You're better off eating smaller amounts of naturally sweetened products than using artificial sweeteners.

If you're a severe type 1 diabetic, consult your doctor and a dietitian before beginning the vegetarian diet.

Type 2 diabetes

Type 2 diabetes is far more common and less threatening than type 1 diabetes. It's referred to as *non-insulin dependent* diabetes. With type 2, your body produces insulin but your body can't metabolize it properly. Though type 2 diabetes has no cure, proper diet and exercise helps keep your insulin levels under control. Sometimes diet and exercise aren't enough and the diabetic has to self-administer insulin shots.

The recommended diet for type 2 diabetics is similar to the diet for type 1 diabetics and blends pretty well with a vegetarian diet if you follow these guidelines:

✔ Diabetics often have an extra accumulation of glucose in the bloodstream, which draws liquid from the tissues; this can lead to dehydration. Drink lots of water and other healthy liquids (like unsweetened tea and low-fat milk) to keep from dehydrating. Though fruit juices are healthy, they also contain natural sugar, so limit the amount of juice you drink to one 6-ounce glass per day.

✔ Eat smaller meals more frequently throughout the day to stabilize your blood sugar level. Rather than three large square meals, try four to five mini meals.

✔ Every day, make sure you have some fruit, vegetables, and whole grains:

- Limit fruits to two to three servings per day because they also contain carbohydrates and natural sugars. Fruits that offer fiber with lower glycemic counts include apples, cantaloupe, berries, pears, plums, and nectarines.

- Eat as many nonstarchy vegetables as you want. Good choices include salad greens, carrots, cucumbers, tomatoes, peppers, radishes, broccoli, cauliflower, mushrooms, asparagus, and zucchini.

- Less refined foods, like whole grains, take longer to digest; consequently, they don't make the blood sugar level spike as much as more refined foods. Whole grains may include whole-grain bread, whole-grain pasta, brown rice, wild rice, whole-grain unsweetened cereal, buckwheat, bulgur, and oatmeal. These grains contain carbohydrates, so you still need to be careful how much you consume, but having two to three servings of whole grains daily is very healthy.

✔ Eat very few sweets.

✔ Limit the amount of carbohydrates you consume (they turn to sugar in your bloodstream). If you're on a 1600-calorie diet, you should have about 200 grams of carbohydrates per day.

✔ Try to eat the same amount of food with the same proportion of carbs, proteins, and fats at the same time every day.

✔ Get plenty of exercise.

✔ Eat foods that have a low *glycemic index*. (See the preceding section, "Type 1 diabetes," for more on the glycemic index.)

Watching weight issues

Mother Nature isn't always kind. Some fortunate people are born with more active metabolisms than others and can burn off calories faster and more efficiently. For the rest of us, what passes our lips reaches our hips. Vegetables can be delicious, but they don't fill you as much as a bowl of pasta or other starchy food. Vegetarian vegetable dishes are often immersed in sauces that add calories to the entrée. Cheese pizza, ice cream, and breaded eggplant parmigiana are all high in calories. Despite these tempting food choices, vegetarians eat a lot of fiber (from fruits, vegetables, beans, nuts, and seeds) and therefore tend to be slimmer than the majority of the population. Vegetarians, just like everyone else in the world, still have to be conscious of what they eat to maintain weight control. This is where you have to be very alert and make wise choices.

In college, you don't have a lot of spare time, so the temptation to grab convenience foods is ever-present. Beware. Some convenience vegetarian foods can be just as fattening (or even more fattening!) than their nonvegetarian counterparts. Plan what you're going to eat ahead of time to avoid bingeing. Keep things in perspective and stay focused.

To lose 1 pound a week, you need to subtract 500 calories per day from the total number of calories you currently consume. At the end of one year, you'll have lost 52 pounds effortlessly. The other alternative is to exercise more and burn 500 more calories each day.

Here are some tips that should help you lose weight while staying healthy on a vegetarian diet:

- Read labels, because some foods are much higher in calories than you would expect. On a weight-loss diet, your total daily fat intake should be 35 grams or less.

- If you're a lacto ovo vegetarian (which means you eat dairy products and eggs), be careful about depending on cheese for added flavor or for snacking. One ounce of cheddar cheese has 10 grams of fat, and 70 percent of its calories are from fat. One ounce of goat cheese has 8.5 grams of fat, and 71 percent of its calories are from fat. Fortunately, you can find low-fat versions of many cheeses so you can still enjoy the flavor without all the fat content.

- Choose complex carbs — like whole-wheat bread, whole-grain cereal, oats, brown rice, and quinoa — over processed carbs (like white bread, white rice, pastries, and white pasta that's not whole grain). These foods fill you up, which keeps you from getting hungry anytime soon and snacking.

- Opt for fat-free salad dressings instead of mayonnaise to use on your salads and wraps. Mayo is 90 percent fat.

Vegetarians or vegans considering going on a strict weight-loss diet should absolutely consult their doctor and/or a nutritionist or dietitian to assure that they're getting the proper nutrition on the diet. Nutritionists and dietitians are trained professionals who can help you balance the carbs, proteins, and fats your body needs to help you reach your weight-loss goals.

Chapter 4

Handling Sticky Social Situations

In This Chapter

▶ Breaking the news to family and friends

▶ Dining outside the comfort of your own home

▶ Taking to the road or the sky

Do you ever feel a little panicky when you realize you don't have a situation under control? When you shop for your own groceries and prepare your own vegetarian meals, you have total control over what you eat. But that all changes when someone else is doing the cooking, whether it's a friend, a family member, or a chef at a restaurant. Don't be intimidated! There are ways to handle each of these situations (and others), as you find out in this chapter.

Relating Your Resolve to Family and Friends

You never quite know how people are going to react when you first tell them you've become a vegetarian. Dad may feel uncomfortable grilling steaks on his new backyard grill at the next family gathering. Friends may hesitate to invite you to join them Friday night to go out for chicken wings.

People understand weight-loss diets. They understand when people restrict certain foods because of a health condition. But when it comes to a voluntary diet that restricts an entire food group, their understanding comes to a sudden halt, and they become perplexed.

Your diet choice may make your friends and family feel uneasy, but the reason doesn't matter. What does matter is how you handle the situation. I provide some helpful guidelines in the following sections.

Using the right tone when you share the news

So how are you going to break the news of your vegetarianism to your family and friends? To see whether you're going to use the right tone, take this quick quiz. Do you plan on

> a. Telling them about the disgusting way farm animals are treated?
>
> b. Explaining in detail how the planet's water and air are being polluted with animal waste?
>
> c. Bringing a diagram that shows how saturated fat from eating meat clogs arteries?
>
> d. None of the above

Please say you chose *d! How* you tell them will make a difference in how they react to the news. Got it? Okay, now take the following quiz — how will you tell parents and siblings about becoming a vegetarian?

> a. Calmly explain your new eating habits
>
> b. Calmly explain why you've chosen this path (no lecturing!)
>
> c. Reassure them that you're still the same person and you still respect their ways
>
> d. All of the above

Now it's okay to choose *d* for your answer. It's important to tell your family and friends (when you have some uninterrupted time with them) that your diet doesn't mean you're turning your back on their traditions and values but that, for personal reasons (like the ones in Chapter 2), you've chosen to eliminate a few things from your diet. For example, you can say something like the following: "I seriously weighed the pros and cons, and I decided to become a vegetarian. The mistreatment of animals has bothered me for so long that I just don't feel right eating meat, fish, or poultry. I'm still going to eat dairy and eggs because they don't involve killing animals. It's a very healthy diet because I eat mostly fruits, vegetables, and lots of beans, and I can still enjoy pasta. I'd like to explain this diet to you. This commitment won't change anything. I'll still be here next week for your barbecue, but I need you to understand why I won't be putting a hamburger on my plate."

Helping your family and friends understand your decision

After you tell your family and friends about your decision to become a vegetarian, you can sit back and wait for them to applaud your selfless contribution to global ecology and your willpower to abstain from eating the spare ribs that are grilling outside . . . but don't count on that happening. Your announcement will more likely leave those around you confused. They probably don't understand what your new diet entails or exactly why you've made the commitment.

Mom has stopped listening because she's thinking ahead to Thanksgiving. Will serving turkey hurt your feelings? Dad is upset that his little fishing buddy doesn't want to go out and catch fish with him anymore. The care and raising of a vegetarian's parents (and other loved ones) is an art form.

Get their attention back by explaining why this diet is so perfect for you, using examples of things they know and understand. Explain that you went for a physical first and that you're in good health. Your doctor said the vegetarian diet is very healthy because it will help prevent high cholesterol and heart problems. (Parents in particular comprehend words like *cholesterol* and *heart problems.*) Tell them how much more energy you have now and that you're so much more alert in class. Stress that now you'll be cooking most of your own meals, which will give you experience in the kitchen; they will interpret that as a good thing.

 Consider giving your folks the book *The China Study: The Most Comprehensive Study of Nutrition Ever Conducted and the Startling Implications for Diet, Weight Loss, and Long-Term Health* by T. Colin Campbell, PhD, and Thomas M. Campbell II, MD (Benbella); it cuts through the maze of misinformation and makes the connection between the foods people eat and diseases. Parents are more likely to understand this approach than an eco-friendly, animal-loving approach.

The dating dilemma for vegetarians

Will you date people who eat meat? The answer to this question gets more convoluted and problematic the more you think about it.

You may think that going out to dinner with an omnivore won't bother you as long as your date doesn't criticize you for being a vegetarian. But picture how it's really going to make you feel to sit across from a potential romantic partner who's salivating when the T-bone steak he or she ordered arrives. This could prove to be a stressful situation.

Vegetarians tend to gravitate toward each other on the dating scene for obvious reasons. But you have to exercise caution. If you're a vegan, will it bother you to go to breakfast with someone who orders eggs? If it does, then consider this — the more limitations you set, the more you're limiting your dating pool options.

Some family members and friends may not remember (or care about) your diet. Don't interpret this as a personal affront and get defensive about it. It's very possible that they just can't understand or handle anything that doesn't fit into their neatly organized preconception of what constitutes a meal or a healthy diet. What you *don't* want to do is criticize or preach. You don't appreciate it if they make derogatory comments about your diet, so don't make cutting remarks about theirs. (And if someone does make a derogatory comment about your diet, simply try to answer with an upbeat, positive response like these: "I'm amazed by how much more energy I have now" or "I'm eating wholesome foods, and that has to be good for my body.")

You may be very surprised to find out which family members and friends support you the most. Give the others time to adjust.

Embarking on Dining Excursions

Never say no to a chance to go out with friends and family (assuming you've finished studying for the day). If friends call you to go out for a hamburger, join them and order French fries and a soda. If the point of destination for a family outing is a pizza shop, learn to love salads and breadsticks. After your family and friends are comfortable with the knowledge that you're a vegetarian, start suggesting places to eat that offer a greater variety of food choices for you.

In the following sections, I provide pointers on how to stick to a vegetarian diet when you're dining outside the comfort of your own home — either in a restaurant, on campus, in someone's home, or at a fancy event.

When you leave your safe bubble at home (where you have control over what you eat) to venture into the real world, keep the following in mind:

- You're *not* going out to fill your stomach. (Repeat this several times.)

- You *are* going out to bond with friends and family.

- Yes, you can get something to eat when you get back home (or you can eat something before you leave so you don't go out starving).

Eating at restaurants

With all the varied menu selections offered at so many different kinds of fast-food joints and sit-down restaurants, you'll inevitably find something to order. When possible, do your homework beforehand with the help of the following guidelines:

- Bring up the restaurant's menu on the Internet (most restaurants now post their menus online). Look it over to see what you can order.

- If you have questions about the menu, call the restaurant ahead of time (*not* during the lunch or dinner rush!). Here are a few sample questions:

  - Does your guacamole contain gelatin?

  - Are the mozzarella sticks fried in the same oil as the fish sticks and fried chicken?

  - Do you use a meat-flavored soup base for the broth when cooking your rice?

  - Where are the bathrooms? (Okay, so this question doesn't have anything to do with the menu, but it might be a nice thing to know.)

The Web site www.vegguide.org lists vegetarian-friendly restaurants throughout the world. When you type in the name of a place, an address, or a city, the site searches by type of food offered, continent, or location (near an airport, near a hotel, and so on) and displays the results of all nearby restaurants that fit the profile you entered, along with contact information for each entry.

Many ethnic restaurants offer vegetarian entrees. Consider going to a Mexican, Chinese, Japanese, Thai, Middle Eastern, Italian, or Indian restaurant.

When you arrive at the restaurant, look at the menu to see what's offered (if you didn't or couldn't look at the menu ahead of time). If you can't find a vegetarian entrée, keep in mind that some chefs are willing to create an entrée out of side dishes, such as pasta aglio olio (pasta with garlic and oil) topped with roasted veggies. Many of the heart-healthy selections on menus are also vegetarian.

Don't be afraid to make simple requests like, "Please leave off the cheese," or, "Can you make this with olive oil instead of butter?" *How* you ask makes a difference on the reply you receive; being polite can get you far. And if you're comfortable with a harmless little fib, instead of saying you're a vegetarian or vegan, it helps to say that you're allergic to dairy (or meat or eggs or whatever).

When you go to a fast-food establishment, finding a complete, nutritionally balanced meal may be challenging. Many franchises now feature veggie options, but many offerings are loaded with saturated fat. You can check out fast-food restaurants' menus and the nutritional value of each item ahead of time on the Internet. Chains are constantly changing their menus and ingredients, so double-check the status of the foods offered each time you place an order.

The worst-case scenario when you go to any restaurant is that you end up ordering a salad . . . again. But that's okay because you're not letting your vegetarian diet keep you from going out and enjoying time spent with your family and friends.

Daring to dine on campus

Are you automatically paying for a meal plan on campus? If you are, try to eat on campus as often as possible. Many colleges are beginning to cater to students who follow special diets, including the vegetarian diet, so maybe cooking all your own food isn't necessary. Here are a few positive steps you can take:

✔ Make an appointment with the head chef and the director of housing and food services. Find out exactly what foods they offer that fit your diet parameters.

✔ On some campuses, the daily or weekly menu is posted online so you can take a look to determine whether they offer foods you can eat.

> ✔ You may have a choice of meal plans. If you don't see a lot of vegetarian offerings, select the plan with the fewest meals and be prepared to cook many of your own meals in your dorm's kitchenette or your apartment kitchen.

> ✔ Your school may offer foods for special diets (including vegetarian and vegan diets), but you may need to sign up for the meals on a weekly basis. Sign-up forms are usually available online and can be submitted online.

Feasting in other people's homes

Suppose your friends invite you over for dinner. You certainly can't dictate to them what to serve. If you're lucky, they may ask ahead of time whether you have any diet restrictions. It's fine to tell them that you're a vegetarian or vegan, then leave it at that.

Whether you're dining with friends or going home for a meal with your family, offer to bring something (chips and dip, a veggie platter or fruit bowl, a pot of vegetable soup, or something for dessert) so you know you'll have at least one thing you can eat. Whatever you decide to bring, make it mainstream — something they'll recognize. This isn't a good time to show off a new marinade you found for tofu or a new brand of seaweed-rolled, bulgur-filled wraps.

If your host makes a vegetarian dish just for you, thank the person wholeheartedly and express your sincere appreciation of the host's thoughtfulness. Keep in mind, though, that many people think of vegetarians as people who don't eat meat. They don't realize that the chicken broth they used to make the rice is a no-no. Or that you may not eat eggs or dairy, or both. Or perhaps that, instead of steak, the salmon they grilled for you still isn't a good alternative. Politely explain that you don't eat fish, and thank the host profusely for trying to do something special for you. Be appreciative of the host's efforts. Etiquette is the art of behaving well under challenging circumstances.

Considering catered events

People plan dinners at most big events (like wedding receptions and graduation parties) well in advance. If you're attending a wedding or any other large, catered event for a close friend or family member, you can ask her to request a special meal for you.

Vegging out with dining clubs

In many towns, especially large cities, vegetarian dining clubs hold potluck dinners, or the members go out together to eat at restaurants. Under the guise of being a foodie function, this doubles as a dating service where like-minded people can meet. Many dinner clubs are informal offshoots from structured vegetarian clubs, so they don't have their own websites. Still, with a little digging and ingenuity, you can find out whether one exists in your area:

✔ Type your city, your state, and the words *vegetarian dinner clubs* into your favorite search engine. When you find a listing that interests you, click on it to see whether it's a dinner club or a group that goes out to eat regularly.

✔ The following website lists many of the veggie clubs in the United States by state: `www.veganfood.com/vegetarian.htm`.

✔ Check out Facebook and Twitter; both have listings of vegetarian and vegan clubs.

✔ If you can't find a dinner club in your area, form your own. Call up fellow vegetarians and ask them whether they're interested in eating out once a month (or twice a month, or weekly). Suggest that a different person be in charge each month for selecting a place.

Luckily, many caterers nowadays offer a vegetarian entrée as a choice for their guests. Besides, they may offer hors d'oeuvres you can snack on, and the meal is bound to include a salad and either a side of vegetables or a starch (potatoes, rice, or pasta). You won't starve! Instead of concentrating on your stomach, focus on bonding with friends and family you haven't seen in a long time. (It won't hurt to carry a package of peanuts or crackers in your pocket, though, just in case your stomach starts to growl too loudly.)

Overcoming the Trials of Traveling

You don't have to be excessively brave to travel into unfamiliar territory as a vegetarian, but it helps to be prepared. In the following sections, I provide some pointers for vegetarians embarking on road trips and flying adventures.

Road trips

Obviously, with a car you're mobile, and that mobility means you can veer off the highway when necessary to find some pretty good food options. Here are some tips for those car trips:

✔ Before you leave, pack a bag in case the hungries hit while you're on the road and you're still 50 miles from any sign of civilization. Here are a few snacks that can be eaten with one hand while driving:

- Peanut butter and jelly sandwiches
- Grape tomatoes
- Cheese cubes and crackers
- String cheese
- Yogurt tubes
- Cut-up veggies with ranch dip
- Roasted nuts
- Trail mix
- Granola bars
- Raisins
- Fresh fruit
- Snack-sized bags of dry cereal

It's even better if you have room to stick a small cooler on the floor of your vehicle. Instead of making room for ice packs in your cooler, freeze a couple of bottles of water the night before, and pack those in your cooler just before you leave home.

✔ If you know the route you'll be traveling, look online for restaurants with vegetarian fare along the way. Print a list of restaurants along with their addresses to take with you; you may be surprised to find vegetarian restaurants that are just off the highway. If you don't have a GPS, print out directions ahead of time showing how to get to the location from the highway. (Find out more about eating vegetarian at restaurants earlier in this chapter.)

✔ Look online for natural food stores. Many of these places have a deli or cafe. While you're there, stock up on vegetarian snacks for the road.

✔ Don't overlook the capability of your cellphone. Many phones can scan for specific kinds of restaurants along the route you're driving. Many apps are GPS-enabled, too. Here are a few of the free apps available: Yelp, Where, Restaurant Nutrition (this one also gives you the nutrition facts for menu items), and Nearby (here you also get reviews of the restaurants).

✔ Grocery stores offer portable foods. Go inside and pick up some deviled eggs (if you eat them), pasta salad, or fruit salad, or make a to-go container from their salad bar or deli case.

Airport adventures

Eating inside the airport isn't an issue. Most have salads, cheese pizza, or veggie wraps available. (I provide general guidance for dining out earlier in this chapter.) After you board the plane, though, your food options change because at 32,000 feet above the ground, you don't have a lot of choices of where to go to eat!

A few airlines offer vegetarian meals, and some even have vegan selections. The major airlines claim that 30 percent to 50 percent of special meal requests are for vegetarian meals. Keep in mind, however, that due to budget cutbacks, meals are offered only on long-distance flights now or, in some cases, have been discontinued altogether.

Take all the right precautions to ensure you receive a vegetarian or vegan meal (if it's available from the airline of your choice):

- ✔ Tell the travel agent or airline that you need a vegetarian or vegan meal.

- ✔ Call just prior to 72 hours before your flight to confirm your special meal request.

- ✔ Call again to confirm the special meal the day before your flight.

- ✔ When you arrive at the airport, tell the attendant behind the check-in desk about needing a vegetarian meal.

- ✔ When you board the plane, identify yourself to the flight attendant, explaining that you're the one who ordered the vegetarian or vegan meal.

If everything goes smoothly, you'll be served a meal that matches your request, but don't count on that happening. If someone forgets to enter your request into the computer system 72 hours before the flight, the caterers have no way of knowing that such a meal needs to be onboard. As the Boy Scout motto so aptly warns, "Be prepared" — stash some food in your pockets to take onboard just in case.

Chapter 5

Shopping with Savvy

. . . .

In This Chapter

▶ Making a list of food staples to keep on hand

▶ Getting around the grocery store

▶ Understanding the lingo on food labels

. . . .

*T*he ideal steps to take before leaving for the grocery store include taking inventory of what you have on hand, planning your meals for the week, writing down the ingredients you need to pick up, and then looking for coupons in the newspaper store ad, the coupon inserts, and online.

Stop at this point for a reality check: You probably don't get the newspaper and don't have a clue if you'll even be home for dinner three days from now, let alone what you're going to cook by then. But even with the *real way* of grocery shopping, taking inventory of what you have on hand and stocking up on staples are still vital steps. Don't skip them! You should also find the location of the healthiest vegetarian products at your local grocery store and figure out how to decipher food labels as you shop so you don't accidentally buy something filled with meat byproducts. In this chapter, I explain what you need to know to shop smart for vegetarian food.

Stocking Up on Vegetarian Staples

Scream, stomp your feet, or just pout, but eventually you're going to realize that making a grocery list makes sense. With a list, you'll have the food items you need when it's time to cook. It's as simple as that. In the following sections, I get you started with lists of vegetarian pantry, refrigerator, and freezer staples to shop for.

If you have obsessive-compulsive tendencies, now's the time to indulge them. Create a form that lists items by grocery store aisles or departments. Make copies so you always have a backup supply, and tape one of the sheets to the refrigerator. Now you can list the food items you need under the proper category (frozen chopped spinach under the *Frozen* heading, carrots under the *Produce* heading, and so on). Seriously, writing foods down in groups saves you a ton of time at the store. When you have a few minutes to run to the store, just grab the list on the fridge and go.

As you make your grocery list, decide on a few dishes you want to make during the week, look carefully at the ingredients you plan to buy, and consider how to use up any leftover ingredients. For instance, if you decide to make a hot veggie dish using half a bag of fresh spinach, plan on making a spinach salad later in the week to use up the other half of the bag. You'll be amazed by how many meals you can create just from odds and ends in the refrigerator. Use these items up before you go out and buy more food; don't let the food you've already paid for go to waste. (Flip to Chapter 15 for plenty of great ideas on resurrecting leftovers.)

Pantry staples

Some things don't spoil (or at least not quickly), like spices and boxed or canned foods. Load your *larder* (now *there's* a word from the past!) with the items in this section.

Cans, jars, and bottles to consider include

- Beans (black, pinto, navy, kidney, garbanzo, and so on)
- Canned artichokes and roasted red peppers
- Diced tomatoes, tomato sauce, and spaghetti or marinara sauce
- Nut and seed butters (such as peanut, almond, and sunflower)
- Olive oil and vegetable oil
- Salad dressings and other flavorful sauces of your choice

    Beware: Caesar salad dressing and Worcestershire sauce are made with anchovies.

- Soups such as lentil soup and vegetable soup

    Watch out for any soups that may look vegetarian but actually contain beef or chicken broth.

- Vinegar (apple cider and balsamic)

Spices and seasonings to consider include

- ✔ Chili powder, ground cumin, dried parsley flakes, Italian seasoning (this takes the place of oregano and basil), dried cayenne red pepper, dried red pepper flakes, salt, pepper, and any other spices you like

- ✔ Minced garlic in oil (and/or a bulb of fresh garlic)

- ✔ Miso (a Japanese seasoning made by fermenting rice, barley, or soybeans)

- ✔ Mustard (and perhaps ketchup), soy sauce or tamari (which has a deeper flavor than soy sauce), and hot pepper sauce (if you really like spice!)

Boxed and packaged staples to consider include

- ✔ Baking mix (Bisquick or Jiffy Baking Mix to use in place of flour, baking powder, and baking soda) and seasoned breadcrumbs

- ✔ Cereals such as Cheerios, Corn Chex, Kashi, and Raisin Bran

- ✔ Dried fruit, nuts, popcorn kernels, and sesame seeds

- ✔ Instant brown rice and whole grains (such as quinoa, bulgur, and oats), plus containers of single-serving cooked brown rice

- ✔ Ramen oriental flavor noodles (the seasoning packets in the other flavors often contain meat flavorings) or GreeNoodles (green noodles that cook in just 2 minutes!)

- ✔ Soba (a thin Japanese noodle made from buckwheat)

- ✔ Sugar or a natural sugar substitute such as Just Like Sugar, date sugar, or agave syrup

- ✔ Whole-wheat pasta

- ✔ Yuba (tofu skin, frequently referred to as *dried bean curd* or *bean skin*)

If you're sensitive to MSG (monosodium glutamate), avoid products (including pantry staples) with HVP (hydrolyzed vegetable protein). MSG is a flavor enhancer that's used in HVP. According to the Mayo Clinic, some people experience adverse reactions to MSG, including headaches; sweating; flushing; facial pressure or tightness; numbness, tingling, or burning in the face and neck (among other areas); heart palpitations; chest pain; nausea; and weakness.

Refrigerator staples

Some products need refrigeration but stay relatively fresh for a while, so you can keep a small inventory without worrying about them spoiling in a few days.

- Cheeses, sour cream, and eggs
- Fresh fruit
- Fresh vegetables
- Hummus
- Seitan (made from wheat gluten)
- Tempeh (fermented soybeans pressed into a cake)
- Tofu (soaked and pressed soybean curd)
- Tortilla wraps

Freezer staples

Consider loading up your freezer with the following goodies.

- Bread items such as pita bread, whole-wheat bread, English muffins, bagels, and pizza crusts
- Cheese pizza
- Frozen fruits, especially berries
- Meatless protein burgers and crumbles, hash brown patties, and breaded eggplant patties
- Pasta or rice dinners
- Textured vegetable protein (TVP)
- Veggies: plain frozen bags and boxes of vegetables, along with some combination vegetables

You have to occasionally rotate or consume items you store in the freezer, or they can get a wicked taste from freezer burn. Use a black marker to write the date on a package before you freeze it. Needless to say, use up the older stuff first.

Mimicking meat

If you really miss the taste of meat, you're in luck, because some very tasty meat substitutes are available and ready to satisfy your craving. They imitate the taste and texture of real meat but have less fat and fewer calories.

✔ Some of the names of meat substitutes sound a little funny, like *Not-So-Sausage, Wheatballs, Fakin' Bacon, Sham Ham, Tofurky, Not-Wurst,* and *Phony Bologna.* These meat substitutes are typically made of soy but differ in ingredients, in price, and definitely in taste. Experiment to find a brand that suits your taste buds and budget. You can buy the pseudo meat in rolls, loaves, patties, and crumbles. Some of the more common brand names you'll find in your grocer's freezer include *Morningstar Farms, Boca, Gardenburger, Garden Gourmet Vegetarian, Imagine Foods, Yves Veggie Cuisine, Lightlife, Gardein,* and *Sunshine Burgers.* You can even find meatless lunchmeat.

✔ Fishless *Skallops* are made from dried fu, which is made from wheat gluten and is similar to seitan. If you have difficulty finding *Skallops* at your local grocery store, check out Asian markets.

✔ If you're not fond of soy products, have you tried a *Walnut Burger*? It's a patty made from chopped walnuts, mozzarella and cheddar cheeses, eggs, onions, tamari, oil, and a slew of spices.

✔ Tofu is often used in cooking to replicate meat as well. It absorbs flavors so it's perfect to use in a stir-fry with tamari or soy sauce, crumbled to make mock sloppy Joes, and in almost every other way that you would use a real meat product.

Navigating a Grocery Store's Layout

If you're not a seasoned shopper, take an hour to walk through your nearest grocery store. Knowing where everything is located saves you a ton of shopping time down the road.

Figure 5-1 depicts a typical grocery store layout. Here are some navigational tips:

✔ You find the fresh produce and fresh dairy items along the store's perimeter. You also find tofu, tempeh, seitan, and vegan nondairy cheeses in the dairy cases.

✔ It's worth taking a look at the deli (which is also along the store's perimeter). In the prepared food cases, you can often find pickled eggs, pasta and veggie salads, and other vegetarian selections.

✔ Stop to check out the bakery (which is also located along the store's perimeter). Here you find French bread that contains no dairy products and no eggs.

✔ In the freezer section, you find packages of frozen meatless veggie burgers and crumbles along with a large selection of frozen veggies. Some stores carry frozen breaded eggplant slices, vegetarian frozen entrées, and other vegetarian convenience foods.

✔ Dried beans, canned beans, grains, pasta, sauces, condiments, cereal, flours, baking mix, and other nonperishable staples are on the shelves in the center of the store.

✔ Nuts, seeds, and dried fruits are sometimes found in the produce section, but often they are in the center aisles with other dry packaged foods.

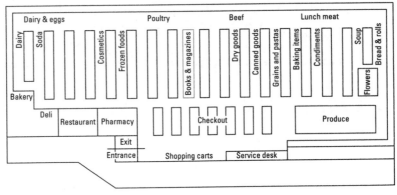

Figure 5-1: A typical grocery store layout.

Splurging on a few vegetarian convenience meals

You can find some marvelous boxed and frozen time-saver meals, but they cost more than preparing the foods from scratch yourself. Still, having a few of these convenience foods in the cupboard or freezer is nice when time is of the essence. Look for

✔ Cans or boxed mixes of vegetarian tacos, vegetarian sloppy Joes, veggie chili, coconut curry, creole dishes, and even veggie BBQ ribs

✔ Boxed and frozen microwavable dinners

✔ Ethnic dinners including Asian, Ethiopian, German, Greek, Indian, Italian, Mexican, Middle Eastern, Slavic, and Spanish

Be sure to compare prices; Asian groceries, outlet groceries, and big-box stores offer these items at a lower cost than a regular grocery store.

Read All about It: Deciphering Food Labels As You Shop

Suppose you're shopping and you spot two soups that look promising: vegetable soup and vegetarian vegetable soup. It turns out that the vegetable soup has beef broth and the vegetarian version doesn't. Then you see baked beans and vegetarian baked beans; the former has pork and the latter doesn't. Picking out the food you need in these examples is fairly easy because the word *vegetarian* appears on the label. Unfortunately, you have to read the list of ingredients — along with the nutrition facts — carefully on most food labels to find out what's inside the package. I provide some pointers on interpreting food labels in the following sections.

Investigating ingredients to steer clear of meat products

When you pick up a package and look at the ingredient list, put it back on the shelf if you see a lot of words that you can't pronounce and certainly can't define; it's probably not vegetarian. So what should you do? Whenever possible, avoid processed foods entirely and stick with the *real thing*. Buy foods that don't need a long list of ingredients (for example, beans, rice, carrots, and bananas).

When you need some processed foods, be on the lookout for ingredients that indicate the inclusion of meat products, and steer clear! The following list is in no way a complete listing of all the terms used on labels that denote the presence of meat, but it includes some of the most common names you'll find:

- **Albumin:** A water-soluble protein found in milk, eggs, muscles, the fiber of many vegetables, and blood plasma

- **Ammonium hydrolyzed protein:** Ammonium salt from animal protein that has been broken down into its component amino acids

- **Bone ash and bone char:** A substance from animals used to turn some brands of sugar white in color

- **Bone meal:** Ground animal bones that are in some vitamins, supplements, and toothpastes

- **Carminic acid (Natural Red Dye #4):** A red dye derived from crushed female beetles that's used in red applesauce, red lollipops, and red food coloring

- **Collagen:** A fibrous protein from animal tissue that's used in gelatin

- **Cystine:** An amino acid found in animals that's used as a nutritional supplement

- **Elastin:** A protein similar to collagen that comes from cows

- **Fatty acids:** Animal-derived acids that are used in foods, cosmetics, and soaps

- **Fish oil:** An oil used in vitamins, supplements, soaps, and milk fortified with vitamin D

- **Gelatin:** A protein from cow and pig bone marrow that's used in cosmetics, as a thickener for fruit gelatins and puddings, and in candy, marshmallows, cakes, ice cream, and some yogurts; also used as a coating for capsules and sometimes in "clearing" wines

- **Glycerines and glycerol:** Byproducts from animal fat that are present in cosmetics, toothpaste, mouthwash, foods, chewing gum, medicines, and more

- **Isinglass:** A form of gelatin from fish used to "clear" wines

- **Lard:** A substance made from rendered pork fat that's present in many baked goods, French fries, refried beans, and many other foods

- **Lecithin:** A substance derived from animal tissues, egg yolks, and occasionally soy that's used in salad dressings to keep oil and vinegar from separating

- **Musk oil:** An oil derived from a wide variety of animals (such as musk deer, beaver, muskrat, and otter) that's used primarily in perfumes but also in food flavorings

- **Natural flavors:** These items can be most anything approved for use in food by the FDA, including meat, seafood, poultry, eggs, and dairy products — check with the product's manufacturer for the exact ingredients

- **Oleic acid:** An omega-9 fatty acid that can come from both plant and animal sources; used in butter and egg substitutes

- **Oleostearine:** A fluid from pressed rendered beef fat that's used primarily in making oleo margarine

- **Pepsin:** A clotting agent that comes from pigs and is used in some cheeses and vitamins

- **Rennet:** Enzymes produced from the stomachs of unweaned calves and sometimes from nonanimal sources; often used in the production of cheese

- **Suet:** A substance made from rendered beef fat and occasionally sheep fat that's used primarily in English dishes such as Yorkshire pudding, English Christmas pudding, and steak and kidney pudding

- **Vitamin D3:** A vitamin derived from fatty fish and/or eggs that can be found in milk, yogurt, margarine, cereal, and bread

In addition to the preceding ingredients, ovo vegetarians have to watch out for dairy products, lacto vegetarians need to watch out for egg products, and vegans have to watch out for both groups! In particular, ovo vegetarians and vegans should steer clear of *casein,* which is the protein found in milk. It's sometimes hidden in pancake syrup, fried food coating mixes, flavored potato chips, textured vegetable protein (TVP), soy cheeses, whipped toppings, and artificial sweeteners. In addition, if you're a lacto vegetarian or a vegan and you see any of the following words in a list of ingredients, it means that egg has been added to the food:

- Apovitellin

- Cholesterol-free egg substitute

- Fat substitutes

- Globulin

- Livetin

- Lysozyme

- Mayonnaise

- Meringue, meringue powder

✔ Ovalbumin

✔ Ovoglobulin

✔ Ovomucin

✔ Ovomucoid

✔ Ovotransferrin

✔ Ovovitellin

✔ Silici albuminate

✔ Vitellin

If you have an iPhone or iPod touch, your shopping experience just got easier: You can download an app that will let you scan an ingredient's label and find out which of the mysterious words actually mean an animal product. You'll immediately get a reply telling you whether the product is vegetarian. Find out more about these apps at www.vegetarianwomen.com/articles/5_ great_iphone_apps.html.

Comparing nutrition facts

Are you ready to be shocked? Look at two different brands of the same product. Turn them over and compare the nutrition numbers. You're going to be surprised at what you find. For example, some salsas have 450 milligrams of sodium, while others have more than 1,000 milligrams of sodium. One cup of whole milk has 5.1 grams of saturated fat, but a cup of 1% milk has only 1.5 grams of saturated fat. A corn tortilla has 52 calories; a flour tortilla has 150 calories.

And that's not all. Did you know that packages labeled *made from real fruit* may have no whole fruit in them at all? *Real fruit* usually translates into a little white grape juice (sugar) mixed with water. The list of ingredients and where in that list the fruit or fruit juice appears indicate exactly how healthy the product is or isn't.

Another example: When buying whole-wheat bread, if *whole wheat* isn't the first or second ingredient listed, then the bread isn't as wholesome as you think it is.

Will you pick up a box of semolina white spaghetti or the healthier multigrain pasta? A head of iceberg lettuce or the healthier bag of spinach or arugula greens? A can of corn or the wiser choice of frozen corn? As a vegetarian, you're eliminating an entire food group from your diet, so getting the proper nutrition from the other foods you eat is very important. Here are some guidelines to follow as you compare the nutrition information on different items

(Figure 5-2 shows a typical label; see Chapter 3 for more information on nutrition):

✔ Start at the top of the label and read the serving size. This information is important to note! For example, a 2-cup package of macaroni and cheese states there are two servings per package. If you plan to eat the entire package for dinner, you have to double all the counts on the label — and that may not be a good thing.

✔ Next up is the category of Total Calories, along with the subcategory Calories From Fat. The recommended number of daily calories (and fat grams) varies for each person. There's a formula from the University of Maryland Medical Center to help you figure out what's right for you at www.umm.edu/heart/caloric.htm.

✔ Fats are listed as Total Fat, Saturated Fat, and Trans Fat. Pick foods with 0 grams of trans fat and no more than 3 to 4 grams of saturated fat per serving. Total fat per day should be around 25 to 27 grams per 1,000 calories consumed; saturated fats should be only 10 percent of the total calories consumed.

✔ Check the Cholesterol category. If it's anything higher than 0, it's not vegan.

✔ Sodium counts are important. The American Heart Association recommends no more than 1,500 milligrams of sodium per day. Compare sodium levels on nutrition labels because they can vary widely. Consider this: One cup of vegetable broth has 1,200 milligrams of sodium; one cup of *low-sodium* vegetable broth has 128 milligrams of sodium. Quite a difference, right?

✔ The category of Total Carbohydrates can be confusing. It's important to eat the right kind of carbs, like whole-grain bread, cereal, pasta, nuts, seeds, legumes, fruits, and vegetables. The carb count on a nutrition label doesn't explain whether the carbs are from good sources, though — you have to read the ingredients label to find that out. The recommended amount of carbs per day should be fewer than 250 grams.

Under Total Carbohydrates is the subcategory of Dietary Fiber. The nutrition label won't tell you whether the fiber in the food is soluble or insoluble, but your body needs both kinds. Your fiber count per day should be more than 20 grams for women and more than 30 grams for men.

✔ Finally, look at the Protein category. The Centers for Disease Control and Prevention recommends that women between the ages of 19 and 70 have 46 grams of protein per day. Men between the ages of 19 and 70 should have 56 grams per day.

Nutrition Facts

Serving Size: About 20g
Servings Per Container: 16

	Amount Per Serving	% Daily Value*
Total Calories	60	
Calories From Fat	15	
Total Fat	2 g	3%
Saturated Fat	1 g	4%
Trans Fat	0 g	
Cholesterol	0 mg	0%
Sodium	45 mg	2%
Total Carbohydrates	15 g	5%
Dietary Fiber	4 g	17%
Sugars	4 g	
Sugar Alcohols (Polyols)	3 g	
Protein	2 g	
Vitamin A		0%
Vitamin C		0%
Calcium		2%
Iron		2%

*Percent Daily Values are based on a 2,000 calorie diet.

Ingredients: Wheat flour, unsweetened chocolate, erythritol, inulin, oat flour, cocoa powder, evaporated cane juice, whey protein concentrate, corn starch (low glycemic), natural flavors, salt, baking soda, wheat gluten, guar gum

Figure 5-2: A typical nutrition label.

You can use the nutrition facts on a food label not only to help limit those items you want to cut back on (like fat) but also to increase those nutrients you need to consume in greater amounts (like fiber).

Chapter 6

Setting the Scene for Vegetarian Cooking

● ●

In This Chapter

▶ Getting necessary kitchen gear

▶ Organizing your kitchen

▶ Distinguishing different cooking methods

● ●

*B*eing a college student, your kitchen is likely minuscule, and you probably share that small kitchen with roommates. If you're lucky, you may have one shelf of the refrigerator to call your own. Not to worry, though — with a little planning, your kitchen can be organized and efficient, which makes cooking on a regular basis a lot easier. In this chapter, I describe the essential gear you need to cook vegetarian meals, provide some tips on how to organize everything in your kitchen, and give you the lowdown on basic cooking methods.

Determining the Tools, Gadgets, and Serving Pieces You Need

As soon as you step into your kitchen, you'll realize very quickly that your shelves can't come close to holding all the cooking gear that's available for purchase, so it's decision time. In the following sections, I describe the cooking tools and gadgets you need, along with the basic serving pieces to have on hand.

 If you want to save big bucks on buying kitchen utensils, check out dollar stores and garage sales. For larger items, you can get good deals at big-box stores and even online stores like www. overstock.com; www.amazon.com offers used appliances for even bigger savings.

Picking out basic cooking tools

No kitchen is complete without basic gear like pots, pans, bakeware, utensils, and more. The following sections cover these requisite items.

Pots and pans

You can never have too many pots and pans, unless, of course, you have a small kitchen. The basic pots and pans you need include the following (see Figure 6-1):

✔ One small (8-inch) and one medium (10-inch) nonstick skillet

✔ One small (2-quart) and one medium (3-quart) nonstick saucepan

✔ One pot large enough to cook pasta and soup (6-quart)

Figure 6-1: Useful pots and pans.

If you're buying new pans for your kitchen, steer clear of aluminum pans; unless the aluminum is coated with an exterior color coating of silicone polyester, the pans will discolor over time and aren't dishwasher-safe. Food sticks more in aluminum pans, so you either have to soak the pans after using them or use a scouring pad to get off the baked-on residue. Instead, look for Teflon-coated stainless-steel pans.

Bakeware

Make room for bakeware, too; either metal or glass will do. Here's what you need:

✔ One 8-inch or 9-inch square baking pan

✔ One 9-x-13-inch baking pan

✔ One 9-inch pie plate

✔ One 10-x-15-inch baking sheet

✔ One 12-cup cupcake/muffin tin

✔ Two large (1-cup) custard cups

✔ One cooling rack

Utensils

If you've ever walked through a fancy kitchen supply store, you know exactly how many kitchen gadgets there are to tempt you. My advice? Keep it simple. With the following items, you can cook most anything:

✔ Spoons: one wooden spoon, one large metal serving spoon, and one large slotted spoon

✔ One wire whisk

✔ Spatulas: one large metal or plastic spatula or turner, and one rubber spatula

✔ Potato masher (if you're not familiar with what this tool looks like, check out Figure 6-2)

potato masher

yikes!

Figure 6-2: A potato masher.

✔ Pasta ladle

✔ Vegetable peeler

✔ Box grater

✔ Tongs

✔ A set of dry measuring cups (¼ cup, ⅓ cup, ½ cup, and 1 cup), and a 1-cup glass measuring cup for liquids

✔ A set of measuring spoons (¼ teaspoon, ⅓ teaspoon, ½ teaspoon, 1 teaspoon, and 1 tablespoon)

✔ Knives: one chef's knife (the workhorse), one paring knife (for small jobs), and one serrated knife (for cutting breads so they don't squish) — check them out in Figure 6-3

Figure 6-3: A set of handy knives for the kitchen.

Other handy cooking gear

Here are a few more things you should have on hand:

✔ A timer (if the one on the stove or microwave doesn't work)

✔ Three glass or ceramic mixing bowls (one small, one medium, and one large)

✔ A strainer or colander (having both a large 10-inch one and a small 6-inch one is helpful)

✔ A can opener

✔ A wood or plastic cutting board

Don't even consider a glass cutting board because it will dull your knives.

✔ Kitchen towels and a couple of potholders

If you're watching pennies, don't go out and buy new plastic food containers for leftovers; a lot of foods come packaged in plastic containers that you can wash out and reuse to store food. But do stock up on aluminum foil, plastic wrap, storage baggies, and paper towels.

Getting by with essential gadgets

The recipes in this book assume that you have three major appliances at your disposal:

✔ A refrigerator with at least a small freezer

✔ A stove with an oven

✔ A microwave

Here are some smaller electric gadgets you should consider:

✔ A blender and a food processor usually produce the same outcome when it comes to chopping, mashing, or totally pulverizing food. The recipes in this book use a blender (because it's less expensive), but you can use a food processor in its place if you already own one (or if your parents gave you a hand-me-down).

✔ A mixer is a necessity, but a big mixer isn't. A hand-held one can do the job and takes less cupboard space (and money!) than a stand mixer.

✔ A toaster oven is multifunctional. You can bake, broil, and toast in it, and that's good. But it's larger than a plain ol' toaster, and that's bad. If your kitchen is small, the toaster oven goes.

✔ A slow cooker (also known as a crockpot) is so easy to use, but it takes up storage space. If you decide to get one, get a small one (2-quart capacity).

If you don't have room to store a slow cooker, most slow-cooker recipes can be made on the stove in a saucepan; cook over medium heat and stir often.

✔ If you're a coffee drinker, get a small 4-cup coffee maker.

Deciding on dishes and silverware

Chances are you won't ever have more than four people over for dinner at one time, so you can limit the number of dishes you have on hand. You need only the following:

✔ Four each: dinner plates, salad plates, soup bowls, mugs or cups, and 8-ounce drinking glasses

✔ One serving platter (no need for serving bowls; good-looking mixing bowls can handle the job)

And though I'm sure that this doesn't apply to you personally, some people use a fork or spoon and then toss it into the sink for a month, or until they get around to washing dishes. These poor souls need *lots* of utensils. You, on the other hand, are wise enough to clean them right away so they're ready to use the next time you need them. Therefore, the following should suffice:

- Six each: forks, knives, soup spoons, and coffee spoons
- One serving fork
- Two serving spoons

Making the Most of Limited Kitchen Space

You have no control over the layout of your kitchen, but you *do* have control over how that space is used. Look at every nook and cranny and think about how to use the space more effectively. In the following sections, I provide pointers on how to organize the food, tools, gadgets, serving pieces, and other essentials in your kitchen.

Before you give your kitchen an organizational makeover, you need to clean up and reduce clutter. Reducing clutter means that you have to find a place to stash kitchen stuff out of sight. Everything needs an assigned place, and you need to make sure that each item is returned to that place after each use. (In case you're wondering what constitutes *clutter,* it's almost everything that's on your counters now.)

Before you drill or hammer even one hole into a wall or cupboard, check with your landlord or read over the dorm regulations to be sure you're allowed to do that. You don't want to risk losing your security deposit or being fined for damaging the premises.

Putting away food

It's time to take charge of your food! You probably have either a small pantry or some cabinets for stashing your ingredients. First, store canned and jarred goods at eye level so you can easily see what you have. Group similar kinds together (soups, canned beans and veggies, pasta sauces, and so on); that way, you'll quickly know when you're running low on a particular item. On the shelf above the canned goods, put the baking products, grains, and other bags and boxed items.

To keep your food supply super organized, try the following: Get two large plastic tubs that will fit on your shelves. In one, put dessert items (cookie mixes, baking mix, brown sugar, and so on). In the other, put other dry food products (such as cereals, pastas, rice, and beans). The tubs will keep everything neat and together.

 Mount a spice rack on the inside of one of the cupboard doors to save some space, or you can nail a narrow shelf on a wall at eye level and store spices there. If you have to keep spices on a shelf in the cupboard (because you're not allowed to put holes in anything), put them on a turntable so you can see what you have with a quick turn. (Whatever you do, don't store your spices in direct sunlight, which can rob them of their flavor.)

 Here's a fun way to store some treats: If your sink is underneath a window, suspend a three-tier hanging basket beside the window (see Figure 6-4). Fill the baskets with teas, packages of pasta, or other goodies — anything that's not too heavy. Just fill them with items that you don't have to store in a cupboard, leaving more cupboard space for large things.

Figure 6-4: A three-tier hanging basket.

Stashing tools and gadgets

Most of the stuff you need to store in your kitchen likely consists of cooking tools and small appliances. Consider the following storage solutions:

- ✔ If the center of your kitchen has a small open space, get a small, rolling kitchen cart; you can order them online from big-box store websites for as little as $25. It gives you more working area on the top and additional storage space underneath. Use this space to store some of your larger appliances (your mixer, blender, and so on), pots, and pans, or put potatoes and onions into attractive bowls and set them on the cart's shelf.

- ✔ If your kitchen has a bar and bar stools rather than a table and chairs, you're in luck; you can use that extra floor space for storage. Check garage sales and secondhand shops for storage units. If money is tight, get a few concrete blocks and spray-paint them the color of your kitchen. Then go to a lumberyard or a home improvement store and get two or three flat, sturdy pieces of wood; lay the wood on top of the blocks to create your own shelving (see Figure 6-5). Everyone will see whatever you choose to store on these shelves, so keep them neat.

Of course, you can use your kitchen's built-in storage for your gear. Stash large, heavy items — such as your pots and pans, mixer, blender or food processor, and crockpot — in the kitchen's lower cupboards. While you're down there, install lid racks inside the cupboard to save a bit of room. One type of rack slides out from the cupboard; another type of rack attaches to the inside of the door of the cupboard (see Figure 6-6).

You probably won't fill some cupboard shelves to the top. Use this air space by getting raised metal- or vinyl-covered racks that stand on the shelves, giving you two tiers to store lids. You can also use this area to store cups, glasses, spices, extra canned goods, or anything else that isn't too tall.

You can also store pans in the pull-out drawer in the bottom of your stove. If it doesn't have one, you can get attractive ceiling racks designed specifically to hold pans. If the kitchen has a blank wall, think about hanging a vinyl or metal grid, or even a trellis, and use it to hang small pots and skillets.

Figure 6-5: Do-it-yourself kitchen storage.

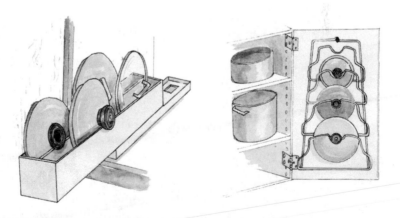

Figure 6-6: Lid racks inside cupboards.

Here are some other ideas for stashing tools and gadgets:

✔ Do you have a pitcher or wide-mouthed vase? Either of these is a perfect container to hold large cooking utensils. Set it next to the stove, where it's both functional and attractive.

✔ If you have dead space above the cabinets or on top of the refrigerator, use it to store nested mixing bowls.

✔ Hang a canvas shoe rack on the back of the kitchen door to store rolled-up kitchen towels, paper towels, and cooking utensils.

Storing dishes and silverware

Stack your plates and bowls on top of one another to save space in your cupboards. You can get hooks (also known as cup hangers) from a home improvement store and install them to hang your cups above the dishes.

Reserve one drawer for silverware, and store your silverware in small drawer organizers. If space is a true problem, though, here's another alternative: Save frozen juice cans. Clean them well, dry them, and cover them with contact paper. Put your silverware inside the cans and set the cans in the center of your kitchen table as a centerpiece.

Stowing other kitchen essentials

If you keep recipes or notes on the counter — don't! Hang a small bulletin board on the inside of one of the cabinet doors and post your notes there.

If you have a collection of cookbooks, stack them on a shelf in your rolling kitchen cart (if you have one) or in a small book rack placed on top of your refrigerator. Another option is to install a box-type frame on a kitchen wall and stack your books in it. You can even buy a vinyl milk crate, turn it on its side, slide your books in there, and then put a comfy stuffed pillow on top of it.

Don't forget to save one drawer for wax paper, aluminum foil, plastic wrap, storage baggies, and paper napkins. In addition, you can mount a paper towel rack under a cabinet near the sink so that it doesn't take up counter space.

What about other stuff for your kitchen, like a trash can and cleaning supplies? Consider the following solutions:

✔ Fill a small corner in the kitchen by putting up a screen. A screen instantly gives a room personality, plus you can hang hooks on the back to hold your mop and broom.

✔ Some older kitchens have a sink that's exposed underneath so the pipes show. Using Velcro, attach a piece of material around the sink to conceal the pipes (see Figure 6-7). You've just created a place to hide household cleaners, a bucket, and a trash can.

Figure 6-7: Hiding stuff under your sink.

Getting a Grip on Cooking Methods

Being a cook, I love to ramble on and on about different cooking methods. You can prepare and cook foods in so many ways that covering all the methods can be a book by itself. But the following is a quick guide to the basic methods you need to get cookin' right away:

✔ **Bake:** Putting something in a pan and dry cooking it in the oven. (This general term refers to anything that's cooked in the oven.)

- ✔ **Beat** or **whip:** Mixing ingredients to incorporate air until the mixture is smooth.

- ✔ **Blanch:** Cooking food briefly immersed in boiling water, then plunging it into ice water to stop the cooking process.

- ✔ **Boil:** Cooking food in liquid that's so hot that it's bubbling vigorously.

- ✔ **Braise:** Browning food slowly on all sides in a pan coated with melted butter or oil, then adding liquid and cooking it, covered, over low heat until it's tender.

- ✔ **Bread:** Coating food with a flour or breadcrumb mix before cooking.

- ✔ **Broil:** Cooking food by exposing it to a flame or another direct source of intense heat, such as over a grill or under an electric element.

- ✔ **Chop:** Cutting food into small pieces (about ½-inch square).

- ✔ **Dice:** Cutting food into small cubes (about ¼-inch square).

- ✔ **Fold:** Using a whisk or rubber spatula to gently incorporate ingredients so they don't deflate.

- ✔ **Fry:** Cooking food in hot oil or fat over direct heat (usually on top of a stove or in a deep fryer).

- ✔ **Grate:** Reducing food to shreds by rubbing it against an abrasive surface that has many sharp-edged openings.

- ✔ **Julienne:** Cutting food into matchstick-size strips.

- ✔ **Marinate:** Coating food with a dry rub or immersing it in an acidic-based liquid to tenderize and flavor it before cooking.

- ✔ **Mince:** Chopping food into very small pieces (about ⅛-inch square).

- ✔ **Mix:** Stirring ingredients together with a spoon to blend them.

- ✔ **Poach:** Slowly cooking food that's submerged in barely boiling liquid. Water is used for eggs, broth or stock is used for vegetables, and red wine or light sugar syrup is used for fruits.

- ✔ **Purée:** Blending foods (usually in a blender) until they're completely smooth.

- ✔ **Reduce:** Boiling a liquid so some of the volume evaporates, which thickens the mixture and intensifies the flavor.

✔ **Roast:** Slowly cooking large pieces of food, uncovered, in the dry heat of the oven. This term typically refers to meats and vegetables (not baked goods), and the food is often placed on a rack so it isn't directly immersed in the pan juices.

✔ **Sauté:** Quickly cooking small pieces of food in oil in a skillet so the food sears (browns).

✔ **Shred:** Cutting food into finer strips than julienning.

✔ **Simmer:** Cooking food slowly in a liquid on the stove at or just below the boiling point.

✔ **Skim:** Removing foam or fat from the surface of broth or soup.

✔ **Slice:** Cutting a thin piece from a large item of food.

✔ **Steam:** Cooking food with moist heat vapors (for example, cooking food over boiling water rather than in boiling water).

✔ **Stew:** Slowly simmering food in a liquid in a pan on top of the stove.

✔ **Stir-fry:** Cooking food super-fast in a small amount of oil in a skillet or wok over high heat.

Part II
Vegetarian Vittles

The 5th Wave   By Rich Tennant

"Do you want the cheese on your sandwich melted or not? Hurry up—the iron's hot."

In this part . . .

This part is where the cooking begins! Breakfast, lunch, and dinner recipes are divided into grab 'n' go recipes (which you can make in about 5 to 10 minutes) and recipes that take 20 to 30 minutes or less. No matter how many commitments you have, no matter what your class schedule is like, and no matter how many items are still on your to-do list, you can find 5 minutes to create a healthy and delicious meal. The recipes use ingredients that you can buy at a regular grocery store, which saves you time and money when you shop. And many recipes suggest substitute ingredients you can use in case you've run out of something called for in the recipe.

Chapter 7

Five Minutes or Less: Grab 'n' Go Breakfasts

*O*n some days (okay, most days), you may not have time to cook breakfast. But even if you have only a few minutes, you can throw something together in the kitchen and eat it on your way to class. (If you drive to school, be sure to grab a napkin for your dashboard dining — not that I recommend dashboard dining as a safe driving practice, mind you.) With the recipes in this chapter, you can't use the excuse that you don't have time to make something to eat.

You've heard it so many times before, but it's for real: *You need to eat breakfast.* Eating good food in the morning, even if it's just a small amount, jump-starts your body so you have more energy all day. Really! Sure, it's a bummer to drag yourself out of bed five minutes early each day just so you have time to eat before going to class, but hey, it's a small price to pay for good nutrition.

Your ideal breakfast includes food from all the following categories:

✔ Whole grains (such as oatmeal, whole-grain bagels, breads, or cereal)

✔ A low-fat protein (such as beans, eggs, or peanut butter)

✔ A low-fat dairy item (such as 1% milk, low-fat yogurt, or low-fat cheese)

✔ Fruits or vegetables (veggies can be added to omelets)

Noshing on No-Cook Breakfasts

If you skip breakfast, you'll be starving by lunchtime, and at that point you'll wolf down any food you can find. Nutritional value will be the last thing on your mind. Be smart! You need to eat the right foods at the right times to keep your body working the way it's supposed to. Take time — *make* time — for breakfast. All you need is a few minutes — honestly! The no-cook recipes in this section are a great start.

Wraps are an excellent no-cook option at breakfast or for any other meal. To wrap any filling in a tortilla, simply lay the tortilla on a flat surface and spoon or lay the filling down the center, about three-fourths of the way down. Fold the bottom flap up over the bottom portion of the filling (so the filling doesn't ooze out at the bottom), and then wrap one side of the tortilla over the filling and tuck the edge under the filling. Now fold the remaining flap of the tortilla over the top, securing the filling inside (see Figure 7-1).

Emergency treats for mornings when you oversleep

If you oversleep, don't panic and think, "What to do . . . what to do?" Have some emergency rations handy that you can stick into your pocket or book bag. These can include:

✔ Protein bars, trail mix, or a bag of nuts with dried fruit

✔ Pita chips, oat bran sesame sticks, flaxseed crackers, or soy crisps with a handful of cheese cubes

✔ Roasted pumpkin seeds with a container of yogurt

Quiz time: What's missing from this list? If you guessed things like toaster tarts, sweet rolls, and donuts, yup, you're right. You are what you eat, so eat healthy!

HOW TO WRAP A TORTILLA

1. PLACE A TORTILLA ON A FLAT SURFACE.

2. PLACE THE FILLING ON THE TORTILLA, CENTER IT AND LEAVE ROOM AT THE BOTTOM.

3. FOLD UP THE BOTTOM FLAP, MAKING SURE YOU FOLD ENOUGH TO HOLD IN THE FILLING.

4. FOLD ONE SIDE UP AND OVER THE FILLING.

5. MAKE A SMALL FOLD WITH THE LEFTOVER SIDE SO THE BOTTOM STAYS FOLDED.

6. FOLD THE LAST SIDE OF THE TOR-TILLA DOWN AND OVER THE FILLING.

Figure 7-1: Wrap any filling in a tortilla for a quick no-cook meal.

Ran-Out-of-Cereal Breakfast

Prep time: 1 min • **Yield:** 1 serving

Ingredients	*Directions*
3 large caramel-corn rice cakes	**1** Crumble the rice cakes into a bowl and pour in the milk.
¾ cup low-fat milk or soymilk	

Per serving: *Calories 228 (From Fat 23); Fat 3g (Saturated 1g); Cholesterol 7mg; Sodium 178mg; Carbohydrate 43g (Dietary Fiber 1g); Protein 8g.*

Tip: Make this breakfast in a plastic bowl or large paper cup if you're going to eat it on the run.

Banana in a Bun

Prep time: 1 min • **Yield:** 1 serving

Ingredients	*Directions*
1 tablespoon honey	*1* Drizzle the honey over the inside of the bun.
1 whole-wheat hot dog bun	
1 tablespoon chopped walnuts	*2* Sprinkle chopped nuts over the honey.
1 medium banana, peeled	
	3 Place the banana over the walnuts. Hold the bun closed and enjoy!

Per serving: Calories 338 (From Fat 63); Fat 7g (Saturated 1g); Cholesterol 0mg; Sodium 207mg; Carbohydrate 70g (Dietary Fiber 8g); Protein 6g.

Vary It! You can enjoy the basic recipe by itself, but you can also go wild and add any of the following toppings: low-fat peanut butter; jam, jelly, or preserves (the flavor is your choice); chocolate hazelnut spread; honey; raisins; coconut; or mini chocolate chips.

Tip: If you really want to be decadent, wrap the banana and bun in wax paper, warm them in the microwave, and drizzle them with chocolate sauce. Wow — we're talking good!

Breakfast in a Cup 1

Prep time: 3 min • **Yield:** 1 serving

Ingredients	Directions
¾ cup low-fat cottage cheese Dash of cinnamon	**1** Spoon the cottage cheese into a large plastic cup and stir in the cinnamon.
2 tablespoons low-fat granola ½ cup fresh blueberries	**2** Sprinkle the cottage cheese mixture with some granola and put the blueberries on top.

Per serving: Calories 203 (From Fat 23); Fat 3g (Saturated 1g); Cholesterol 7mg; Sodium 720mg; Carbohydrate 23g (Dietary Fiber 3g); Protein 22g.

Vary It! Feel free to use whole-grain cereal in place of the granola and either strawberries, raspberries, or peaches in place of the blueberries.

Breakfast in a Cup II

Prep time: 3 min • **Yield:** 1 serving

Ingredients	Directions
1 small banana, sliced	**1** Place the banana slices in the bottom of a large plastic cup. Spread the jam over the bananas.
1 teaspoon all-fruit strawberry jam	
1 container (6 ounces) low-fat strawberry yogurt or soy yogurt	**2** Top the bananas and jam with the yogurt and sprinkle the top with the crackers.
¼ cup crumbled cinnamon graham crackers	

Per serving: Calories 378 (From Fat 40); Fat 5g (Saturated 2g); Cholesterol 11mg; Sodium 241mg; Carbohydrate 78g (Dietary Fiber 3g); Protein 10g.

Note: Cinnamon graham crackers need to be a staple in your kitchen cupboard — seriously. They're great to grab for a snack, to crumble on top of a cobbler, or in this case, to sprinkle over a breakfast parfait of sorts.

Peanut Butter Stick

Prep time: 3 min • **Yield:** 1 serving

Ingredients	Directions
2 tablespoons low-fat peanut butter	*1* Spread the peanut butter over the entire surface of the tortilla.
1 (8-inch) whole-wheat flour tortilla	
2 tablespoons whole-grain oat cereal	*2* Sprinkle the cereal over the peanut butter so it sticks and doesn't fall out of the tortilla as you're eating it.
1 teaspoon pancake syrup	*3* Drizzle the tortilla with the syrup, roll it into a stick, and enjoy!

Per serving: Calories 304 (From Fat 117); Fat 13g (Saturated 2g); Cholesterol 0mg; Sodium 347mg; Carbohydrate 41g (Dietary Fiber 4g); Protein 12g.

Vary It! A good oat cereal to use in this recipe is Cheerios; if you're out of Cheerios, you can use a flake-type cereal.

Vary It! To add fiber, sprinkle on some flaxseeds, sunflower seeds, and/or crushed peanuts before rolling.

Date Roll-ups

Prep time: 5 min • **Yield:** 1 serving

Ingredients	Directions
2 slices soft whole-wheat bread 3 tablespoons low-fat soft cream cheese 6 pitted dates 1 tablespoon chopped walnuts	**1** Using a rolling pin, roll the bread slices flat. If you don't have a rolling pin, give the bread slices a few quick pounds with the palm of your hand to flatten them so that they roll easier without cracking.
	2 Spread the cream cheese on one side of each bread slice.
	3 Lay 3 dates on one edge of each bread slice.
	4 Sprinkle the walnuts over the dates, dividing evenly.
	5 Roll each slice of bread, starting with the side where the dates are lined up. After it's rolled, press down lightly so that the cream cheese seals the bread seam.

Per serving: Calories 421 (From Fat 131); Fat 15g (Saturated 6g); Cholesterol 23mg; Sodium 480mg; Carbohydrate 65g (Dietary Fiber 8g); Protein 12g.

Tip: If you don't have soft cream cheese that comes in a tub, use solid block cream cheese. Soften 3 tablespoons quickly by putting it on a dish and nuking it for 10 seconds.

Banana Wrap

Prep time: 5 min • **Yield:** 1 serving

Ingredients	Directions
⅓ cup low-fat cottage cheese	**1** In a small bowl, stir together the cottage cheese, granola, cranberries, brown sugar, cinnamon, and honey. Spread this mix on the tortilla.
2 tablespoons low-fat granola	
1 teaspoon dried cranberries	
2 teaspoons brown sugar	**2** Lay the banana on top of the cottage cheese mixture.
Dash cinnamon	
1 tablespoon honey	
1 (10-inch) whole-wheat flour tortilla	**3** Wrap the tortilla by folding up the bottom and folding in the sides (refer to Figure 7-1).
1 small banana, peeled and cut in half lengthwise	

Per serving: Calories 470 (From Fat 43); Fat 5g (Saturated 2g); Cholesterol 3mg; Sodium 420mg; Carbohydrate 96g (Dietary Fiber 5g); Protein 19g.

Tip: If you're really running short on time, just put dollops of the cottage cheese on the tortilla and then put the rest of the ingredients on top in layers; forget about mixing everything together in a bowl first.

Vary It! If you don't have cottage cheese, use ¼ cup cream cheese or Greek yogurt. If you don't have granola, use whole-wheat cereal. If you don't have brown sugar, you can probably make this recipe without it. But if you're out of cinnamon and honey, seriously consider making another breakfast!

Blending Breakfast Beverages

Sure you need to eat breakfast, but you can also drink it! A drinkable breakfast is perfect for a college student on the run. It saves you time in the morning because you dump everything into a blender at the same time. It also pumps you full of nutrition to get you through the day. Try one of the recipes in this section to discover how great a breakfast beverage can be.

Milk, yogurt, berries, bananas, vanilla or almond flavoring, and ice are the basic ingredients in a breakfast beverage. You can choose what else to include in your slushie, smoothie, or shake:

- ✔ If you like drinks that are jazzed up a bit, add something extra like peanut butter, cocoa, papaya, or mango.

- ✔ If you want more fiber, add oatmeal, flaxseed (or flaxseed meal), nuts, and/or protein powders. (See the sidebar "The skinny on vegetable protein powder" for more information.)

- ✔ If you really want a power-packed drink, make a smoothie instead of a slushie (a *smoothie* is just a thicker slushie that usually has a milk base instead of an ice base). In addition to or instead of some of the preceding ingredients, you can toss in spinach leaves, baby carrots, sliced apples, ginger root, sunflower or sesame seeds, and even some salsa.

The skinny on vegetable protein powder

Vegetable protein powder can be made from all sorts of natural foods, including some or all of the following: peas, whey, soy, rice, potato, barley, bran, and more. Protein powder is available at almost all drug stores and health food stores. Protein powders sound like a great idea in theory, but keep in mind that no more than ¼ of your daily protein should come from powders. You're much better off getting nutrition from whole foods than from powders because a whole food gives you a complete package of nutrition that a powder can't deliver.

If you work out, the most effective protein powder is a casein-whey combination. *Casein* is very high in the important amino acids that you need, but it's absorbed very slowly into your system, so it doesn't act fast enough when you're exercising. That's why you need a powder that also contains *whey*, which is absorbed very quickly and helps give you the energy you need when you work out. Drink the protein drink immediately after you exercise, because that's when your muscles are like sponges; they soak up nutrients quickly, which helps the strained muscles repair and recover.

Raspberry Smoothie

Prep time: 1 min • **Yield:** 2 servings

Ingredients	Directions
1½ cups frozen raspberries	*1* Combine the raspberries, yogurt, milk, and vanilla in a blender; whip for 30 seconds or until smooth.
12 ounces low-fat lemon yogurt	
¾ cup low-fat milk	
1 tablespoon vanilla	

Per serving: Calories 242 (From Fat 32); Fat 4g (Saturated 2g); Cholesterol 12mg; Sodium 159mg; Carbohydrate 39g (Dietary Fiber 6g); Protein 12g.

Note: If you don't have a blender, make this smoothie with a hand mixer or an immersion blender (also called a wand or a hand blender), but in any case, make it! It's wonderfully delicious.

Tip: If you don't have a dishwasher and don't have time to wash out the blender container after making the smoothie, at least fill it with water so the leftover sticky stuff doesn't adhere like concrete.

High Protein Shake

Prep time: 1 min • **Yield:** 1 serving

Ingredients	*Directions*
1 cup vanilla almond milk	*1* Place all ingredients in a blender and blend on high speed for about 30 seconds or until smooth.
1 tablespoon flaxseed meal	
1 serving vanilla vegetable protein powder (follow the recommended amount from package directions)	
¾ cup frozen strawberries	
¼ teaspoon vanilla	
10 drops agave syrup	

Per serving: Calories 344 (From Fat 87); Fat 10g (Saturated 0g); Cholesterol 0mg; Sodium 558mg; Carbohydrate 38g (Dietary Fiber 9g); Protein 28g.

Vary It! If you don't have frozen strawberries, it's okay to use fresh or frozen blackberries, raspberries, or blueberries instead.

Note: Agave (uh-gah-vay) syrup is made from the same plant that tequila comes from. Agave is the nectar from the plant. It has a low glycemic level (11 to 30) and has a sweeter taste than honey. It doesn't break down when heated so you can use it in baking without fear of a bitter aftertaste. Agave comes in different colors, but most agave nectar is a shade of toasty brown. You can find the nectar in a bottle at most grocery stores where pancake and maple syrup is sold.

Note: Flaxseed meal is made from ground-up flaxseeds. The dark meal has a distinctive taste, but the golden meal is virtually tasteless so you can add it to any food. Flax is exceptionally high in omega-3 fatty acids, fiber (both soluble and insoluble), and protein. It's packaged in bags and sold at most grocery stores where you find wheat flour and alternative flours. Because flaxseed meal has no preservatives, be sure to keep it frozen so it doesn't turn rancid.

Protein Punch Smoothie

Prep time: 1 min • **Yield:** 1 serving

Ingredients	*Directions*
1 cup low-fat milk	**1** Place all the ingredients in a blender and blend on high for 30 seconds or until the mixture is a thick purée.
1 serving vanilla vegetable protein powder (follow the recommended amount from package directions)	
1½ tablespoons unsweetened cocoa	
1 medium banana, peeled and sliced	
1 tablespoon low-fat peanut butter	
½ teaspoon vanilla	
8 drops agave syrup	
4 to 5 ice cubes	

Per serving: Calories 441 (From Fat 87); Fat 10g (Saturated 4g); Cholesterol 10mg; Sodium 301mg; Carbohydrate 61g (Dietary Fiber 9g); Protein 35g.

Vary It! As with most recipes that call for milk, if you're dairy-free, you have several other choices, such as milk made from almonds, rice, soy, hemp, or coconut.

Throwing Together Quick-Cook Breakfasts

A hot breakfast that can be made in 5 or so minutes to warm your tummy on a cold morning — what a radical idea. The following recipes are proof that it can be done.

 Just know that some of these breakfasts don't have all four food groups that you need as a vegetarian (I describe them at the start of this chapter). But if you grab a piece of fruit or have a glass of orange juice with breakfast, or maybe add a hard-boiled egg or a slice of wheat toast, you'll get all the good stuff your body needs in the morning. (See the sidebar "The easy way to make hard-boiled eggs" for tips on whipping up a batch of eggs.)

The easy way to make hard-boiled eggs

If you have a few free minutes on the weekend, boil a batch of hard-boiled eggs to have handy during the week. Eat them for breakfast, make an egg salad sandwich for lunch, and cut them into salads for dinner. Hard-boiled eggs are easy to grab when you don't have time to cook.

If you're wondering how to make hard-boiled eggs that are cooked inside but don't have that yucky, ugly, gray ring around the yolk, here's a way that works.

1. **Put the eggs in a small pan and add enough cold water to totally cover them. Set the pan on the stove and bring the water to a boil.**

2. **When the water comes to a boil, lower the heat to medium high and cook the eggs for exactly 11 minutes.** (Not 10 minutes or 12 minutes; timing here is crucial.)

3. **Immediately drain off the boiling water and run cold tap water over the eggs until they're cool when you touch them (about 1 minute).**

4. **Remove the eggs from the water and refrigerate them.**

Hint: If you add a couple drops of vinegar to the boiling water as the eggs cook, it softens the shells just enough that the eggs are easier to peel.

Deluxe PB&J

Prep time: 1 min • **Cook time:** 1 min • **Yield:** 1 serving

Ingredients	*Directions*
2 slices whole-grain bread	*1* Toast the bread and then spread the peanut butter on one slice of toast; spread the cream cheese on the second slice of toast.
1 tablespoon low-fat peanut butter	
1 tablespoon low-fat soft cream cheese or tofu cream cheese	*2* Lay the strawberries on top of the cream cheese and cover with the other piece of toast, peanut-butter side down.
3 large fresh strawberries, sliced thin	

Per serving: Calories 278 (From Fat 113); Fat 13g (Saturated 5g); Cholesterol 16mg; Sodium 386mg; Carbohydrate 34g (Dietary Fiber 6g); Protein 11g.

Vary It! No strawberries on hand? No problem. Use blueberries, blackberries, raspberries, or thinly sliced peaches or nectarines in place of the strawberries. You can substitute the peanut butter with a different kind of nut or seed butter, too.

Tip: If you slip in a few mini chocolate chips, no one will ever know; just be sure to put them right on the peanut butter so they stick and don't fall out.

Chocoholic Pancake Sandwich

Prep time: 2 min • **Cook time:** 30 sec • **Yield:** 1 serving

Ingredients	*Directions*
2 frozen whole-wheat pancakes	*1* Place the pancakes side by side on a large dish, cover with damp paper towels, and microwave on high for 30 seconds, or until the pancakes are warmed.
1 tablespoon chocolate hazelnut spread (such as Nutella)	
2 tablespoons chocolate syrup	*2* Spread one pancake with chocolate hazelnut spread. Drizzle the chocolate sauce over the top.
	3 Place the second pancake on top, and then cut the sandwich in half.

Per serving: Calories 333 (From Fat 77); Fat 9g (Saturated 2g); Cholesterol 14mg; Sodium 331mg; Carbohydrate 61g (Dietary Fiber 4g); Protein 5g.

Vary It! Because you can't even pretend that this is a healthy breakfast, you may as well splurge even more by sprinkling the spread with mini chocolate chips before drizzling the syrup. Thinly sliced bananas are another great addition; they add flavor and may help give the illusion that this sandwich has some health benefits!

Morning Rice Salad

Prep time: 2 min • **Cook time:** 45 sec • **Yield:** 1 serving

Ingredients	Directions
1 container (1 cup) instant, ready-to-serve brown rice	**1** Spoon the rice into a small, microwave-safe bowl and nuke for 30 seconds.
¼ teaspoon cinnamon	
1 apple, cored and diced	**2** Stir the cinnamon, apple, orange, cranberries, dates, and coconut into the rice. Heat in the microwave on high for 15 more seconds.
½ navel orange, diced	
½ cup dried cranberries	
¼ cup chopped dates	**3** Remove the bowl from the microwave and spoon the yogurt on top before serving.
¼ cup shredded sweetened coconut	
½ cup low-fat vanilla yogurt or soy yogurt	

Per serving: Calories 980 (From Fat 122); Fat 14g (Saturated 9g); Cholesterol 6mg; Sodium 164mg; Carbohydrate 208g (Dietary Fiber 17g); Protein 17g.

Note: Ready-to-serve brown rice containers come in 1-cup serving portions. They're great to create a spur-of-the-moment breakfast cereal, to nuke at lunchtime to add to a tortilla, or to stir into cut-up veggies for dinner.

Vary It! Chopped pecans or walnuts are good to add to this breakfast. And if you don't have any dates, you can substitute raisins.

Tip: This concoction is not only great for breakfast but also makes a nice side dish at dinnertime.

Microwave Oatmeal

Prep time: 2 min • **Cook time:** 1 min • **Yield:** 1 serving

Ingredients	Directions
⅓ **cup plain instant oatmeal**	*1* Place the oats and water in a microwave-safe bowl that can hold 2 cups of liquid. Stir to mix well.
⅔ **cup water**	
¼ **teaspoon cinnamon**	
1 tablespoon brown sugar	*2* Microwave uncovered on high for 1 minute, or until the oatmeal is thick and almost all the water has been absorbed.
2 tablespoons dried cranberries	
1 tablespoon chopped walnuts	*3* Stir in the cinnamon, brown sugar, cranberries, walnuts, and milk. Let the mixture stand for 1 minute.
¼ **cup low-fat milk or soymilk**	

Per serving: Calories 280 (From Fat 65); Fat 7g (Saturated 1g); Cholesterol 2mg; Sodium 320mg; Carbohydrate 48g (Dietary Fiber 5g); Protein 8g.

Tip: If you like thinner oatmeal, stir in a little more milk after the mixture has set for 1 minute.

Cheesy Eggs

Prep time: 1 min • **Cook time:** 3 min • **Yield:** 1 serving

Ingredients	*Directions*
⅓ cup condensed, low-sodium, cheddar cheese soup	**1** In a small saucepan, stir together the soup and milk. Cook over medium heat, stirring often, until the mixture is smooth and warm, about 3 minutes.
1½ tablespoons low-fat milk	
1 slice whole-grain bread	**2** While the soup mixture is cooking, toast the bread and put it on a plate. Lay the egg slices on top of the toast and spoon the soup over the eggs.
1 hard-boiled egg, peeled and sliced	

Per serving: Calories 212 (From Fat 106); Fat 12g (Saturated 4g); Cholesterol 223mg; Sodium 617mg; Carbohydrate 20g (Dietary Fiber 2g); Protein 12g.

Tip: Even though this breakfast takes only 5 minutes from start to finish, you can make it even quicker by using the microwave. Put the soup and milk in a microwave-safe bowl and nuke it for 45 seconds, stirring once halfway through the cooking time.

Quick Grits

Prep time: 1–2 min • **Cook time:** 3 min • **Yield:** 1 serving

Ingredients	Directions
⅔ cup water	*1* Bring the water to a boil in a saucepan over high heat. Add the butter.
1 teaspoon butter	
2½ tablespoons quick grits	*2* Stir in the grits. Reduce heat to medium, cover the pan, and cook, stirring occasionally, for 3 minutes, or until the grits are nearly done and most of the water has been absorbed. (Cook 1 minute longer if you like thicker grits.)
2½ tablespoons shredded low-fat cheddar cheese or nondairy cheese	
Dash salt	*3* Add the cheese, salt, and pepper and stir until the cheese is melted.
Dash black pepper	

Per serving: Calories 160 (From Fat 48); Fat 5g (Saturated 3g); Cholesterol 14mg; Sodium 348mg; Carbohydrate 21g (Dietary Fiber 0g); Protein 7g.

Breakfast Pizza

Prep time: 3 min • **Cook time:** 1½ min • **Yield:** 1 serving

Ingredients	Directions
½ piece whole-wheat pita bread 1 tablespoon olive oil ½ teaspoon Italian seasoning 4 slices tomato	**1** Place the pita bread on a microwave-safe plate. Drizzle the top with oil and sprinkle on the Italian seasoning. Lay the tomato slices on top.
1 egg Dash salt Dash black pepper	**2** In a small, microwave-safe bowl, whisk the egg with the salt and pepper. Microwave it on high for 30 seconds, stir the egg, and then continue to nuke it for 30 seconds or until the egg is set. Remove the bowl and spoon the egg on top of the tomatoes.
¼ cup shredded low-fat sharp cheddar cheese or nondairy cheese	**3** Sprinkle the top of the egg mixture with cheese. Microwave for 30 to 40 seconds to melt the cheese.

Per serving: Calories 347 (From Fat 195); Fat 22g (Saturated 5g); Cholesterol 219mg; Sodium 553mg; Carbohydrate 23g (Dietary Fiber 4g); Protein 17g.

Note: You have several options for a crust when making any kind of pizza. Pre-made crusts (both vacuum-sealed and frozen) are great, or you can use bagel halves or even tortillas as a base. If you're really ambitious and plan to make a large portion, you can piece together refrigerated crescent rolls as a pizza base.

Vary It! What's in the fridge? If you have sliced olives left over from last night's salad, or chopped onions and/or green peppers, add them. Or you can quickly nuke a small amount of meatless sausage crumbles to add to your breakfast pizza (sneak them in under the cheese).

Bagel Broil

Prep time: 3 min • **Cook time:** 1½ min • **Yield:** 1 serving

Ingredients	Directions
1 bagel, cut in half 6–8 thin slices of apple	*1* Preheat the broiler to a high setting. Line a baking sheet with foil.
2 thin slices low-fat American or cheddar cheese or nondairy cheese	*2* Place the bagel halves on the baking sheet, cut side down, and broil for 20 seconds until the tops are slightly toasted.
	3 Turn the bagels cut side up. Lay apple slices on the bagel halves and cheese slices on top of the apples.
	4 Broil about 1 minute to melt the cheese.

Per serving: Calories 192 (From Fat 24); Fat 3g (Saturated 1g); Cholesterol 10mg; Sodium 539mg; Carbohydrate 28g (Dietary Fiber 3g); Protein 13g.

Tip: You can use any flavor of bagel, but a cinnamon-raisin bagel is really, really good (though whole-wheat or whole-grain bagels are healthier choices).

Vary It! If you don't have any bagels, substitute a ciabatta roll, English muffin, or even whole-wheat bread in a pinch.

Cinnamon Almond Milk Toast

Prep time: 3 min • **Cook time:** 1½ min • **Yield:** 1 serving

Ingredients	*Directions*
2 slices whole-grain bread	*1* Toast the bread well until it's deep brown on both sides; spread butter or margarine on one side of each of the toast slices and sprinkle with sugar and cinnamon.
1 teaspoon butter or nondairy margarine	
½ teaspoon sugar	
½ teaspoon cinnamon	*2* Tear the toast into bite-sized pieces and put them in a cereal bowl, sprinkling the almonds on top.
1 tablespoon slivered almonds	
¼ cup low-fat milk or almond milk	*3* Heat the milk in a small saucepan on medium heat or in a bowl in the microwave until it's really warm but not simmering, about 30 seconds. Remove the pan from the stove (or bowl from the microwave) and stir in the vanilla.
¼ teaspoon vanilla	
	4 Pour the warm milk mixture over the toast pieces.

Per serving: Calories 242 (From Fat 89); Fat 10g (Saturated 3g); Cholesterol 13mg; Sodium 286mg; Carbohydrate 32g (Dietary Fiber 5g); Protein 9g.

Vary 1t! For really special milk toast, use half and half in place of the low-fat milk.

Lemon-Filled Pancakes

Prep time: 4 min • **Cook time:** 45 sec • **Yield:** 1 serving

Ingredients	*Directions*
3 tablespoons small-curd, low-fat cottage cheese	*1* In a small bowl, stir together the cottage cheese and lemon curd.
3 tablespoons lemon curd	
2 frozen whole-grain pancakes	*2* Microwave the pancakes for 45 seconds or the time indicated on the package's directions.
2 tablespoons blueberries or sliced strawberries	
	3 Place one pancake on a dish, top with the cheese mixture, sprinkle with the berries, and then top with the second pancake.

Per serving: Calories 394 (From Fat 67); Fat 8g (Saturated 2g); Cholesterol 15mg; Sodium 509mg; Carbohydrate 69g (Dietary Fiber 3g); Protein 9g.

Vary It! You can drizzle maple or pancake syrup over the top . . . or not. This combo is sweet enough all by itself.

Tip: If you buy a can of lemon curd (sold where they sell pie fillings), you'll obviously have some left over. Don't throw it out! Stir some into oatmeal, spoon it over ice cream or yogurt, substitute it as part of the liquid when you bake a cake or muffins, or just get a spoon and eat it right out of the can when you're up late studying.

Chocolate Peanut Butter Oatmeal

Prep time: 2 min • **Cook time:** 3 min • **Yield:** 1 serving

Ingredients	*Directions*
½ cup plain, quick-cooking oats	**1** Put all the ingredients in a medium saucepan. Cook over medium heat, stirring frequently, until the mixture is thick and all the ingredients are well blended, about 3 minutes.
1 envelope instant cocoa mix	
1½ teaspoons low-fat peanut butter	
1 cup water	
Dash salt	
1 teaspoon vanilla	

Per serving: Calories 325 (From Fat 67); Fat 7g (Saturated 2g); Cholesterol 3mg; Sodium 375mg; Carbohydrate 52g (Dietary Fiber 5g); Protein 10g.

Brown Rice Cereal

Prep time: 4 min • **Cook time:** 1 min • **Yield:** 1 serving

Ingredients	Directions
1 container (1 cup) instant, ready-to-serve brown rice	**1** In a microwave-safe bowl, stir together all the ingredients until they're blended.
2 tablespoons chopped pecans	
2 tablespoons raisins	**2** Microwave for 30 seconds on high; stir the mixture and microwave for another 30 seconds. For a creamier texture, let the mixture sit for 2 to 3 minutes after removing it from the microwave.
½ cup low-fat milk or soymilk	
3 tablespoons maple syrup	
¼ teaspoon vanilla	
¼ teaspoon cinnamon	

Per serving: Calories 716 (From Fat 137); Fat 15g (Saturated 2g); Cholesterol 5mg; Sodium 94mg; Carbohydrate 133g (Dietary Fiber 7g); Protein 14g.

Tip: You don't have to toast the pecans before adding them to the cereal, but toasting sure does give them added flair.

Vary It! Feel free to swap the raisins for dried cranberries and the maple syrup for pancake syrup.

Apple English Muffin

Prep time: 3 min • **Cook time:** 2 min • **Yield:** 1 serving

Ingredients	*Directions*
1 English muffin	**1** Split the English muffin in half horizontally and toast both halves in a toaster.
1 tablespoon peanut butter	
⅛ large apple, peeled, cored, and sliced thin	**2** Spread the peanut butter on one toasted English muffin half. Lay the apple slices on top.
½ teaspoon butter or nondairy margarine	
¾ teaspoon brown sugar	**3** In a small, microwave-safe bowl, heat the butter in the microwave on high for 15 seconds. Stir in the brown sugar and cinnamon, and then nuke for another 15 seconds. Stir until smooth. (If necessary, pop the mixture back into the microwave until the brown sugar melts.)
⅛ teaspoon cinnamon	
	4 Drizzle the cinnamon mixture over the apple slices, and then place the second half of the English muffin on top.

Per serving: Calories 267 (From Fat 100); Fat 11g (Saturated 3g); Cholesterol 5mg; Sodium 339mg; Carbohydrate 35g (Dietary Fiber 3g); Protein 9g.

Vary It! Sure, this apple topping is great on an English muffin, but you can assemble it on almost any bread product — bagel, sliced bread, croissant, or biscuit (no, last night's garlic bread won't work). If you're out of apples, use a pear, ripe peach or nectarine, mango, or even a banana.

Pancake Roll-ups

Prep time: 3 min • **Cook time:** 2 min • **Yield:** 1 serving

Ingredients	Directions
2 tablespoons raisins	**1** In a small bowl, stir together the raisins, pear, cinnamon, and walnuts.
½ medium pear, chopped	
¼ teaspoon cinnamon	**2** Lightly toast the pancakes in a toaster or in the microwave.
2 tablespoons chopped walnuts	
2 frozen whole-grain pancakes	**3** Spoon half of the pear mixture down the center of each pancake and drizzle each with 1 teaspoon syrup.
2 teaspoons pancake syrup	
	4 Fold the sides of each pancake over to enclose the filling.

Per serving: Calories 405 (From Fat 128); Fat 14g (Saturated 2g); Cholesterol 13mg; Sodium 314mg; Carbohydrate 68g (Dietary Fiber 7g); Protein 7g.

Note: Toast the pancakes long enough so that they're very warm, but don't toast them so long that the edges get crunchy or they may crack when you fold them.

Vary It! If you don't have pancake syrup on hand, you can substitute honey.

Tip: If you're going to eat en route to class, wrap the bottom part of each folded pancake in foil to keep it together and to keep the filling from oozing out.

Egg-cellent Wrap

Prep time: 3 min • **Cook time:** About 2 min • **Yield:** 1 serving

Ingredients	*Directions*
1 meatless sausage-flavored link	*1* Place the meatless link on a piece of wax paper and cook it in the microwave for 20 seconds, or until the center is hot. Cut the link into small pieces.
2 eggs	
Dash salt	
Dash black pepper	*2* Put the eggs in a small, microwave-safe bowl. Add the salt and pepper and whisk it all together. Stir in the veggie link pieces.
1 (10-inch) whole-wheat flour tortilla	
2 tablespoons taco sauce or salsa	*3* Microwave the bowl on high for 40 seconds. Stir the eggs and then microwave for another 30 seconds, or until the eggs are set.
2 tablespoons low-fat shredded pepper jack cheese or nondairy sharp cheddar-flavored cheese	
	4 Lay the tortilla on a microwave-safe dish. When the eggs are done cooking, immediately remove them from the bowl (so they don't stick) and spread them down the center of the tortilla. Spoon on the taco sauce or salsa, and then sprinkle with the cheese.
	5 Microwave for 30 seconds to melt the cheese; then roll up the tortilla.

Per serving: *Calories 409 (From Fat 144); Fat 16g (Saturated 5g); Cholesterol 428mg; Sodium 781mg; Carbohydrate 40g (Dietary Fiber 2g); Protein 29g.*

Chapter 8

20 Minutes till Mealtime: Breakfasts

In This Chapter

► Enjoying a sweet meal in the morning
► Making savory breakfasts

*W*hen you're in a hurry to rush out the door, breakfast isn't always a top priority. Still, it's nice to eat something that tastes pretty terrific and doesn't involve a lot of pots, pans, or time. The recipes in this chapter take 20 minutes or less to fix (with preparation and cooking time combined), and they offer you choice and variety. Keep reading; you'll see for yourself that a vegetarian breakfast can be more than a bowl of cereal.

Color is the secret to eating a good breakfast. Look at the colors on your plate. The more colors you see, the more variety you're getting, and the more variety, the more nutrition. Who knew it could be so simple?

Indulging Your Sweet Tooth at Breakfast

Sure, you can have oatmeal for breakfast every day. It's healthy, inexpensive, and super simple to prepare. But once in a while, wouldn't you like to really splurge and have something special and sweet for breakfast? The recipes in this section are sweet but not totally decadent; each one has some nutritionally redeeming ingredients.

Fried Bananas

Prep time: 2 min • **Cook time:** 4 min • **Yield:** 1 serving

Ingredients	*Directions*
½ tablespoon butter or nondairy margarine	**1** Melt the butter in a small skillet over medium-high heat.
1 large banana, cut into ½-inch crosswise slices ⅛ teaspoon cinnamon ¼ teaspoon brown sugar 1 (10-inch) whole-wheat tortilla	**2** Stir the banana slices into the butter just as the butter begins to brown. Sprinkle the bananas with cinnamon and brown sugar and cook over medium-high heat about 3 minutes, turning once, until the banana slices are golden brown on each side.
	3 Spoon the bananas down the center of the tortilla. Bring up the bottom of the tortilla and fold in the sides to form a wrap.

Per serving: Calories 355 (From Fat 84); Fat 9g (Saturated 5g); Cholesterol 15mg; Sodium 87mg; Carbohydrate 66g (Dietary Fiber 5g); Protein 10g.

Tip: You can eat the bananas in a wrap, but they're also great on top of ice cream or served over pancakes or oatmeal.

Waffles with "Ice Cream"

Prep time: 4 min • **Cook time:** 2 min • **Yield:** 1 serving

Ingredients	Directions
1 medium ripe banana, peeled 1 teaspoon orange juice 1 tablespoon shredded sweetened coconut 1 frozen whole-grain waffle ¼ cup pancake syrup 4 strawberries, halved 1 teaspoon chocolate chips	*1* The night before, put the banana, orange juice, and coconut in a sandwich-size self-seal bag. Mash the banana well until almost no lumps are left. As best you can, push the contents to the center to form a ball, and then freeze overnight.
	2 The next morning, toast the waffle. Pour the syrup into a small bowl and heat it in the microwave for 20 seconds, or until the syrup is very warm to the touch.
	3 Place the waffle on a dish, top with the banana "ice cream," sprinkle the berries and chocolate chips over the top, and then drizzle with syrup.

Per serving: Calories 487 (From Fat 71); Fat 8g (Saturated 4g); Cholesterol 37mg; Sodium 155mg; Carbohydrate 105g (Dietary Fiber 7g); Protein 5g.

Note: This recipe requires you to do Step 1 the night before! If you think you'll forget, put a sticky note on the refrigerator to remind yourself.

Tip: Should you forget to make the banana ice cream in advance, the good news is you'll still be able to eat breakfast. Just brush the banana with the juice, slice the banana, put the slices on top of the waffle along with the strawberries, and then sprinkle the coconut over the top.

Breakfast Polenta

Prep time: 3 min, plus 2 min rest time • **Cook time:** 1 min • **Yield:** 2 servings

Ingredients	Directions
1 cup water	**1** In a small saucepan, bring the water and salt to a boil. Stir in the polenta and cook for 1 minute. Remove from heat.
⅛ teaspoon salt	
¼ cup quick-cooking polenta (coarse cornmeal)	**2** Stir in the almonds, dates, cranberries, cinnamon, and nutmeg and let the mixture sit for 2 minutes so the flavors can blend.
1 tablespoon slivered almonds	
2 pitted dates, chopped	
1 tablespoon dried cranberries	**3** After spooning the polenta into a bowl, drizzle honey over the top.
¼ teaspoon cinnamon	
Dash nutmeg	
2 tablespoons honey	

Per serving: Calories 199 (From Fat 16); Fat 2g (Saturated 0g); Cholesterol 0mg; Sodium 147mg; Carbohydrate 46g (Dietary Fiber 3g); Protein 3g.

Tip: Toasting the almonds before adding them to the mix adds a nice toasty flavor. You can toast them on a small baking pan or even a piece of foil in the oven, keeping a close eye on them so they don't burn, or you can toast them in a skillet on the stove (spray the pan first with nonstick spray). The stove method is faster because you don't have to sit around while the oven heats.

Vary It! You can use 1 tablespoon raisins in place of dates in a pinch.

Tip: For a true grab 'n' go breakfast, spoon hot polenta into a plastic bowl or cup and grab a plastic spoon to take along with you.

Coconut French Toast Casserole

Prep time: 5 min • **Cook time:** 2 min • **Yield:** 1 serving

Ingredients	*Directions*
2 tablespoons low-fat cream cheese, softened	**1** Spread the cream cheese on one side of each slice of bread. Spread the jam over the cream cheese, and then sprinkle with coconut. Cut the bread into ¾-inch cubes.
2 slices whole-wheat bread	
2 tablespoons strawberry jam	
2 tablespoons shredded sweetened coconut	**2** Spray a small ramekin very well with nonstick cooking spray. Place half of the bread cubes in the ramekin and press the cubes down with the back of a spoon.
Nonstick cooking spray	
½ apple, peeled, cored, and sliced thin	**3** Lay the apple slices on top of the bread cubes, and then sprinkle the sugar on top of the apples. Add the rest of the bread cubes and press them down lightly.
¼ teaspoon granulated sugar	
1 egg	**4** In a small bowl, whip together the egg, milk, cinnamon, and vanilla. Pour the egg mixture over the bread cubes.
2 tablespoons low-fat milk	
¼ teaspoon cinnamon	
¼ teaspoon vanilla	**5** Microwave for 2 minutes, or until the egg is absorbed and the mixture is set.

Per serving: Calories 496 (From Fat 167); Fat 19g (Saturated 10g); Cholesterol 235mg; Sodium 476mg; Carbohydrate 70g (Dietary Fiber 5g); Protein 16g.

Tip: Depending on the brand of jam, sometimes it just clumps together and is kind of hard to spread. If you want the jam to spread more easily, stick a fork into the jar and stir it around a bit to break it up and make it looser.

Vary It! If strawberry isn't your flavor of choice, use any jam you like. If coconut turns you off, substitute chopped nuts.

Cherry French Toast Sticks

Prep time: 3 min • **Cook time:** 5 min • **Yield:** 1 serving

Ingredients	Directions
2 tablespoons whipping cream	*1* In a small saucepan, bring the cream, pancake syrup, brown sugar, butter, cherries, and cinnamon to a boil over medium heat, stirring constantly. Cook, stirring, for 2 minutes. Remove from heat and stir in the vanilla.
2 tablespoons pancake syrup	
1 tablespoon brown sugar	
2 teaspoons butter	
1 tablespoon dried cherries	*2* Toast the French toast in a toaster.
⅛ teaspoon cinnamon	
⅛ teaspoon vanilla	*3* Dip the sticks into the syrup mixture to eat.
4 pieces (¼ of a 16-ounce package) frozen French toast sticks	

Per serving: Calories 575 (From Fat 222); Fat 25g (Saturated 13g); Cholesterol 123mg; Sodium 761mg; Carbohydrate 83g (Dietary Fiber 2g); Protein 10g.

Vary It! You can substitute half and half for the whipping cream if you have to, but regular milk just doesn't do it for this syrup. It's too thin and the consistency won't be right.

Spiced Fruit

Prep time: 4 min • **Cook time:** 5 min • **Yield:** 6 servings

Ingredients	*Directions*
One 20-ounce can sliced peaches, packed in juice	*1* Drain the peaches, pineapple, and pears, reserving ⅓ cup of peach juice.
One 8-ounce can pineapple tidbits or chunks, packed in juice	*2* Put the fruits and reserved juice, the cinnamon, and the brown sugar into a medium saucepan. Warm over medium heat, stirring occasionally, for 5 minutes.
One 15-ounce can pears, packed in juice	
½ teaspoon cinnamon	
1 tablespoon brown sugar	

Per serving: Calories 81 (From Fat 1); Fat 0g (Saturated 0g); Cholesterol 0mg; Sodium 9mg; Carbohydrate 21g (Dietary Fiber 2g); Protein 1g.

Tip: Canned fruits packed in heavy or even light syrup are loaded with extra sugars. Look for fruits packed in water or in juice as a healthier alternative.

Note: The beauty of this dish is its versatility: You can eat it warm when it's done cooking; you can enjoy it cold from the refrigerator; you can spoon it cold over cold cereal or ice cream; or you can reheat it to spoon over oatmeal or waffles. And it will hold in the refrigerator (in a covered plastic container) for an entire week. Now that's awesome!

Trail Mix Couscous

Prep time: 2 min, plus 6 min rest time • **Cook time:** 1 min • **Yield:** 1 serving

Ingredients	*Directions*
⅔ **cup low-fat milk or soymilk**	*1* In a small saucepan, bring the milk to a simmer over medium heat, about 1 minute. Remove the pan from the heat.
¼ **cup dry couscous**	
2 tablespoons dried cranberries	*2* Stir in the couscous, cranberries, raisins, walnuts, brown sugar, cinnamon, and salt. Cover the pan and let it rest for 6 minutes, or until thickened.
2 tablespoons raisins	
2 tablespoons chopped walnuts	
2¼ **teaspoons brown sugar**	*3* Spoon the mixture into a bowl and drizzle maple syrup over the top of the hot cereal.
¼ **teaspoon cinnamon**	
Dash salt	
1 teaspoon maple or pancake syrup	

Per serving: Calories 498 (From Fat 107); Fat 12g (Saturated 2g); Cholesterol 7mg; Sodium 95mg; Carbohydrate 87g (Dietary Fiber 5g); Protein 14g.

Vary It! You can exchange some of the fruits in this recipe, or add to them. Almost any dried fruit (chopped dates, prunes, dried blueberries, and so on) works well, or fold in fresh blueberries, strawberries, or raspberries.

Fruity Chimichanga

Prep time: 8 min • **Cook time:** 10 min • **Yield:** 1 serving

Ingredients	Directions
1 ounce (⅓ of a 3-ounce package) cream cheese, softened	*1* Preheat the oven to 475 degrees.
2 tablespoons small-curd, low-fat cottage cheese	*2* In a small bowl, stir together the cream cheese, cottage cheese, and sugar. Spoon the cheese mixture down the center of the tortilla.
½ teaspoon granulated sugar	
1 whole-wheat flour tortilla	*3* Lay the strawberry slices over the cheese mixture, and then spoon 1 tablespoon of the preserves over the strawberries.
3 fresh strawberries, sliced	
2 tablespoons strawberry preserves	*4* Fold one end of the tortilla up about 1 inch over the mixture, and then fold in the sides of the tortilla to overlap. Brush the edges with water to seal.
Nonstick cooking spray	
1 teaspoon honey	
	5 Spray a small baking pan with nonstick spray. Lay the tortilla in the pan, and then spray the top of the tortilla with the nonstick spray. Bake about 10 minutes, or until the filling is hot and the outside begins to brown.
	6 In a small bowl, stir together 1 tablespoon of the preserves and the honey. Microwave on high for 20 seconds, or until the preserves have melted.
	7 Place the tortilla on a dish and drizzle the honey mixture over the top.

Per serving: *Calories 321 (From Fat 99); Fat 11g (Saturated 7g); Cholesterol 32mg; Sodium 378mg; Carbohydrate 53g (Dietary Fiber 3g); Protein 9g.*

Vary It! For added fiber, sprinkle sunflower seeds, flaxseeds, or chopped walnuts over the cheese mixture before rolling.

Serving Up Savory Breakfasts

The recipes in this section show you so many different and tasty ways to cook an egg. I also include recipes using bagels, tofu, and other savory breakfast foods that give your body the fuel it needs to get started in the morning.

Omelets are a classic breakfast and perfectly acceptable if you're a lacto ovo vegetarian (ovo vegetarians can eat omelets without cheese). They're really not hard to make when you know the following tricks (see Figure 8-1):

✔ Whip or whisk the eggs thoroughly before cooking them. The more you whisk, the more air gets into them and the fluffier they'll be.

✔ Use a spatula to push the edges of the egg mixture into the center as they set. This way the uncooked portion can flow underneath, directly onto the skillet, to cook. Keep repeating this until the egg is completely cooked. You can also tilt the pan so that the uncooked egg runs down onto the pan. Some people like to flip the egg over so the top side browns, too; that's your choice.

✔ The final step is what makes an omelet so special — after the egg is cooked, fold it in half or into thirds.

HOW TO FOLD AN OMELET

1. STIR THE EGG MIXTURE OVER HIGH HEAT.

2. REMOVE THE PAN FROM THE HEAT AND LET IT REST FOR A FEW SECONDS.

3. USING A SPATULA, GENTLY FOLD A THIRD OF THE OMELET ON ITSELF.

4. USING THE SPATULA, GENTLY FOLD THE FAR SIDE OF THE OMELET OVER THE TOP.

Figure 8-1: Making an omelet is a snap.

If you don't have a nonstick pan to use on your stovetop, it helps to spray the pan with nonstick spray before cooking. Soak the pan immediately after cooking so that foods don't stick to it. For foods you need to cook in the oven, don't forget to preheat the oven for 10 minutes before baking.

Mediterranean Omelet

Prep time: 3 min • **Cook time:** 2½ min • **Yield:** 1 serving

Ingredients	Directions
3 egg whites	**1** In a medium bowl, whisk the egg whites until they're frothy. Add the spinach, artichoke heart, cheese, salt, pepper, and Italian seasoning.
¼ cup fresh spinach, sliced into thin strips	
1 canned artichoke heart, drained and chopped	
2 tablespoons crumbled feta cheese	**2** Spray a medium skillet with nonstick spray and add the oil. Pour in the egg mixture and cook it over medium heat, without stirring, until the bottom is lightly browned and the top is beginning to set, about 1½ to 2 minutes. Flip the omelet over and cook until the other side is lightly browned, about 30 seconds more. (Refer to Figure 8-1 for help.)
Dash salt	
Dash black pepper	
Dash Italian seasoning	
Nonstick cooking spray	
1 teaspoon olive oil	

Per serving: Calories 152 (From Fat 78); Fat 9g (Saturated 3g); Cholesterol 17mg; Sodium 608mg; Carbohydrate 4g (Dietary Fiber 1g); Protein 14g.

Vary It! If you don't have feta cheese on hand, use goat cheese, shredded white cheddar, or most any other cheese you have in the fridge. You can use asparagus tips in place of the artichoke heart and chopped broccoli in place of the spinach.

Tip: If it's a busy morning and you don't have time to sit down to enjoy this omelet, wrap it in a tortilla or spoon it into a pita pocket so you can eat it on the way to class.

Apple Waffles

Prep time: 4 min • **Cook time:** 2 min • **Yield:** 1 serving

Ingredients	*Directions*
1 frozen meatless sausage-flavored link	*1* Microwave the meatless link for 30 seconds, or as directed on the package. Cut the link in half lengthwise.
1 frozen low-fat whole-grain waffle or vegan waffle	
	2 Toast the waffle and cut it in half.
1 slice low-fat sharp cheddar cheese or nondairy cheese	
3 thin medium apple slices	*3* Fold the cheese slice in half and lay it on one half of the waffle. Place the two sausage pieces on the cheese. Put the apple slices on top of the sausage and cover with the remaining waffle half.

Per serving: Calories 220 (From Fat 76); Fat 9g (Saturated 3g); Cholesterol 43mg; Sodium 470mg; Carbohydrate 21g (Dietary Fiber 3g); Protein 16g.

Note: A meatless sausage link (also known as TVP, or textured vegetable protein) is used in this recipe. TVP is basically soy flour, water, and flavoring. Because of the way it's processed, you can keep it in the refrigerator for about three days. That's not a long time, so it's best to keep veggie meats frozen until shortly before you're ready to cook them. If you need to thaw them fast, wrap them in wax paper and nuke them for 30 seconds. Don't overcook veggie meats or they'll become tough, and be careful taking them out of the microwave because they'll be really hot.

Garden in a Mug

Prep time: 4 min • **Cook time:** About 2 min • **Yield:** 1 serving

Ingredients	Directions
Nonstick cooking spray	*1* Spray a microwave-safe, 10-ounce coffee mug or bowl well with nonstick spray.
2 large eggs	
2 tablespoons low-fat milk	*2* In a small bowl, whisk together the eggs, milk, salt, and pepper. Stir in the green onion, green pepper, tomatoes, and cheese. Pour the mixture into the mug or bowl.
Dash salt	
Dash black pepper	
1 teaspoon minced green onion	
1 teaspoon minced green pepper	*3* Microwave on high for 45 seconds. Remove the mug or bowl and stir the egg mixture. Continue to microwave the eggs another 30 seconds, and then stir again. Cook in the microwave for a third time for 30 seconds, or until the eggs are set.
2 grape tomatoes, minced	
2 tablespoons crumbled feta cheese	

Per serving: Calories 221 (From Fat 131); Fat 15g (Saturated 6g); Cholesterol 443mg; Sodium 491mg; Carbohydrate 5g (Dietary Fiber 0g); Protein 16g.

Tip: If all you have are small mugs or cups, you can cook the garden in a small, microwave-safe bowl or custard cup.

Tip: Are you awake enough to make choices? You can eat breakfast right out of the mug, or run a knife around the edge and slide it onto a plate.

Note: The advantage to eating out of the mug is that you only have one container to clean. But some egg will stick to the bottom, so after you eat, you need to soak the mug for about 15 minutes to loosen the stuff that's still stuck to the bottom.

South of the Border Omelet

Prep time: 5 min • **Cook time:** 4 min • **Yield:** 1 serving

Ingredients	*Directions*
½ **cup low-fat refried beans** **4 tablespoons salsa or taco sauce** **2 large eggs**	*1* In a small saucepan, stir together the beans and 2 tablespoons of salsa. Heat over medium heat until the mixture is hot, about 1 minute.
2 tablespoons water **Nonstick cooking spray**	*2* In a small bowl, whisk together the eggs and water.
2 tablespoons low-fat shredded cheddar cheese or nondairy cheddar-flavored cheese	*3* Spray a small skillet with nonstick spray and warm over medium-high heat. When a drop of water sizzles in the pan, pour in the eggs. With an inverted turner, carefully push the cooked portions at the edges toward the center so the uncooked portions can reach the hot pan surface, tilting the pan as needed. Cook until the top is thickened and the eggs are cooked through, about 3 minutes. (Refer to Figure 8-1 for additional help on making an omelet.)
	4 Slide the omelet onto a serving plate. Spread the hot bean mixture over the omelet and top it with the remaining 2 tablespoons of salsa and the cheese.

Per serving: Calories 346 (From Fat 101); Fat 11g (Saturated 4g); Cholesterol 428mg; Sodium 1,082mg; Carbohydrate 34g (Dietary Fiber 7g); Protein 27g.

Vary It! You definitely have control over the heat level in this recipe. If you're ravenous for something spicy and hot, slather your omelet with hot salsa. If you can't tolerate really hot food, use the mild salsa or taco sauce.

Vary It! This breakfast is a wrap just waiting to happen. For variety, spread the bean/salsa mixture inside a tortilla. Add the cooked egg, and then drizzle with the remaining salsa and cheese. Wrap it up and enjoy!

Note: Did you know that adding water to eggs before scrambling them makes the eggs lighter — even lighter than adding a little milk? (That's a rhetorical question; you don't have to answer it.)

Mock Sausage Gravy

Prep time: 4 min • **Cook time:** 5 min • **Yield:** 1 serving

Ingredients	*Directions*
Nonstick cooking spray 3 tablespoons meatless sausage-flavored crumbles	*1* Spray a small saucepan with nonstick spray and cook the sausage crumbles for 1½ minutes, stirring frequently. Remove the sausage from the pan and set aside.
1½ tablespoons butter or nondairy margarine 1 tablespoon baking mix ½ cup whole milk or soymilk	*2* Melt the butter or margarine in the same saucepan used to cook the crumbles. Stir in the baking mix and cook, stirring constantly over low heat, until the flour begins to brown, about 30 seconds.
⅛ teaspoon salt ⅛ teaspoon pepper 1¼ teaspoons maple or pancake syrup	*3* Stir in the milk. Continue to cook, stirring, until the mixture thickens, about 3 minutes.
2 frozen biscuits, thawed as directed on package (see the note after this recipe's directions)	*4* Stir in the sausage, salt, pepper, and maple syrup. (Add a little more milk if the mixture is too thick.) Spoon over the biscuits.

Per serving: Calories 598 (From Fat 235); Fat 26g (Saturated 14g); Cholesterol 63mg; Sodium 1,655mg; Carbohydrate 74g (Dietary Fiber 1g); Protein 18g.

Note: Refrigerated biscuits come four or eight to a package. You only need two biscuits for this recipe. You can buy frozen biscuits and then just thaw two of them so there's no waste.

Note: Most recipes in this book recommend using low-fat milk; this recipe is an exception. You need to use whole milk if you want the gravy to be thick and creamy.

Vary It! You can spoon the gravy over toast, but in my opinion, biscuits are so much better!

Bagel Deluxe

Prep time: 5 min • **Cook time:** 4 min • **Yield:** 1 serving

Ingredients	Directions
1 bagel, cut in half horizontally	*1* Toast the bagel halves and set them on a dish.
3 tablespoons low-fat ricotta cheese or nondairy cottage cheese Dash of dried dill	*2* Spread the ricotta cheese on one of the bagel halves and sprinkle with dill and Parmesan cheese.
1 tablespoon grated Parmesan cheese or nondairy Parmesan-type cheese ¼ cup arugula	*3* Lay the arugula over the ricotta layer, drizzle with ½ teaspoon of oil, and then top that with the tomato slice.
1½ teaspoons olive oil 1 slice tomato 1 large egg Dash salt Dash black pepper	*4* In a small skillet, heat 1 teaspoon of oil. Carefully break the egg into the skillet, sprinkle it with salt and pepper, and fry for 2 minutes. Turn the egg over gingerly with a spatula and fry it another minute, or until the white is set.
	5 Put the egg on top of the tomato. Add the lid of the bagel and enjoy!

Per serving: Calories 280 (From Fat 141); Fat 16g (Saturated 5g); Cholesterol 228mg; Sodium 479mg; Carbohydrate 18g (Dietary Fiber 1g); Protein 15g.

Vary It! If you're short on funds, use baby spinach in place of the arugula, cottage cheese in lieu of the ricotta, and two slices of whole-wheat bread to replace the bagel.

Eggs a la King

Prep time: 6 min • **Cook time:** 4 min • **Yield:** 2 servings

Ingredients	Directions
1 tablespoon butter	*1* Melt the butter in a medium saucepan over medium-high heat. Sauté the green pepper, onion, and mushrooms in melted butter until the vegetables are soft, about 3 minutes, stirring occasionally.
2 tablespoons chopped green pepper	
2 tablespoons chopped onion	
¼ cup sliced mushrooms	
2 slices whole-grain bread	*2* While the vegetables cook, toast the bread slices in a toaster.
¾ cup low-fat cream of celery or cream of mushroom soup	*3* Stir in the soup, cheese, and milk. Lower heat to medium and cook, stirring constantly, until the cheese has melted, about 1 minute.
½ cup shredded low-fat American or cheddar cheese	
¼ cup milk	
2 hard-boiled eggs, sliced	*4* Fold in the eggs. Spoon the mixture over the toast, dividing evenly.

Per serving: Calories 323 (From Fat 147); Fat 16g (Saturated 8g); Cholesterol 246mg; Sodium 970mg; Carbohydrate 26g (Dietary Fiber 3g); Protein 19g.

Tip: See Chapter 7 for tips on making a perfectly cooked batch of hard-boiled eggs to have on hand all week.

Tip: If you're cooking for one, you can either make half the recipe or cover and refrigerate the leftover egg mixture and reheat it tomorrow; that'll be one morning you don't have to worry about what's for breakfast.

Eggs in a Roll

Prep time: 3 min • **Cook time:** 8 min • **Yield:** 1 serving

Ingredients	Directions
1 slice whole-wheat hoagie roll ½ cup sliced bell peppers (green, red, orange, yellow, or a combination of all four) 2 teaspoons olive oil 2 large eggs 2 tablespoons water ⅛ teaspoon salt Dash pepper 1 slice low-fat Swiss cheese, cut in half	**1** Preheat the oven to 400 degrees (or use a toaster oven). Cut the roll in half and toast it in the oven (or toaster oven) about 2 minutes, turning it over once so both sides get golden. Remove the roll from the oven and set it on a dish. **2** In a small, nonstick skillet, sauté the peppers in 1 teaspoon of oil over medium-high heat for about 2 minutes, or until barely tender. Remove the peppers and set aside. Wipe out the pan with a paper towel. **3** In a small bowl, whisk together the eggs, water, salt, and pepper. Warm the remaining 1 teaspoon of oil in the pan and add the egg mixture. **4** As the eggs cook, use a spatula to pull the cooked edges toward the center of the pan so the uncooked egg rolls out to the side of the pan and cooks. Continue cooking until the top surface of the eggs is thickened and the eggs are cooked through, about 3 minutes (refer to Figure 8-1 for help). **5** Lay the cheese slices on top of the eggs. Spoon the peppers onto one half of the eggs. Fold the omelet in half and slide it onto the bottom half of the roll. Cover the sandwich with the top of the roll.

Per serving: Calories 461 (From Fat 209); Fat 23g (Saturated 5g); Cholesterol 430mg; Sodium 929mg; Carbohydrate 41g (Dietary Fiber 6g); Protein 24g.

Vary It! Instead of peppers, you can sauté onions or mushrooms. In place of the Swiss cheese, you can use almost any other cheese. For Italian Eggs in a Roll, spoon 2 tablespoons of pizza sauce or spaghetti sauce on one half of the omelet before folding it over. Make Mexican Eggs in a Roll by spooning 2 tablespoons of salsa or taco sauce over the egg and using pepper jack cheese in place of the Swiss.

Potato Melt

Prep time: 5 min • **Cook time:** 6 min • **Yield:** 1 serving

Ingredients	*Directions*
1½ teaspoons olive oil	*1* Preheat the broiler to high.
½ cup canned sliced potatoes, drained	*2* Warm the oil in a medium skillet. Add the potatoes, mushrooms, onion, jalapeño pepper, salt, pepper, paprika, and Italian seasoning. Cook over medium-high heat for about 5 minutes, turning the potatoes fairly often, until they begin to get crusty.
3 button mushrooms, sliced	
¼ medium onion, sliced thin	
1 small jalapeño pepper, seeded and diced	
2 dashes salt	*3* While the potatoes cook, toast the bread in a toaster. Set the toasted bread on a foil-lined baking sheet.
2 dashes black pepper	
¼ teaspoon paprika	
⅛ teaspoon Italian seasoning	*4* Spoon the potato mixture on the toast, and then lay the slice of cheese on top.
1 slice whole-wheat bread	
1 slice provolone or nondairy cheese	*5* Broil for about 1 minute, or until the cheese melts.

Per serving: Calories 318 (From Fat 143); Fat 16g (Saturated 6g); Cholesterol 20mg; Sodium 994mg; Carbohydrate 33g (Dietary Fiber 5g); Protein 14g.

Tip: The bummer about cooking for one person is that there will be times when you only use half of a can of an ingredient, like the potatoes in this recipe. But with the part that's left over, you have a jump-start on tomorrow's meal. Cover the unused potatoes and put them in the fridge. Tomorrow, either fry up some onions and peppers to add to the potatoes as a side dish with dinner, or chop up the potatoes and add chopped celery, green pepper, onions, and mayo to make a potato salad.

Note: Take precautions when working with hot peppers. Wear latex gloves to protect your hands and keep your hands away from your face to avoid burning your eyes. After you take off the gloves and toss them out, wash your hands thoroughly with soap. The oil on the skin of hot peppers clings and can irritate your skin if you're not careful.

Scrambled Tofu

Prep time: 6 min • **Cook time:** 6½ min • **Yield:** 1 serving

Ingredients	*Directions*
2 teaspoons olive oil 2 slices onion, chopped 3 button mushrooms, sliced	**1** In a small skillet, heat the oil over medium heat. Stir in the onion and mushrooms and sauté, stirring often, for 3 minutes, until the vegetables are soft and begin to brown.
Dash salt Dash pepper ⅛ teaspoon garlic powder ½ teaspoon low-sodium soy sauce ⅓ cup firm tofu	**2** Add the salt, pepper, garlic powder, soy sauce, and tofu. Stir-fry the mixture, stirring occasionally, until the tofu begins to brown, about 3 minutes.
1 slice tomato, diced	**3** Stir in the tomato and cook just until the tomato is heated through, about 30 seconds.
½ avocado, peeled, pitted, and chopped	**4** Spoon the scrambled tofu onto a serving dish and top with the avocado.

Per serving: Calories 353 (From Fat 255); Fat 28g (Saturated 5g); Cholesterol 0mg; Sodium 256mg; Carbohydrate 16g (Dietary Fiber 10g); Protein 17g.

Tip: This is another one of those breakfasts that you can convert to a carry-it-as-you-walk-to-class meal. Just pile the scramble into a pita pocket or tortilla wrap.

Waffle Sandwich

Prep time: 3 min • **Cook time:** 10 min • **Yield:** 1 serving

Ingredients	*Directions*
Nonstick cooking spray **2 frozen whole-grain waffles** **1 large egg** **Dash salt** **Dash black pepper** **1 slice low-fat cheddar or American cheese or nondairy cheddar cheese**	*1* Preheat the oven to 400 degrees. Generously spray a baking sheet with nonstick spray. Place the waffles on the baking sheet.
	2 In a small bowl, whip the egg, salt, and pepper until frothy. Spoon the egg over the waffles, dividing evenly, spreading to fill the cavities.
	3 Bake about 10 minutes, or until the egg is set and the waffles are crisp.
	4 Place the cheese over 1 waffle and cover with the second waffle, egg side down; press together. Let stand for 1 minute to allow the cheese to melt.

Per serving: Calories 335 (From Fat 144); Fat 16g (Saturated 5g); Cholesterol 293mg; Sodium 640mg; Carbohydrate 27g (Dietary Fiber 2g); Protein 20g.

Tip: Add even more pizzazz to this by slicing the baked waffles into strips and dipping the strips into pancake syrup for a salty/sweet combo.

Tip: If you're out of eggs, forgo the egg/cheese filling altogether. Toast the waffles, and then spread them with peanut butter and jelly. Voilà! Another vegetarian waffle sandwich!

Chapter 9

Five Minutes or Less: Grab 'n' Go Lunches

• •

In This Chapter

▶ Creating quick lunches without any cooking
▶ Fixing a hot lunch in only a few minutes

• •

Don't fall into the short-on-time trap of grabbing a bag of potato chips for lunch to hold you over till dinnertime. Eat something hearty at noon to keep your energy levels up throughout the afternoon. Pop a dish into the microwave to reheat leftovers from last night's dinner, or quickly throw together a no-cook or quick-cook mini meal. The grab 'n' go lunches in this chapter can be ready in five minutes or less.

Pick up some convenient, individually-packed foods like applesauce, puddings (without gelatin), and fruit to have with your homemade lunches. If you're watching your pennies, you can find some of these items at discount stores.

Keeping Cool with No-Cook Lunches

You're in college, and that means you don't have time to fuss in the kitchen at lunchtime preparing a big meal. And swinging through a fast-food drive-through isn't much of an option for a vegetarian (and besides, fast food isn't a healthy food choice). The no-cook recipes that follow are easy to put together. All you have to do is grab ingredients from the fridge or pantry, chop, and assemble. You'll have a delicious meal in no time. As an added convenience, you can make a lot of these no-cook lunches ahead of time.

Some of the recipes in this section use avocados, which are delicious and great in a vegetarian diet. You can tell whether an avocado is ripe by holding it in your hand. If it's hard, it's not ripe. If it's really soft, put it back. It should have just a slight give when you squeeze it if it's perfectly ripe. When you get home, keep it stored in the refrigerator so that it doesn't keep ripening too fast. When it's time to pit an avocado, just follow the directions in Figure 9-1.

How to Pit and Peel an Avocado

Slice avocado in half lengthwise and pull apart.

Hold the avocado half with the pit, and firmly strike the pit with a chef's knife in your other hand.

Lift the pit out with a gentle twist of the knife.

GENTLY scoop out the meat with a spoon.

Chop or slice according to your recipe.

Figure 9-1: Pitting an avocado.

Wrap it up!

Some of the recipes in this chapter are wraps. Have you ever had a wrap break apart in your hands? Oh man, what a mess! Here are the three things that usually cause this catastrophe and what you can do to avoid it:

- **Heating the wrap too long:** Bake a filled wrap in a preheated, 350-degree oven for a maximum of 8 minutes, or just until the filling is warmed. To warm a filled wrap in the microwave, cook it on high for a maximum of 20 to 30 seconds. To warm the tortilla wrap alone, before you fill it, microwave it for 15 seconds — just long enough that it softens a bit so it's easier to roll without cracking or breaking.

- **Letting the wrap cool before wrapping it:** If you heat a tortilla and then allow it to cool before you wrap it around a filling, it gets brittle and cracks. Fill the tortilla as soon as you remove it from the microwave while it's still warm.

- **Adding too much liquid to the filling (making the wrap soggy):** The filling needs to be more on the dry side than the moist side or the wrap will get soggy and the filling may start to ooze out. Use more rice than guacamole, more refried beans than salsa . . . you get the idea.

Mandarin Salad

Prep time: 3 min • **Yield:** 1 serving

Ingredients	Directions
2 cups baby spinach leaves	*1* Put the spinach on a dish and sprinkle the oranges on top.
½ cup canned mandarin oranges, drained	
1 tablespoon olive oil	*2* In a cup or small bowl, use a fork to whisk together the oil, vinegar, and soy sauce.
1 teaspoon balsamic vinegar	
1 teaspoon low-sodium soy sauce	*3* Pour the dressing over the salad and sprinkle on the sesame seeds.
½ teaspoon sesame seeds	

Per serving: Calories 196 (From Fat 12g); Fat 14g (Saturated 2g); Cholesterol 0mg; Sodium 282mg; Carbohydrate 18g (Dietary Fiber 5g); Protein 2g.

Vary It! This salad is just the start of your creation. Add other cut-up fruits (kiwi, blueberries, and strawberries are especially good). Toss in sunflower seeds, slivered almonds, raisins, onion slices, and any other ingredients you have on hand.

Tip: Use a plastic container rather than a dish if you're going to eat this salad in transit.

Watermelon Salad

Prep time: 5 min • **Yield:** 1 serving

Ingredients	*Directions*
2 cups arugula leaves	*1* In a medium bowl, toss together the arugula, pepper, and dressing.
Dash black pepper	
2 tablespoons balsamic vinaigrette salad dressing	*2* Add the watermelon and feta cheese to the salad and toss again.
½ cup watermelon cut into small cubes	
3 tablespoons crumbled feta cheese crumbles	

Per serving: Calories 165 (From Fat 101); Fat 11g (Saturated 5g); Cholesterol 25mg; Sodium 577mg; Carbohydrate 13g (Dietary Fiber 1g); Protein 5g.

Vary It! You can use spinach in place of the arugula, and if you don't have balsamic vinaigrette salad dressing, mix together 2 tablespoons olive oil with 2 teaspoons balsamic vinegar.

Cucumber Dilly Delight

Prep time: 5 min • **Yield:** 1 serving

Ingredients	Directions
½ piece whole-wheat pita pocket bread	**1** Open the pocket in the pita and spread it liberally with the dill dip.
¼ cup prepared dill dip	
6 thin slices cucumber	**2** Stuff the cucumber slices, onion, tomato, and green pepper inside the pita pocket, close up, and enjoy!
3 thin slices onion	
3 thin slices tomato	
3 thin strips green pepper	

Per serving: Calories 498 (From Fat 370); Fat 41g (Saturated 6g); Cholesterol 30mg; Sodium 497mg; Carbohydrate 31g (Dietary Fiber 4g); Protein 4g.

Tip: To convert this to a vegan sandwich, omit the dill dip. Instead, stir ¼ teaspoon dried dill into nondairy sour cream or cream cheese.

Deviled Egg Delight

Prep time: 5 min • **Yield:** 1 serving

Ingredients	Directions
1 hard-boiled egg, diced	**1** In a small bowl, use the back of a fork to mix together the egg, mayonnaise, mustard, salt, and pepper. Spread this mixture on one half of the bagel.
¾ teaspoon low-fat mayonnaise	
2 drops mustard	
Dash salt	**2** Lay the tomato slice and spinach on top of the egg mixture and cover with the other half of the bagel.
Dash black pepper	
1 whole-grain bagel, cut in half horizontally	
1 large tomato slice	
¼ cup baby spinach leaves	

Per serving: Calories 383 (From Fat 66); Fat 7g (Saturated 2g); Cholesterol 212mg; Sodium 856mg; Carbohydrate 65g (Dietary Fiber 11g); Protein 19g.

Vary It! If you want to make this a bit more fancy, add some chopped green pepper or thin slices of avocado.

Hurry Up Hero

Prep time: 5 min • **Yield:** 1 serving

Ingredients	Directions
½ piece whole-wheat pita pocket bread	**1** Open the pocket in the pita bread and spread the mustard inside the pocket.
½ teaspoon yellow mustard	
1 slice pepper jack cheese or nondairy cheese	**2** Place the cheese, green pepper, cucumber, onion, tomato, avocado, and lettuce inside the pocket.
3 thin slices green pepper	
3 slices cucumber	
2 thin slices onion	
2 slices tomato	
¼ avocado, peeled, pitted, and sliced thin	
¼ cup shredded lettuce	

Per serving: Calories 285 (From Fat 147); Fat 16g (Saturated 7g); Cholesterol 30mg; Sodium 347mg; Carbohydrate 27g (Dietary Fiber 7g); Protein 11g.

Vary It! Use mayo if you don't have mustard, or drizzle a little olive oil and vinegar over the filling. If you're out of tomatoes, medium salsa works great as a substitute. In a pinch, you can use cooked asparagus spears or tiny broccoli florets if you're avocado-less. And you can use spinach in place of the lettuce.

Maple Syrup Salad

Prep time: 5 min • **Yield:** 1 serving

Ingredients	Directions
1 teaspoon apple cider vinegar	**1** In a small bowl, whisk together the vinegar, oil, mustard, syrup, salt, and pepper.
2 teaspoons olive oil	
¼ teaspoon spicy brown mustard	**2** Add the greens, beet slices, and onion rings; toss to coat evenly.
1 teaspoon maple syrup	
Dash salt	
Dash black pepper	
2 cups mixed greens	
½ cup canned beet slices, drained	
3 thin slices onion, separated into rings	

Per serving: Calories 153 (From Fat 85); Fat 10g (Saturated 1g); Cholesterol 0mg; Sodium 351mg; Carbohydrate 16g (Dietary Fiber 4g); Protein 3g.

Vary It! If you're out of canned beets, substitute other canned (and drained) veggies: artichoke hearts, corn, peas, asparagus tips, or even mixed vegetables. You can also use plain ol' pancake syrup if you don't have maple syrup on hand.

Tip: The maple syrup dressing is fabulous on this salad, but you can use it on other salads as well or to marinate vegetables before grilling, broiling, or pan-frying them.

Broccoli Slaw Sandwich

Prep time: 5 min • **Yield:** 1 serving

Ingredients	*Directions*
⅓ cup prepared broccoli slaw	**1** In a small bowl, mix together the broccoli slaw, mayonnaise, brown mustard, and pepper.
1½ tablespoons mayonnaise or vegan mayonnaise	
⅛ teaspoon spicy brown mustard	**2** Lay the tomato, onion, and cheese slice inside the pita pocket.
2 dashes black pepper	
2 slices tomato	**3** Spoon in the broccoli slaw mixture.
2 thin slices onion	
1 slice pepper jack cheese or nondairy cheese, cut in half	
½ piece whole-wheat pita pocket bread	

Per serving: Calories 368 (From Fat 234); Fat 26g (Saturated 8g); Cholesterol 38mg; Sodium 486mg; Carbohydrate 23g (Dietary Fiber 3g); Protein 11g.

Tip: Broccoli slaw is sold in bags in the produce section of the grocery store where you find other bagged salads.

Tip: It's fine to use ⅓ cup prepared broccoli slaw for this sandwich, but what are you supposed to do with the rest of the slaw mix that's left in the bag? One thing's for sure — you don't want to let it rot in the refrigerator while you're trying to decide. Add the broccoli slaw to casseroles and soups at dinnertime, add some to scrambled eggs in the morning, or sprinkle it on top of salads for lunch. If you still have some left over, steam it, add a little olive oil and lemon juice, and eat it as a side dish with dinner.

Hummus Wrap

Prep time: 5 min • **Yield:** 1 serving

Ingredients	Directions
3 tablespoons hummus	**1** Spread the hummus down the center of the tortilla. Lay the cheese slices on top of the hummus.
1 whole-wheat 8-inch tortilla	
1 slice pepper jack cheese or nondairy cheese, cut in half	
2 thin slices onion, separated into rings	**2** Put the onion rings, red pepper, green pepper, pepperoncini, and spinach leaves over the cheese.
1 roasted red pepper, cut in half lengthwise	**3** Fold up the bottom of the tortilla and fold in the sides to make a wrap. (Check out Chapter 7 for more information on folding a wrap.)
2 thin slices green pepper	
2 pepperoncini, sliced in half lengthwise	
¼ cup baby spinach leaves	

Per serving: Calories 313 (From Fat 142); Fat 16g (Saturated 6g); Cholesterol 25mg; Sodium 911mg; Carbohydrate 36g (Dietary Fiber 6g); Protein 13g.

Tip: You can pay a premium price for fresh red bell peppers, roast them till they just begin to char, carefully remove the skins, remove the seeds inside, and then place them in a bowl and marinate them . . . or you can take the easy way out and just buy a jar of prepared roasted red peppers sold at almost all grocery stores (usually where olives and pickles are sold).

Note: Hummus is made mostly from chickpeas (also known as garbanzo beans), so it's loaded with fiber, iron, and protein and is a great source of magnesium — all things vegetarians need. The fat in hummus is the good kind of fat because it comes from olive oil.

Avocado Pita

Prep time: 5 min • **Yield:** 1 serving

Ingredients	*Directions*
½ ripe avocado, pitted	*1* Use a spoon to scoop out the avocado pulp into a small bowl. Add the lemon juice, olive oil, Italian seasoning, salt, pepper, hot pepper sauce, and onion. Using a fork, gently mash the ingredients together.
½ teaspoon lemon juice	
1 teaspoon olive oil	
Dash Italian seasoning	
Dash salt	
Dash black pepper	*2* Add the cheese and tomatoes and gently stir to blend.
2 drops hot pepper sauce	
1 slice onion, minced	*3* Open the pocket of the pita bread and spoon in the avocado mixture.
3 tablespoons crumbled feta cheese	
4 grape tomatoes, halved	
½ piece whole-wheat pita pocket bread	

Per serving: Calories 347 (From Fat 215); Fat 24g (Saturated 7g); Cholesterol 25mg; Sodium 632mg; Carbohydrate 29g (Dietary Fiber 10g); Protein 10g.

Vary It! If spicy is your thing, shake in a few extra drops of the hot sauce. A few spinach leaves are also good to add to this sandwich.

Greek Hummus Wrap

Prep time: 5 min • **Yield:** 1 serving

Ingredients	Directions
3 tablespoons hummus	*1* Spread the hummus down the center of the tortilla.
1 whole-wheat 8-inch tortilla	
1 tablespoon fat-free plain Greek yogurt or soy yogurt	*2* Spread the yogurt over the hummus and sprinkle the yogurt with dill and mint.
Dash dried dill	
Dash dried mint flakes	*3* Sprinkle the cheese over the yogurt.
2 tablespoons crumbled feta cheese or nondairy mozzarella cheese, crumbled	*4* Place the cucumber, onion, and tomato slices over the feta cheese.
4 thin slices cucumber	*5* Fold up the bottom of the tortilla and fold in the sides to make a wrap. (Flip to Chapter 7 if you need extra help on folding a wrap properly.)
2 very thin slices onion, separated into rings	
3 thin slices tomato	

Per serving: Calories 260 (From Fat 93); Fat 10g (Saturated 4g); Cholesterol 17mg; Sodium 516mg; Carbohydrate 35g (Dietary Fiber 6g); Protein 11g.

Vary It! This wrap is delicious as is, but feel free to add some beans (garbanzo are great but any other kind of beans will do, too), pitted kalamata olives, and shredded lettuce.

South of the Border Wrap

Prep time: 5 min • **Yield:** 1 serving

Ingredients	Directions
2 tablespoons low-fat cream cheese or tofu cream cheese	**1** Spread the cream cheese down the center of the tortilla.
1 whole-wheat 8-inch tortilla	
¼ cup guacamole dip	**2** Spread the guacamole over the cream cheese, and then spread the sour cream over the guacamole.
1 tablespoon low-fat or nondairy sour cream	
2 thin slices onion, separated into rings	**3** Sprinkle the onion rings, sunflower seeds, and pepper cheese over the sour cream.
½ teaspoon sunflower seeds	
1 tablespoon shredded pepper jack or nondairy cheese	**4** Drizzle the salsa on top of the pepper cheese, and then sprinkle the alfalfa sprouts over the salsa.
4 teaspoons salsa	
½ cup alfalfa sprouts	**5** Fold up the bottom of the tortilla and fold in the sides to make a wrap. (Head to Chapter 7 for full details on properly folding a wrap.)

Per serving: Calories 335 (From Fat 161); Fat 18g (Saturated 7g); Cholesterol 33mg; Sodium 632mg; Carbohydrate 36g (Dietary Fiber 5g); Protein 10g.

Vary It! If you have any leftover rice, put a few spoonfuls on this sandwich before rolling it up. And if you don't have alfalfa sprouts, substitute shredded lettuce.

Tip: If you don't have prepared guacamole dip, you can make your own in a couple of minutes. Put ¼ peeled, ripe avocado into a small bowl. Add 2 teaspoons minced onion, 1 teaspoon lemon juice, and a dash of salt and black pepper, and then mash everything together with a fork.

Making Heat-It-and-Eat-It Lunches

College life conjures up images of campus activities, going out on weekends with friends, enjoying a social dorm life — and oh, yes, studying. What you don't usually picture is a college student spending hours in a kitchen cooking. You'll have plenty of time later in life to do that. What you need now is healthy vegetarian food that's quick and easy . . . heat-it-and-eat-it foods. The lunches that follow are just that.

Some of the recipes in this section require you to preheat the broiler. When time is of the essence, make these dishes in the microwave instead. Just put the food on a paper plate and pop it in the microwave on full power for about a minute or so, until the cheese melts and the filling is warmed.

Stocking your kitchen with prepared lunches

Your intention to come home and make a nice lunch for yourself every day is a great goal, but you know that's not always going to happen. Keep a few prepared foods on hand (like the ones in the following list) for those days when you really don't have time to spend in the kitchen (or when you forget to shop for fresh foods):

✔ Amy's Garden Vegetable Lasagna (in the freezer section)

✔ Campbell's Tomato or Vegetarian Vegetable Soup

✔ Individual-sized containers of heat-and-eat, cheese-filled ravioli and macaroni and cheese

✔ Lean Cuisine Santa Fe-Style Rice & Beans and Vegetable Eggrolls (in the freezer section)

✔ MorningStar Farms Buffalo Wings Veggie Wings (in the freezer section)

✔ Smucker's Uncrustables (in the freezer section)

✔ Vegetable sushi, rice-stuffed grape leaves, hummus, and tabbouleh in the deli section (these are handy to keep in the fridge for a quick lunch with crackers or pita bread)

Burrito Roll

Prep time: 3 min • **Cook time:** 40 sec • **Yield:** 1 serving

Ingredients	Directions
2 meatless sausage-flavored links, cut in half lengthwise	*1* Set the meatless links on a dish, cover the dish with wax paper, and microwave on high for 40 seconds, or until heated through.
2 low-fat mozzarella or nondairy string cheese sticks, cut in half lengthwise	
1 whole-wheat 10-inch tortilla	*2* Place the cheese sticks on the tortilla, drizzle with mustard, and add the meatless links. Drizzle taco sauce over the links.
¾ teaspoon spicy brown mustard	
1 tablespoon taco sauce	*3* Fold the bottom fourth of the tortilla up over the filling to prevent the taco sauce from dripping out. Then fold in one side of the wrap to cover the filling and fold over the other side of the wrap to secure the filling inside.

Per serving: Calories 416 (From Fat 136); Fat 15g (Saturated 5g); Cholesterol 10mg; Sodium 1,077mg; Carbohydrate 41g (Dietary Fiber 3g); Protein 33g.

Tip: If you have a few extra moments, wrap the tortilla in a damp paper towel and warm it in the microwave for a few seconds before adding the filling. Heating the tortilla makes it more flexible and less likely to crack when you roll it.

Vary It! If the filling seems a bit plain to you, toss in some leftover corn, add a scrambled egg, or spoon on some leftover rice. The combinations are limited only by the amount of time you have to prepare lunch and what's left over in the fridge.

Open-faced Pseudo Turkey Sandwich

Prep time: 2 min • **Cook time:** 2 min • **Yield:** 1 serving

Ingredients	*Directions*
⅓ cup vegetarian gravy 3 slices vegetarian turkey lunchmeat 1 slice whole-wheat bread	*1* Pour the gravy into a small saucepan. Add the lunchmeat and warm over medium-high heat about 2 minutes, or until heated through.
	2 While the gravy mixture is heating, toast the bread. Place the toast on a dinner plate and top with the lunchmeat and gravy.

Per serving: Calories 365 (From Fat 77); Fat 9g (Saturated 0g); Cholesterol 0mg; Sodium 1,774mg; Carbohydrate 29g (Dietary Fiber 8g); Protein 49g.

Tip: If you're looking for a can of vegetarian gravy, Imagine Foods has canned, organic Wild Mushroom Gravy, and it's available in many grocery stores. Franco-American's canned Mushroom Gravy is vegan.

Pesto Roll-up

Prep time: 3 min • **Cook time:** 1 min • **Yield:** 1 serving

Ingredients	Directions
1 whole-wheat 8-inch tortilla	*1* Preheat the broiler.
3 tablespoons pesto sauce	
3 thin slices tomato	*2* Lay a piece of foil on a baking pan and lay the tortilla on top of the foil.
2 tablespoons shredded low-fat mozzarella cheese	
	3 Spread the pesto sauce evenly over the tortilla, lay the tomato slices on top, and sprinkle the cheese over the tomatoes.
	4 Bake for 1 minute, or until the cheese melts. Quickly roll the tortilla into a log shape.

Per serving: Calories 343 (From Fat 204); Fat 23g (Saturated 7g); Cholesterol 18mg; Sodium 644mg; Carbohydrate 26g (Dietary Fiber 4g); Protein 16g.

Tip: Pesto sauce is made from some really good stuff: crushed fresh basil leaves, Parmesan cheese, olive oil, pine nuts, and minced fresh garlic. You can find it in the grocery store where spaghetti sauce is sold. Pesto is great to use as a spread. When you open a jar of pesto, stir it well because, as it sits, the oil can separate.

Vary It! The variety of toppings you can add to this roll-up is limited only by your imagination . . . and weight (weight of the toppings — not your weight!). A tortilla is thin and can tear under too much weight. Some tasty items to add include alfalfa sprouts, baby spinach leaves, thin slices of avocado, sautéed mushrooms, caramelized onions, thin slices of zucchini, sliced black olives, sliced pimento-stuffed green olives, sliced pepperoncini, minced broccoli, chopped sun-dried tomatoes, slivers of roasted red pepper, feta cheese crumbles, shredded cheddar cheese, crumbled blue cheese, minced green pepper, and even minced garlic. I'm sure you can come up with more, but this list will get you started.

Tantalizing Taco

Prep time: 4 min • **Cook time:** 25 sec • **Yield:** 1 serving

Ingredients	*Directions*
⅓ cup canned pinto beans, rinsed and drained	**1** In a small bowl, stir together the beans, chili powder, salt, and pepper. Heat bean mixture in the microwave for 25 seconds. Spoon this mixture into the taco shell.
⅛ teaspoon chili powder	
Dash salt	
Dash black pepper	**2** Layer the red pepper, onion, avocado, and cheese on top of the beans. Drizzle the taco sauce on top.
1 hard corn taco shell	
½ roasted red pepper, sliced lengthwise	
2 thin slices onion	
¼ avocado, peeled, pitted, and sliced	
1 tablespoon low-fat shredded sharp cheddar cheese or nondairy cheese	
3 tablespoons taco sauce	

Per serving: Calories 258 (From Fat 89); Fat 10g (Saturated 2g); Cholesterol 2mg; Sodium 588mg; Carbohydrate 31g (Dietary Fiber 9g); Protein 8g.

Vary It! This is one of those lunches where it's super easy to improvise. If you have black beans or kidney beans or most any other kind of beans left over in the refrigerator, use them up in place of the pinto beans. No corn taco shell? Wrap the contents in a soft corn or whole-wheat flour tortilla. No red peppers on hand? Substitute sliced tomatoes. No cheddar cheese? Use provolone or mozzarella or most any cheese you have in the fridge.

Simple Cheese Toast

Prep time: 2 min • **Cook time:** 2½ min • **Yield:** 1 serving

Ingredients	Directions
1 slice whole-grain bread	**1** Preheat the broiler.
½ teaspoon yellow or brown spicy mustard	**2** Lay the bread on a piece of foil and toast it lightly in the broiler for about 1 minute. Turn it over and toast it about 30 more seconds for the second side to brown.
3 strips (each ¾-inch wide) roasted red pepper	
1 slice low-fat American or Swiss cheese or nondairy cheese	**3** Spread mustard on one side of the bread. Top with the red pepper strips and cheese slice.
	4 Broil the toast for 1 minute, or until the cheese has melted.

Per serving: Calories 110 (From Fat 20); Fat 2g (Saturated 1g); Cholesterol 5mg; Sodium 397mg; Carbohydrate 15g (Dietary Fiber 2g); Protein 8g.

Blue Cheese Bonanza

Prep time: 2 min • **Cook time:** 3 min • **Yield:** 1 serving

Ingredients	Directions
2 tablespoons crumbled blue cheese 2 slices whole-grain bread ¼ ripe pear (with skin), cored and sliced thin 2 tablespoons shredded low-fat mozzarella cheese Nonstick cooking spray	*1* Spread the blue cheese on one slice of bread. Lay the pear slices over the blue cheese and sprinkle the mozzarella cheese over the pears. Lay the second piece of bread on top. *2* Warm a small skillet on the stove over medium-high heat. Spray one side of the sandwich with nonstick spray and place it, sprayed-side down, in the pan. Now spray the top of the sandwich. *3* Cook over medium-high heat for about 1½ minutes per side, or until the sandwich is golden brown on both sides.

Per serving: Calories 250 (From Fat 75); Fat 8g (Saturated 4g); Cholesterol 15mg; Sodium 641mg; Carbohydrate 33g (Dietary Fiber 5g); Protein 13g.

Vary It! If you hate blue cheese, shame on you, but you can substitute hot pepper cheese.

Broiled Open-faced Sandwich

Prep time: 3 min • **Cook time:** 2 min • **Yield:** 1 serving

Ingredients	*Directions*
1 slice whole-grain bread	*1* Preheat the broiler. Lightly toast the bread in a toaster.
¼ teaspoon olive oil	
Dash Italian seasoning	*2* Place the toast on a baking sheet or piece of foil. Brush one side of the toast with oil and sprinkle with Italian seasoning.
3 slices tomato	
2 fresh white mushrooms, sliced thin	*3* Lay the tomato slices on the bread and cover the surface with the mushrooms. Sprinkle the cheese on top of the mushrooms.
2 tablespoons grated Parmesan cheese or nondairy cheese	
	4 Broil for 1 minute, or until the cheese melts. Watch closely so the bread and cheese don't burn.

Per serving: Calories 143 (From Fat 49); Fat 5g (Saturated 2g); Cholesterol 8mg; Sodium 320mg; Carbohydrate 17g (Dietary Fiber 3g); Protein 8g.

Vary It! If you don't feel like buying and slicing fresh mushrooms, you can use 3 tablespoons of canned sliced mushrooms; just make sure to drain them first. You can also use provolone, Swiss, or mozzarella cheese in place of the Parmesan.

Vary It! Add delicacies to your sandwich like roasted red peppers, sliced olives, or even sliced artichoke hearts or asparagus tips.

Vegetarian Hot Dogs and Beans

Prep time: 3 min • **Cook time:** 2 min • **Yield:** 1 serving

Ingredients	Directions
Nonstick cooking spray	*1* Spray a small saucepan with nonstick spray. Add the hot dog slices and cook for about 1 minute over medium-high heat, stirring frequently.
1 meatless hot dog, sliced into thin circles	
⅓ cup canned vegetarian baked beans, partially drained	*2* Add the beans to the pan and continue to cook about 1 minute, or until heated through.
½ teaspoon brown mustard	
1 whole-wheat hot dog bun	*3* Spread mustard inside both halves of the bun and lay the onion slices on one half.
2 thin slices onion	
3 tablespoons crushed tortilla chips	*4* Spoon in the hot dogs and beans and top with tortilla chips.

Per serving: Calories 314 (From Fat 43); Fat 5g (Saturated 0g); Cholesterol 0mg; Sodium 654mg; Carbohydrate 46g (Dietary Fiber 5g); Protein 21g.

Vary It! You can add lots of toppings to this sandwich, including coleslaw, sauerkraut, dill pickle relish, and/or shredded cheddar cheese. You can also toast the hot dog bun if you like.

Black Bean Tortilla

Prep time: 3 min • **Cook time:** 2 min • **Yield:** 1 serving

Ingredients	Directions
3 tablespoons low-fat refried beans	**1** Spread the refried beans down the middle of the tortilla. Top with the spinach, salsa, and cheese.
1 whole-wheat 8-inch tortilla	
¼ cup baby spinach leaves	**2** Fold the bottom fourth of the tortilla up over the filling and then, starting at one side, roll the tortilla so the filling is sealed inside.
3 tablespoons corn salsa	
2 tablespoons shredded low-fat sharp cheddar cheese or Mexican cheese blend or nondairy cheese	**3** Heat a small, nonstick skillet on medium-high heat. Spray the pan lightly with nonstick spray.
Nonstick cooking spray	**4** Cook the tortilla, turning occasionally, for 2 minutes, or until heated through.

Per serving: Calories 195 (From Fat 29); Fat 3g (Saturated 1g); Cholesterol 3mg; Sodium 737mg; Carbohydrate 35g (Dietary Fiber 4g); Protein 9g.

Tip: If you're really in a hurry and can't spare 2 quick minutes to cook the tortilla, you can skip Steps 3 and 4 and just eat it as is.

Tip: The leftover salsa makes a perfect midnight snack with tortilla chips.

Blue Cheese Onion Ring Pizza

Prep time: 3 min • **Cook time:** 2 min • **Yield:** 1 serving

Ingredients	Directions
1 small individual store-bought pizza crust	**1** Preheat the oven to 425 degrees.
½ teaspoon olive oil	**2** Set the crust on a piece of foil and brush the top of the crust with oil.
3 thin slices tomato	
2 tablespoons canned fried onions	**3** Lay the tomato slices on top of the crust and sprinkle the fried onions over the tomatoes.
3 tablespoons crumbled blue cheese	
	4 Sprinkle the blue cheese on top of the onions.
	5 Bake the pizza for 2 minutes, or until the cheese has melted.

Per serving: Calories 531 (From Fat 151); Fat 17g (Saturated 7g); Cholesterol 19mg; Sodium 1,095mg; Carbohydrate 76g (Dietary Fiber 3g); Protein 18g.

Tip: If you're in a rush, you can bake the pizza in the microwave for 30 seconds instead of using the oven.

Vary It! I'm talking divine taste here, something you just can't stop eating. If you honestly don't like blue cheese, learn to like it! (Or, you know, just substitute any cheese of your choice.)

Chapter 10

25 Minutes till Mealtime: Lunches

In This Chapter

▶ Mixing up yummy salads

▶ Putting together sandwiches and burgers

▶ Serving up pizza and tacos

▶ Cooking soup in a jiffy

*Y*ou're probably looking at the title of this chapter and thinking, "I don't have 25 free minutes at noon to make lunch." Think for a minute of the alternatives — would you prefer to spend your money buying unhealthy junk food out each day? Or go without lunch and then get sluggish mid-afternoon? A day has 24 hours. Twenty-five minutes or less of your time is a good trade for a great lunch.

The key to fun lunches is variety. Keep foods on hand to have with your lunch that don't take extra time to prepare, like hard-boiled eggs, cut-up raw veggies with ranch dressing for dipping, flavored yogurt, and cheese cubes. Muffins make a great side dish for a salad lunch. Dip fruit slices in something fun, like peanut butter or another nut butter, honey, cream cheese, all-fruit preserves, or apple butter.

Going to the grocery store for lunch

If you can't get home for lunch, consider going to a grocery store and creating your own salad from the salad bar rather than stopping at a fast-food drive-through. Check out the deli while you're there; most grocery delis now offer entire meals, and you can pick up all kinds of scrumptious vegetarian foods.

Finally, keep a supply of things in the kitchen cupboard you can grab after lunch to satisfy your sweet tooth. Good choices include natural fruit leathers, low-fat fruit and cereal bars, granola bars, dried fruit mixed with nuts and seeds, individual containers of applesauce or small fruit cups, graham crackers, bagel crisps, and fruit-sweetened cookies.

Going Green with Salads and Vegetables

Vegetables are pretty close to being perfect foods. They're readily available and affordable, and they're full of vitamins, minerals, and fiber. They have zero cholesterol and are almost completely fat-free. Vegetables come in every size, shape, and color imaginable, so you'll never get bored with them. And you can eat most of them boiled, steamed, microwaved, sautéed, braised, baked, roasted, broiled, grilled, and even raw.

Veggie Pita

Prep time: 4 min • **Cook time:** 2 min • **Yield:** 1 serving

Ingredients	Directions
½ **teaspoon butter or nondairy margarine**	**1** Put the butter, cauliflower, and broccoli in a small, microwave-safe bowl, cover with wax paper, and microwave on high for 2 minutes, stirring once after 1 minute.
¼ **cup sliced cauliflower**	
¼ **cup sliced broccoli**	
2 slices onion	**2** Stir in the onions, tomatoes, Italian seasoning, and cheese. Spoon the mixture into the pita pocket.
3 tablespoons chopped tomato	
Dash Italian seasoning	
2 tablespoons shredded low-fat sharp cheddar cheese or nondairy cheddar cheese	
½ **whole-wheat pita pocket bread**	

Per serving: Calories 152 (From Fat 36); Fat 4g (Saturated 2g); Cholesterol 8mg; Sodium 273mg; Carbohydrate 23g (Dietary Fiber 4g); Protein 8g.

Vary It! You can exchange the cauliflower and/or the broccoli with any leftover veggies you have in the fridge. No cheddar cheese? Use whatever cheese you have on hand.

Tip: If you're vegan, use olive oil in place of the butter.

Pita Garden

Prep time: 7 min • **Yield:** 1 serving

Ingredients	*Directions*
½ whole-wheat pita pocket bread	**1** Open the pocket of the pita bread gingerly. Spread the mustard inside the pita.
½ teaspoon brown mustard	
1 slice pepper jack or nondairy cheese	**2** Put the cheese, green pepper, onion, cucumber, tomato, and avocado slices into the pita pocket. You've just built yourself a pita garden!
2 slices green pepper	
2 slices onion, separated into rings	
3 slices cucumber, unpeeled	
2 slices tomato	
3 slices avocado, peeled and pitted	

Per serving: Calories 281 (From Fat 143); Fat 16g (Saturated 6g); Cholesterol 30mg; Sodium 412mg; Carbohydrate 27g (Dietary Fiber 6g); Protein 12g.

Vary It! This, like so many other recipes, can be adjusted depending on what you have in the fridge. For example, you can use roasted red peppers in place of the tomato slices. Add sliced hot peppers, banana pepper rings, sliced zucchini, or yellow squash. If you have hummus or pesto, spread that (rather than mustard) inside the pita bread before filling it with veggies, or really live life on the edge and use mayonnaise.

Tip: One advantage to eating cucumbers is that you can leave on the skin, and that means you're getting more nutrition and more fiber. Baby cucumbers (also known as pickling cucumbers) are a good choice because their skins are so tender.

Taco Salad

Prep time: 8 min • **Cook time:** 1 min • **Yield:** 1 serving

Ingredients	*Directions*
½ cup light red kidney beans, rinsed and drained	*1* In a small saucepan, stir together the kidney beans, water, and seasoning mix. Cook over medium heat and simmer about 1 minute, or just until the liquid is absorbed. Remove the pan from the heat.
3 tablespoons water	
¾ teaspoon taco seasoning mix	
2 cups shredded lettuce	*2* Place the lettuce on a plate or in a large soup bowl. Drizzle with the Italian dressing.
2 tablespoons fat-free Italian dressing	
2 tablespoons sliced black olives	*3* Spoon the kidney bean mixture over the lettuce, and then add the olives, onions, and tomatoes. Top off the salad with the cheese, salsa, and crushed chips.
1 green onion, sliced	
3 grape tomatoes, halved	
2 tablespoons shredded low-fat sharp cheddar cheese or nondairy cheese	
2 tablespoons salsa	
5 tortilla chips, crumbled	

Per serving: Calories 276 (From Fat 57); Fat 6g (Saturated 1g); Cholesterol 4mg; Sodium 1,165mg; Carbohydrate 42g (Dietary Fiber 12g); Protein 15g.

Vary It! This recipe has no mock meat, but you can easily cook up a few meatless beef-flavored crumbles and stir them into the kidney bean mixture. I don't list sour cream either, but if you have any on hand, add a dollop or two on top of the salad.

Eggless Tofu Salad

Prep time: 10 min • **Yield:** 1 serving

Ingredients	Directions
⅔ cup firm tofu	*1* Drain the tofu well between paper towels. Press on the towels to get out as much moisture as possible from the tofu.
½ rib celery, diced	
2 tablespoons minced green pepper	*2* Crumble the tofu into a bowl, and then mash it with the back of a fork.
2 tablespoons minced green onion	
1 tablespoon vegan mayonnaise	*3* Add the celery, green pepper, green onion, mayonnaise, mustard, cayenne, parsley (if using), dill, salt, and pepper. Stir until everything is well mixed.
¼ teaspoon spicy brown mustard	
Dash cayenne pepper	*4* Spoon the salad onto a piece of bread, and top with spinach leaves and another piece of bread.
1 teaspoon minced fresh parsley (optional)	
⅛ teaspoon dried dill	
⅛ teaspoon salt	
¼ teaspoon black pepper	
2 slices whole-grain bread	
6 spinach leaves	

Per serving: Calories 414 (From Fat 204); Fat 23g (Saturated 3g); Cholesterol 0mg; Sodium 744mg; Carbohydrate 35g (Dietary Fiber 9g); Protein 25g.

Tip: If you have time to make this ahead so it can chill in the refrigerator for a half hour, the taste is even better.

Tip: Make a larger batch of this salad if you like to snack in the evenings. Put a dollop of the salad on top of crackers, and if you still have some left over the next day, make a lettuce wrap.

Building Vegetarian Burgers and Sandwiches

With so many choices of ingredients and methods of preparation, you'll never get bored eating sandwiches. You can build them on so many different kinds of breads, bagels, rolls, pita pockets, tortilla wraps, and even pancakes or waffles. Fillings can be cold or hot, chopped or whole slices of foods, and mixed with a variety of condiments (ketchup, mustard, mayo, salsa, and stuff like that). You can fry, grill, or broil sandwiches, or heat them in a microwave. The best part about a sandwich is that you can usually carry it in one hand so you can eat it en route to class.

Turning leftovers into a tasty lunch

In a perfect world, your lunch would consist of whole grains, vegetables, and fruit, and you'd have plenty of time to eat it. (If you're a lacto or lacto ovo vegetarian, you may want to add dairy to this list of ingredients.) In your world, however, you're probably lucky to grab whatever you can and inhale it before rushing out the door again. Here are two ideas for making lunch when you don't have time to make lunch:

✔ When you make dinner, double the recipe. Rewarm the leftovers in the microwave for lunch the next day and eat them as is or pile them into a pita pocket.

✔ If you have leftover carbs (rice, pasta, or potatoes), heat up something in the microwave to pour or spoon on top of the food to add flavor, such as spaghetti sauce, drained black beans and salsa, leftover cooked vegetables, a small can of vegetarian beans, or canned cheddar cheese soup with a little milk added.

Pan-fried Eggplant Sandwich

Prep time: 2 min • **Cook time:** 4 min • **Yield:** 1 serving

Ingredients	*Directions*
Nonstick cooking spray ¼ teaspoon olive oil 2 slices frozen breaded eggplant 1 teaspoon mayonnaise	*1* Spray a medium skillet with nonstick spray. Add the oil and warm the pan for 20 seconds. Add the eggplant slices and cook over medium heat, turning once, about 3 minutes, or until they're browned on both sides and hot in the center.
1 kaiser roll, split in half horizontally 1 slice tomato Dash Italian seasoning	*2* Spread the mayonnaise on the bottom half of the roll. Lay the tomato on top and sprinkle the tomato with Italian seasoning. Sprinkle the feta cheese on top.
1½ tablespoons feta cheese crumbles	*3* Lay the eggplant on top of the feta cheese and cover with the roll lid.

Per serving: Calories 311 (From Fat 125); Fat 14g (Saturated 4g); Cholesterol 15mg; Sodium 529mg; Carbohydrate 37g (Dietary Fiber 2g); Protein 9g.

Tip: You can get a box of breaded eggplant slices in the freezer section of the grocery store. They're really convenient because you don't have to make a breading mix, add the seasonings, or dip the eggplant in oil or egg and then into the crumb mix. And you don't have to think about what you're going to do with all the leftover fresh eggplant.

Vary It! If you're out of feta cheese, goat cheese or even Swiss or pepper cheese will work. No kaiser roll? Use any roll you have on hand, or even two slices of toasted Italian bread.

Melted Marvel

Prep time: 4 min • **Cook time:** 2 min • **Yield:** 1 serving

Ingredients	Directions
1 whole-wheat English muffin, cut in half	*1* Set the broiler rack one position down from the top, or about 6 to 7 inches from the heat source. Preheat the broiler.
1 hard-boiled egg, sliced	
1 thin slice tomato	*2* Toast the English muffin halves in a toaster.
¼ teaspoon fat-free Italian dressing	
1 thin slice onion, separated into rings	*3* Place one half of the English muffin on a baking pan or piece of foil and lay the egg slices on top.
2 thin slices dill pickle	
1 slice low-fat sharp cheddar cheese	*4* Lay the tomato slices on top of the egg and drizzle the dressing over the tomato.
	5 Lay the onion and pickle on top of the tomato and cover it all with a slice of cheese.
	6 Broil the sandwich for 1 minute, or until the cheese melts, and then cover the sandwich with the remaining English muffin half.

Per serving: Calories 263 (From Fat 76); Fat 9g (Saturated 3g); Cholesterol 218mg; Sodium 650mg; Carbohydrate 29g (Dietary Fiber 3g); Protein 18g.

Vary It! If you don't have an English muffin, do you have a bagel, a loaf of French bread you can slice, or a ciabatta or sub roll you can cut in half? You can use any of these breads in place of the English muffin.

Potato Pocket

Prep time: 4 min • **Cook time:** 3 min • **Yield:** 1 serving

Ingredients	Directions
1 teaspoon olive oil	*1* Warm the oil in a medium skillet over medium-high heat, and then add the potatoes, onion, green pepper, and chili powder. Sauté over medium-high heat, turning the potatoes frequently, for about 3 minutes, or until the potatoes begin to get crusty.
¾ cup canned sliced potatoes, drained	
¼ onion, sliced thin	
⅛ green pepper, chopped	
2 dashes chili powder	
½ whole-wheat pita pocket bread	*2* Open the pita pocket and line the inside with the cheese and the tomato slices.
1 slice pepper jack or nondairy cheese	*3* Spoon the potato mixture into the pocket.
3 thin slices tomato	

Per serving: Calories 340 (From Fat 134); Fat 15g (Saturated 6g); Cholesterol 30mg; Sodium 937mg; Carbohydrate 42g (Dietary Fiber 7g); Protein 13g.

Tip: You're going to be left with a half can of unused potato slices. What to do? Cover the can with plastic wrap and refrigerate it. In the morning, drain the potatoes and fry them with some chopped green pepper to eat with a scrambled egg or scrambled tofu and toast. Yum!

Pesto Grilled Cheese Sandwich

Prep time: 4 min • **Cook time:** 4 min • **Yield:** 1 serving

Ingredients	Directions
1 tablespoon pesto 2 slices whole-grain bread 2 slices pepper jack cheese 2 oil-packed sun-dried tomatoes, diced Nonstick cooking spray	**1** Spread the pesto on one slice of bread. Put a slice of cheese on top of the pesto, and then top with the diced tomatoes. Lay the other piece of cheese on top, and complete the sandwich with the other slice of bread.
	2 Spray a small skillet with nonstick spray. Lay the sandwich in the skillet and spray the top slice of bread with nonstick spray.
	3 Cook the sandwich over medium heat, turning it over once, for about 4 minutes, or until both sides are golden.

Per serving: Calories 443 (From Fat 253); Fat 28g (Saturated 15g); Cholesterol 65mg; Sodium 670mg; Carbohydrate 29g (Dietary Fiber 4g); Protein 20g.

Vary It! Almost any cheese will work with this sandwich, so use whatever you have on hand.

Vegetarian Sloppy Joe

Prep time: 5 min • **Cook time:** 6 min • **Yield:** 1 serving

Ingredients	Directions
1 teaspoon olive oil	**1** Heat the oil in a small skillet over medium-high heat. Add the crumbles, onion, and green pepper. Sauté, stirring frequently, about 2 minutes, until the onion is soft and the crumbles are cooked.
1 cup meatless beef-flavored crumbles	
2 tablespoons chopped onion	
2 tablespoons chopped green pepper	**2** Stir in the sloppy Joe sauce and simmer for 3 minutes. Spoon the mixture onto a bun.
¼ cup sloppy Joe sauce	
1 hamburger bun	

Per serving: *Calories 456 (From Fat 177); Fat 20g (Saturated 4g); Cholesterol 0mg; Sodium 1,138mg; Carbohydrate 42g (Dietary Fiber 9g); Protein 28g.*

Almost Reuben

Prep time: 8 min • **Cook time:** 4 min • **Yield:** 1 serving

Ingredients	Directions
1 teaspoon olive oil	*1* Heat the oil in a medium skillet over medium-high heat. Add the cabbage, onions, green pepper, and lemon juice. Cook, stirring frequently, about 4 minutes, or until the vegetables are tender. (Add a little water if needed to prevent the veggies from sticking to the pan.)
¾ cup finely shredded cabbage	
3 tablespoons thinly sliced onions	
3 tablespoons minced green pepper	
1 teaspoon lemon juice	*2* Spread the dressing on one slice of bread and lay the cheese on top of the dressing. Spoon the hot cabbage mixture over the cheese and cover with the remaining slice of bread.
1 teaspoon Thousand Island dressing	
2 slices rye bread	
1 slice low-fat Swiss or nondairy cheese	

Per serving: Calories 304 (From Fat 91); Fat 10g (Saturated 2g); Cholesterol 11mg; Sodium 875mg; Carbohydrate 40g (Dietary Fiber 6g); Protein 14g.

Tip: You can buy a small head of cabbage and shred the portion you need, or you can buy a bag of preshredded slaw mix. Use the leftover cabbage in casseroles, to make cole slaw, to toss into stews and soups, or boil it with potato wedges and make steamed cabbage and potatoes for dinner.

Vary It! Feel like toasting your rye bread? Go for it! It's a great twist on this recipe.

Vary It! For a classic vegetarian Reuben, add baked or smoked tempeh strips to this sandwich.

Note: Some commercial Thousand Island dressings contain propylene glycol alginate, a natural thickener extracted from seaweed. Calcium disodium EDTA may also be present in commercial dressings. This is a quality protector (flavor enhancer) derived from salts, not to be confused with disodium guanylate (a flavor enhancer derived from fungal sources) or disodium inosinate (a flavor enhancer derived from mineral, animal, vegetable, or fungal sources). Read the label to make sure that the dressing you buy is vegetarian. You don't want to buy anything with disodium inosinate unless you first find out what it's made from by checking with the manufacturer.

Burger a la Greque

Prep time: 10 min • **Cook time:** 2 min • **Yield:** 1 serving

Ingredients	Directions
1 tablespoon feta cheese crumbles	*1* In a small bowl, stir together the feta cheese, yogurt, cucumber, mint, parsley (if using), and garlic. Set aside.
1 tablespoon fat-free plain yogurt	
3 thin slices cucumber, peeled and chopped fine	*2* Spray a nonstick pan with nonstick spray. Cook the burger over medium heat for 1 minute on each side, or just until browned.
⅛ teaspoon dried mint flakes	
¼ teaspoon dried parsley flakes (optional)	*3* Set the patty on the bottom half of the hamburger bun. Top it with the tomato and onion slices. Spoon the feta cheese sauce on top, cover it with the bun lid, and enjoy!
¼ teaspoon minced garlic	
Nonstick cooking spray	
1 meatless burger	
1 whole-wheat hamburger bun	
1 slice tomato	
2 thin onion slices	

Per serving: *Calories 290 (From Fat 66); Fat 7g (Saturated 3g); Cholesterol 20mg; Sodium 612mg; Carbohydrate 44g (Dietary Fiber 9g); Protein 612g.*

Vary It! If you don't have (or don't want!) plain yogurt, use low-fat sour cream instead. Also, shredded lettuce or leaf spinach is a good addition to this sandwich.

Tip: If you have time to make the topping ahead and refrigerate it for a few hours so the flavors can blend, it tastes even better.

Tip: Crumbled feta cheese costs more than buying the cheese in bulk and crumbling it yourself.

Italian Hero

Prep time: 5 min • **Cook time:** 8 min • **Yield:** 1 serving

Ingredients	Directions
1 teaspoon + ¾ teaspoon olive oil	*1* Preheat the broiler.
1 Italian meatless sausage-flavored link, partially thawed	*2* Heat 1 teaspoon oil in a small, nonstick skillet over medium heat. Add the sausage link and broth or water and simmer, covered, for 4 minutes, turning the sausage occasionally.
½ cup vegetable broth or water	
½ medium onion, sliced thin	
¼ green pepper, sliced thin	*3* While the sausage cooks, heat ¾ teaspoon oil over medium heat in a second small skillet. Add the onion and green pepper and cook, stirring occasionally, about 6 minutes, or until the peppers are tender, adding water if needed to keep the veggies from sticking.
Nonstick cooking spray	
1 whole-grain hoagie roll, cut in half horizontally	
1 slice pepper jack or nondairy cheese, cut in half	
	4 Spray the cut sides of the roll with cooking spray. Place the rolls, cut-side up, on a baking pan or piece of foil. Broil the bread about 2 minutes, or just until the top is crispy. (Watch closely so the bread doesn't burn.)
	5 Cut the sausage in half lengthwise. Lay the onions and peppers on the bottom roll. Place the sausage and cheese on top and cover with the roll lid.

Per serving: Calories 521 (From Fat 217); Fat 24g (Saturated 9g); Cholesterol 30mg; Sodium 1,251mg; Carbohydrate 60g (Dietary Fiber 8g); Protein 21g.

Vary It! In a pinch, you can use a hot dog bun in place of the hoagie roll. If you have a little leftover spaghetti sauce in the fridge, warm that up and drizzle it over the sausage just before eating.

Tip: If you're really short on time, cut the sausage links in half, set them on a dish, and nuke them for about 45 seconds instead of cooking them in the skillet.

Parmesan Bean Toast

Prep time: 7 min • **Cook time:** 6 min • **Yield:** 1 serving

Ingredients	Directions
2 teaspoons grated Parmesan or nondairy cheese	**1** Preheat the oven to 450 degrees.
2 slices French or Italian bread	**2** Sprinkle the cheese on one side of each of the bread slices. Put the bread on a piece of foil or a baking sheet and bake for 1 minute. Remove the bread from the oven and sprinkle one side with the cheese. Return the bread to the oven and bake for 1 more minute to melt the cheese.
2 teaspoons olive oil	
1 clove garlic, minced	
1 plum or Roma tomato, diced	
¼ cup canned navy beans, rinsed and drained	**3** While the bread bakes, heat the oil for 20 seconds in a medium skillet over medium heat; add the garlic and sauté for 1 minute. Stir in the tomatoes and beans and cook, stirring constantly, for 1 minute.
1 cup fresh spinach, coarsely chopped	
Dash salt	
Dash black pepper	**4** Stir in the spinach, salt, pepper, and Italian seasoning. Cook, stirring, for 1 more minute.
¼ teaspoon Italian seasoning	
	5 Place the toasted bread on a plate and top with the bean mixture.

Per serving: Calories 546 (From Fat 131); Fat 15g (Saturated 3g); Cholesterol 3mg; Sodium 1,185mg; Carbohydrate 85g (Dietary Fiber 9g); Protein 19g.

Vary It! Navy beans are good in this recipe because they're small, but black beans work just as well.

Tip: This can double as an appetizer when friends come over. Put the bean mixture into a bowl and surround it with slices of the cheese toast. It's like a hot bean bruschetta.

Vegetarian BBQ Sloppy Joe

Prep time: 11 min • **Cook time:** 5 min • **Yield:** 1 serving

Ingredients	Directions
¼ **cup barbecue sauce** ½ **cup plain or barbecue tempeh**	*1* Pour the barbecue sauce into a small bowl. Crumble the tempeh into the sauce and let it marinate for 10 minutes.
¼ **teaspoon olive oil** ¼ **green pepper, chopped** ¼ **medium onion, chopped** **1 kaiser roll, split in half horizontally**	*2* Heat the oil in a small skillet over medium heat. Add the green pepper and onion. Cook over medium-high heat, stirring frequently, about 4 minutes, or until the onion is tender. Stir in the tempeh and sauce and heat through.
	3 Wrap the kaiser roll in a paper towel and heat it in the microwave on high for 20 seconds to warm it. Spoon the barbecue mixture into the roll.

Per serving: Calories 381 (From Fat 116); Fat 13g (Saturated 3g); Cholesterol 0mg; Sodium 831mg; Carbohydrate 49g (Dietary Fiber 3g); Protein 20g.

Tip: Tempeh is made from cooked and slightly fermented soybeans. Commercial brands often have other ingredients added such as other grains (often barley). The taste is different from tofu; tempeh has more of a textured and nutty flavor. Even so, tempeh is almost flavorless — it gets its flavor from strong sauces or marinades. That's why it's good to let it marinate for a few minutes before cooking it, so it can absorb as much flavor as possible.

Roasted Asparagus Sandwich

Prep time: 8 min • **Cook time:** 8½ min • **Yield:** 1 serving

Ingredients	Directions
4 stalks asparagus with tough bottom ends removed	*1* Preheat the broiler.
5 white or baby bella mushrooms, sliced	*2* Lay the asparagus and mushrooms on a foil-lined baking sheet. Drizzle them with oil, sprinkle with salt and pepper, and then sprinkle with the minced garlic. Roast for 6 to 8 minutes, until the vegetables are tender-crisp and slightly toasted. Remove them from the oven and sprinkle them with the vinaigrette.
1 tablespoon olive oil	
Dash salt	
Dash black pepper	
1 clove garlic, minced	
1 tablespoon vinaigrette salad dressing	*3* Place the hoagie roll on a piece of foil and toast it lightly under the broiler for about 1 minute.
1 hoagie roll, cut in half lengthwise	
2 tablespoons grated low-fat Swiss cheese or nondairy cheese	*4* Lay the asparagus and mushrooms on top of the bottom bun. Sprinkle the cheese on top. Place this bread on the baking sheet and put it back under the broiler for 30 seconds, until the cheese has melted. Put the remaining bread lid on top.

Per serving: Calories 386 (From Fat 178); Fat 20g (Saturated 4g); Cholesterol 5mg; Sodium 592mg; Carbohydrate 42g (Dietary Fiber 5g); Protein 14g.

Tip: When preparing asparagus, hold a stalk (or several stalks) in your hands, one hand at each end of the stalk(s). Bend them and they'll break at a natural point, separating the tender part from the woody ends. Throw the bottom parts out because they're too tough to chew.

Vary It! If you don't have vinaigrette, use fat-free Italian dressing.

Tip: If you can't find grated Swiss cheese or don't feel like grating your own, simply use 1 slice of Swiss cheese cut in half.

Adding Variety to Your Lunch with Pizzas and Tex-Mex Dishes

When you think of fun foods for lunch, pizza and Tex-Mex dishes like tacos, nachos, and quesadillas top the list. These comfort foods are quick to fix, and you can add almost any toppings and fillings to them. Obviously, you can make pizza using a pizza crust, but you can also build a pizza on a bagel half, English muffin half, or sliced French bread. Following are some new ideas on how to make old favorites.

Famous vegetarians and vegans through the ages

You're definitely not alone in your diet of choice. Some very well-known people have also chosen the vegetarian (or vegan) lifestyle. You probably recognize many of the names in the following list:

- Hank Aaron, baseball player
- Pamela Anderson, actress
- Aristotle, Greek philosopher
- Kim Basinger, actress
- Michael Bolton, musician
- Christie Brinkley, model
- Pierce Brosnan, actor
- Charles Darwin, scientist
- Leonardo da Vinci, Italian painter and inventor
- Ellen DeGeneres, TV personality
- Emily Dickinson, writer and poet
- Thomas Alva Edison, inventor
- Albert Einstein, scientist
- Prince Fielder, baseball player
- Mahatma Gandhi, Hindu spiritual leader
- Melanie Griffith, actress
- Woody Harrelson, actor and environmental activist
- George Harrison, musician
- Dustin Hoffman, actor
- Billy Idol, musician
- Michael Jackson, musician
- Samuel L. Jackson, actor
- Diane Keaton, actress
- B. B. King, musician
- Coretta Scott King, wife of Martin Luther King Jr.
- John Lennon, musician
- Carl Lewis, Olympic runner
- Paul McCartney, musician
- Sir Isaac Newton, physicist
- Robert Parish, basketball player
- River Phoenix, actor
- Plato, Greek philosopher
- Prince, musician
- Eric Roberts, actor
- J. D. Salinger, novelist
- Seal, musician
- Ringo Starr, musician
- Oliver Stone, film director
- Mark Twain, writer
- Vincent van Gogh, painter
- Kate Winslet, actress

Easy Quesadilla

Prep time: 2 min • **Cook time:** 3½ min • **Yield:** 1 serving

Ingredients	*Directions*
1 teaspoon butter	*1* Heat a large skillet over medium heat. Melt the butter in the skillet, tipping the skillet to coat the bottom evenly.
Dash garlic powder	
1 whole-wheat 8-inch tortilla	
3 tablespoons shredded pepper jack or nondairy cheese	*2* Sprinkle the garlic powder evenly over the bottom of the pan.
1 teaspoon chopped green onion	*3* Place the tortilla in the pan. Immediately sprinkle the cheese, green onion, and chili peppers over half of the tortilla, and fold the other side over the cheese. Cook about 1½ minutes, or until the underside is golden.
¼ teaspoon chopped chili peppers	
	4 Carefully flip the tortilla over and continue to cook for another minute, until the bottom is golden.
	5 Remove the quesadilla and cut it in half.

Per serving: *Calories 228 (From Fat 113); Fat 13g (Saturated 7g); Cholesterol 33mg; Sodium 241mg; Carbohydrate 24g (Dietary Fiber 2g); Protein 8g.*

Vary It! This quesadilla is a simple version; feel free to toss in leftover veggies (chopped small) or even a scrambled egg.

Tip: If you have some salsa, pour some in a bowl and dip your quesadilla into the sauce. Yum!

Rolled Margherita Pizza

Prep time: 5 min • **Cook time:** 1 min, 20 sec • **Yield:** 1 serving

Ingredients	Directions
1 whole-wheat 8-inch tortilla	**1** Lay the tortilla on a microwave-safe dish, brush the oil on one side of the tortilla, and sprinkle the garlic over the oil.
½ teaspoon olive oil	
¼ teaspoon minced garlic	
3 large, thin slices ripe tomato	**2** Microwave the tortilla on high for 40 seconds.
3 very thin slices onion	
⅛ teaspoon Italian seasoning	**3** Lay the tomato slices on the tortilla, and then the onion slices. Sprinkle on the Italian seasoning, red pepper flakes, and vinegar.
⅛ teaspoon red pepper flakes	
½ teaspoon balsamic vinegar	
¼ fresh mozzarella ball, sliced thin	**4** Lay the mozzarella slices over the top of the pizza, and then sprinkle with Parmesan cheese.
1 tablespoon grated Parmesan cheese	
	5 Microwave for 40 seconds, or until the cheese has melted, and then roll up the tortilla like a burrito.

Per serving: Calories 260 (From Fat 111); Fat 12g (Saturated 5g); Cholesterol 26mg; Sodium 277mg; Carbohydrate 30g (Dietary Fiber 3g); Protein 11g.

Note: This is one of the few recipes in this book where it's not advisable to switch or substitute ingredients. The tomato slices, seasonings, and mozzarella cheese are all crucial in creating the delectable result.

Note: A traditional margherita pizza has a very thin crust. In your spare time, you can certainly make a homemade, wait-till-the-yeast-rises crust for this creation, but in an effort to save time, I use a tortilla for the base here.

Layered Nachos

Prep time: 4 min • **Cook time:** 3 min • **Yield:** 1 serving

Ingredients	Directions
15 tortilla chips	*1* Preheat the oven to 425 degrees.
1 tablespoon sliced black olives, drained	*2* Lay the tortilla chips on a small baking pan.
½ cup canned kidney beans, rinsed and drained	*3* Sprinkle the olives, kidney beans, and onion over the chips, and then sprinkle the cheese on top.
1 green onion, sliced	
3 tablespoons low-fat shredded Mexican cheese blend or low-fat shredded sharp cheddar cheese or shredded nondairy cheese	*4* Bake the chips for 3 minutes, or until the cheese melts.
2 tablespoons salsa	*5* Drizzle the salsa over the cheese.

Per serving: Calories 320 (From Fat 89); Fat 10g (Saturated 2g); Cholesterol 4mg; Sodium 632mg; Carbohydrate 44g (Dietary Fiber 10g); Protein 16g.

Note: Even though nachos seem to be more of a snack item, these nachos will definitely fill you at lunchtime, and they're something different — a fun alternative to always eating a sandwich.

Vary It! If spicy is your thing, slice a few jalapeño peppers and sprinkle them on top of the nachos just before adding the cheese.

Tempting Taco

Prep time: 10 min • **Cook time:** 1 min • **Yield:** 1 serving

Ingredients	Directions
2 tablespoons salsa	**1** In a small bowl, stir together the salsa, beans, corn, and cheese. Set aside.
2 tablespoons canned black beans, rinsed and drained	
2 tablespoons canned corn, drained	**2** Spray a small skillet with nonstick spray. Cook the crumbles for 1 minute over medium heat, stirring occasionally. Sprinkle the crumbles with lemon juice and chili powder halfway through cooking.
1 tablespoon shredded low-fat sharp cheddar cheese or nondairy cheese	
Nonstick cooking spray	**3** Spoon the crumbles into the bottom of the tortilla shells, spoon on the salsa mixture, and then top with shredded lettuce.
¼ pound meatless beef- or sausage-flavored crumbles	
½ teaspoon lemon juice	
⅛ teaspoon chili powder	
2 corn tortilla shells	
⅓ cup shredded lettuce	

Per serving: Calories 435 (From Fat 141); Fat 16g (Saturated 4g); Cholesterol 2mg; Sodium 955mg; Carbohydrate 46g (Dietary Fiber 11g); Protein 31g.

Tip: If the crumbles begin to stick to the pan during cooking, add a few tablespoons of water.

Pizza Roll

Prep time: 5 min • **Cook time:** 7 min • **Yield:** 1 serving

Ingredients	Directions
Nonstick cooking spray	**1** Preheat the oven to 425 degrees.
2 teaspoons olive oil	
⅛ green or red pepper, sliced thin	**2** Spray a small skillet with nonstick spray and add the oil. Heat the oil for 20 seconds and then add the pepper, onion, and mushrooms; sauté over medium-high heat, stirring frequently, for 4 minutes, or until the onions are soft and the mushrooms are beginning to brown.
¼ onion, sliced	
¼ cup sliced white or baby bella mushrooms	
¼ cup meatless beef- or sausage-flavored crumbles	**3** Stir in the crumbles and continue to cook for 1 more minute. Remove the pan from the heat.
1 whole-wheat 10-inch tortilla	
3 tablespoons spaghetti sauce	
¼ teaspoon Italian seasoning	**4** Bake the tortilla on a piece of foil for 30 seconds, or just until it's slightly toasted but still very pliable. (This will keep the wrap from getting soggy.)
⅓ cup shredded low-fat mozzarella cheese or nondairy cheese	
	5 Spread the spaghetti sauce evenly over the surface but not quite to the edges. Sprinkle the Italian seasoning and then the cheese over the sauce. Return the pizza to the oven for 1 more minute, or until the cheese melts.
	6 Spoon the crumble mixture about three-fourths of the way down the center of the tortilla. Fold up the bottom and then, starting on one side, roll up the tortilla.

Per serving: Calories 428 (From Fat 173); Fat 19g (Saturated 5g); Cholesterol 13mg; Sodium 664mg; Carbohydrate 50g (Dietary Fiber 7g); Protein 19g.

Tip: You can make this recipe even easier by warming the tortilla in a damp paper towel in the microwave for a few seconds instead of baking it. Baking it gives it more of a toasted taste versus nuking it, which just warms it.

Souping It Up

Hot soup is a bowl of miracles. It's inexpensive to create because it's mostly water. You can usually chop up any leftovers you have in the fridge and add them to the soup. If you make a large pot, you'll have plenty left over to freeze, so you'll have a head start on another meal. Depending on the ingredients you choose to use, soup can be full of carbs and protein, and it's an easy way to add more fiber to your diet. All that's missing is a bowl of crackers to go along with it! Try one of the following recipes to see just how easy it is to make great homemade soup.

The directions *heat oil in a skillet* seem simple enough, but they can also be the formula for a stovetop fire if you're not careful. Watch oil closely as you warm it. Heat it about 20 seconds, and then add whatever it is you're going to cook in the oil. If oil gets too hot, it smokes or, worse yet, catches on fire. If you ever have a stovetop fire, here's what to do:

- ✔ *Do not* throw water on the fire. Water is heavier than oil, so it sinks to the bottom of the pan, below the oil, and turns into steam, causing an eruption and a much larger fire.

- ✔ *Do* turn off the stove and leave the pan right where it is.

- ✔ If the pan has a lid, put the lid on the pan to help smother the fire.

- ✔ Soak a dish towel with water, ring it out, and place it over the pan (or over the lid if you've put a lid on the pan). This will suffocate the fire.

- ✔ If the kitchen towel method doesn't work and you have a fire extinguisher, use it now.

- ✔ If the fire continues, call 911 immediately.

Tortellini Soup

Prep time: 4 min • **Cook time:** 11 min, 20 sec • **Yield:** 4 servings

Ingredients	Directions
2 tablespoons olive oil	*1* Heat the oil in a medium saucepan for 20 seconds. Add the garlic and sauté over medium heat, stirring frequently, about 1 minute, or just until it begins to brown.
2 teaspoons minced garlic	
3 cups vegetable broth	
1 can (15 ounces) diced tomatoes, undrained	*2* Stir in the broth and tomatoes and heat to boiling. Reduce the heat to simmer and stir in the tortellini; cook for 8 minutes, or until the pasta is tender but not overcooked and mushy.
1 cup dried cheese tortellini	
1 bag (10 ounces) fresh spinach, chopped	
1 teaspoon Italian seasoning	*3* Stir in the spinach, Italian seasoning, salt, and pepper. Cook 1 more minute. Stir in the cheese.
⅛ teaspoon salt	
⅛ teaspoon black pepper	
¼ cup grated Parmesan cheese	

Per serving: Calories 217 (From Fat 106); Fat 12g (Saturated 3g); Cholesterol 10mg; Sodium 1,210mg; Carbohydrate 22g (Dietary Fiber 4g); Protein 10g.

Hot Black Bean Soup

Prep time: 4 min • **Cook time:** 20 min • **Yield:** 2 servings

Ingredients	Directions
1 can (15 ounces) black beans, undrained	*1* Place half of the beans, with their liquid, and the broth in a blender or food processor and whip until smooth. If you don't have a blender, mash the beans, liquid, and broth well with the back of a fork.
1 cup vegetable broth	
½ tablespoon olive oil	
1 small onion, chopped	
½ teaspoon minced garlic	*2* In a medium saucepan, heat the oil for 20 seconds and then add the onion and garlic and sauté over medium-high heat, stirring frequently, for about 4 minutes, or until the onion is tender.
¾ cup medium chunky salsa	
1 teaspoon cumin	
¼ teaspoon crushed red pepper	
2 tablespoons chopped parsley (optional)	*3* Add the whipped (or mashed) beans and the remaining whole beans with their liquid, salsa, cumin, red pepper, and parsley (if using). Bring to a boil. Reduce the heat to low, cover, and simmer for 15 minutes, stirring occasionally.

Per serving: Calories 300 (From Fat 109); Fat 12g (Saturated 1g); Cholesterol 0mg; Sodium 1,435mg; Carbohydrate 41g (Dietary Fiber 13g); Protein 14g.

Vary It! "Hot" is a relative term, but by anyone's definition, this soup will definitely tingle your tongue! If you like soups a bit more mellow, just reduce or eliminate the crushed red pepper and use mild salsa instead of medium.

Chapter 11

Ten Minutes or Less: Grab 'n' Go Suppers

Cooking a meal for dinner usually takes more than five minutes because people have been programmed to think that supper is supposed to be more than a bowl of cereal or a quick sandwich. But you can still make dinner when you're in a hurry; all you need is ten minutes or less. Check out this chapter for quick 'n' easy dinners that focus on pasta, rice, and vegetables — and taste delicious!

Oodles of Noodles: Preparing Vegetarian Pasta Dishes

Ah, pasta — it's a staple of college students everywhere, and for good reason. It's cheap, really easy to find, and nearly foolproof to make. In this section, I provide a bunch of pasta recipes that work well for busy (and hungry!) college-age vegetarians.

Here are a couple ways to cut down on the cooking time of pasta:

✔ The directions on a box of spaghetti say to fill a large pot with water and bring the water to a boil. But if you're cooking spaghetti or another type of pasta for one person, why would you want to wait until a full pot of water comes to a boil? For one serving, 4 cups of water in a medium saucepan is enough to cook the pasta. The less water you use, the quicker it will boil.

✔ Directions on a box of spaghetti also usually say to cook the spaghetti for approximately 10 minutes. Regular spaghetti really does have to cook for 10 minutes to soften, but thinner spaghetti doesn't! Using angel hair pasta can cut that cooking time by 5 or 6 minutes.

Lazy Day Ravioli Casserole

Prep time: 2 min • **Cook time:** 2½ min • **Yield:** 1 serving

Ingredients	*Directions*
Nonstick spray	*1* Spray a 1-quart, microwave-safe dish with nonstick spray and place the crumbles in the dish. Microwave on high for 30 seconds.
1 cup meatless crumbles	
1 microwavable bowl (7.5 ounces) cheese ravioli	
1 can (15 ounces) spinach, drained and chopped	*2* Stir in the ravioli, spinach, and Italian seasoning. Cover with wax paper and microwave on high for 2 minutes, or until the casserole is warmed.
¼ teaspoon Italian seasoning	
2 tablespoons grated Parmesan cheese	*3* Spoon the dinner onto a dish and sprinkle with cheese.

Per serving: Calories 507 (From Fat 172); Fat 19g (Saturated 7g); Cholesterol 50mg; Sodium 2,202mg; Carbohydrate 43g (Dietary Fiber 11g); Protein 40g.

Vary It! If you have a small can of sliced mushrooms in the cupboard (8-ounce size), drain the mushrooms and stir them in with the ravioli, spinach, and Italian seasoning.

Green Beans with Macaroni and Cheese

Prep time: 3 min • **Cook time:** 2 min • **Yield:** 1 serving

Ingredients	*Directions*
1 microwavable bowl (7.5 ounces) macaroni and cheese (such as Chef Boyardee)	*1* In a microwave-safe bowl, stir together the macaroni and cheese, green beans, and chili powder.
1 can (8 ounces) French cut green beans, drained	*2* In a small bowl, use a fork to mix the breadcrumbs and oil until the crumbs are evenly coated. Sprinkle the crumbs over the macaroni mixture.
¼ teaspoon chili powder	
¼ cup seasoned breadcrumbs	
¾ teaspoon olive oil	*3* Cover the bowl with wax paper and microwave on high for 2 minutes.

Per serving: Calories 333 (From Fat 82); Fat 9g (Saturated 3g); Cholesterol 6mg; Sodium 2,116mg; Carbohydrate 51g (Dietary Fiber 6g); Protein 12g.

BBQ Pasta

Prep time: 3 min • **Cook time:** 3 min • **Yield:** 1 serving

Ingredients	*Directions*
4 cups water	*1* Bring the water to a boil in a medium saucepan over high heat.
1 package Top Ramen Soup (without the enclosed seasoning packet)	*2* Break the noodles into smaller pieces and add them to the water. Cook over high heat for about 3 minutes, or until tender; as they cook, separate the noodles with a fork. Drain, and then return them to the pan.
1 cup meatless beef-flavored crumbles	
¼ cup barbecue sauce	
⅔ cup shredded low-fat sharp cheddar cheese	*3* As the noodles cook, put the crumbles in a small, microwave-safe bowl. Cover the bowl with wax paper and microwave on high for 40 seconds.
	4 Stir the crumbles, barbecue sauce, and cheese into the noodles.

Per serving: Calories 776 (From Fat 194); Fat 22g (Saturated 7g); Cholesterol 16mg; Sodium 1,449mg; Carbohydrate 91g (Dietary Fiber 6g); Protein 52g.

Tip: To convert this recipe to vegan, use nondairy cheese in place of the cheddar cheese.

Vary It! If you like foods that are really spicy, add a few drops of hot pepper sauce when you stir in the barbecue sauce.

The Orient Express

Prep time: 2 min • **Cook time:** 5 min • **Yield:** 1 serving

Ingredients	*Directions*
¾ cup vegetable broth	*1* In a large skillet, bring the broth to a boil over high heat.
1 package Top Ramen Oriental Soup with half of the enclosed seasoning packet	*2* Add the ramen, seasoning packet, soy sauce, and veggies to the broth. Cook for about 3 minutes over high heat, or until the noodles are cooked, stirring frequently with a fork to break up the noodles and vegetables.
½ teaspoon low-sodium soy sauce	
¾ cup frozen peas and carrots	
1 egg	*3* In a small bowl, whisk the egg and oil together well. Drizzle this slowly into the noodle mixture, stirring quickly to scramble the egg as it cooks. Cook another 2 minutes over medium-high heat.
2 teaspoons olive oil	

Per serving: Calories 578 (From Fat 239); Fat 27g (Saturated 11g); Cholesterol 213mg; Sodium 1,538mg; Carbohydrate 71g (Dietary Fiber 6g); Protein 17g.

Note: The flavor packet that comes with Top Ramen Oriental Soup is the only one that's vegetarian. Ramen cooks quickly so it's great to keep on hand for emergency dinners when you have nothing in the fridge to eat.

Vary It! If you don't have peas and carrots in the freezer, substitute any other frozen vegetable (corn, broccoli, lima beans, Brussels sprouts, green beans, spinach, and so on), or chop up leftover veggies that are hiding in the refrigerator. Also, if you don't have any veggie broth on hand, you can definitely use water instead.

Noodles and Asparagus à la Crème

Prep time: 2 min • **Cook time:** 7 min • **Yield:** 2 servings

Ingredients	*Directions*
3 cups water	*1* Put the water into a medium saucepan and bring it to a boil over high heat.
1 package Top Ramen Soup (without the enclosed seasoning packet)	
1 can (10.75 ounces) condensed broccoli cheddar cheese soup	*2* Add the noodles, breaking them up as you add them. Cook for 3 minutes over high heat, or until the noodles are soft. Drain.
1 cup low-fat milk	*3* Stir the soup and milk together in the saucepan used to boil the noodles. Fold in the asparagus, pepper, chili powder, and noodles and cook over medium heat about 2 minutes, or until mixture is hot.
1 can (14.5 ounces) cut asparagus spears, drained	
Dash black pepper	
¼ teaspoon chili powder	

Per serving: *Calories 356 (From Fat 47); Fat 5g (Saturated 2g); Cholesterol 11mg; Sodium 1,058mg; Carbohydrate 61g (Dietary Fiber 3g); Protein 16g.*

Garlic Pasta with Peas

Prep time: 3 min • **Cook time:** 6 min • **Yield:** 1 serving

Ingredients	Directions
4 cups water	**1** Bring the water to a boil in a medium saucepan over high heat.
2 ounces angel hair pasta	
2 small garlic cloves, crushed	**2** Add the pasta to the water and cook over medium-high heat for about 4 minutes. Drain the pasta and return it to the pan.
2 tablespoons olive oil	
Dash salt	
Dash black pepper	**3** While the pasta cooks, sauté the garlic in the oil in a small saucepan over medium heat, stirring frequently, for about 40 seconds, or until the garlic starts to turn golden. Remove from heat and stir in the salt and pepper.
½ cup frozen peas, thawed	
2 tablespoons grated Parmesan cheese	
	4 Stir the peas and the oil-garlic mixture into the pasta and toss well to coat evenly. Just before serving, sprinkle the cheese on top.

Per serving: Calories 562 (From Fat 279); Fat 31g (Saturated 6g); Cholesterol 8mg; Sodium 399mg; Carbohydrate 56g (Dietary Fiber 6g); Protein 16g.

Tip: To convert this recipe to vegan, use nondairy grated cheese in place of the Parmesan cheese.

Garlic Gnocchi

Prep time: 3 min • **Cook time:** 6 min • **Yield:** 1 serving

Ingredients	Directions
4 cups water	*1* Bring the water to a boil in a medium saucepan over high heat.
1 cup (4 ounces) gnocchi	
2 teaspoons olive oil	*2* Add the gnocchi to the water and cook over medium-high heat for 3 minutes, or until tender. (Note: After about 1 minute, the gnocchi will rise to the surface of the water.) Drain.
2 cloves garlic, minced	
⅛ teaspoon chili powder	
⅛ teaspoon salt	
⅛ teaspoon black pepper	*3* While the gnocchi is cooking, warm the oil in a medium skillet for 20 seconds over medium-high heat. Add the garlic and sauté it for 40 seconds, or until the garlic is just beginning to brown. Remove pan from heat until the gnocchi is finished cooking.
1 tablespoon lemon juice	
2 tablespoons shredded low-fat mozzarella cheese	
	4 Return the pan with the garlic back to the stove and stir in the chili powder, salt, pepper, lemon juice, and gnocchi. Stir until heated through, about 1 minute.
	5 Stir in the cheese until it's melted.

Per serving: Calories 281 (From Fat 162); Fat 18g (Saturated 7g); Cholesterol 26mg; Sodium 480mg; Carbohydrate 26g (Dietary Fiber 2g); Protein 5g.

Note: Gnocchi technically isn't pasta; it's actually dumplings that can be made of potatoes, flour, or other ingredients. However, gnocchi cooks up just like pasta does. It's the perfect choice when you have little or no time to cook because it cooks so fast. That's the easy part. The hard part is learning to pronounce it correctly (***nyo***-kee).

Mexican Medley

Prep time: 3 min • **Cook time:** 6 min • **Yield:** 2 servings

Ingredients	Directions
4 cups water	**1** Bring the water to a boil in a medium saucepan over high heat.
1 package Top Ramen Oriental Soup (without the enclosed seasoning packet)	**2** Add the noodles to the water and cook over medium-high heat for about 3 minutes, or until the noodles are tender. Drain, and then return the noodles to the pan.
1 cup meatless beef-flavored crumbles	
1 cup salsa	
1 cup frozen corn	**3** While the noodles cook, put the crumbles in a microwave-safe bowl or dish, cover with wax paper, and microwave for 40 seconds.
⅔ cup canned black beans, rinsed and drained	
2 teaspoons taco seasoning mix	**4** Stir the crumbles, salsa, corn, beans, seasoning mix, salt, and pepper into the noodles. Cook over medium-high heat for 1 minute, or until all ingredients are blended and hot.
Dash salt	
Dash black pepper	
⅓ cup shredded low-fat sharp cheddar cheese	**5** Spoon the pasta onto dinner dishes and sprinkle the cheese on top.

Per serving: Calories 431 (From Fat 84); Fat 9g (Saturated 3g); Cholesterol 4mg; Sodium 1,495mg; Carbohydrate 60g (Dietary Fiber 9g); Protein 28g.

Tip: To convert this recipe to vegan, use nondairy cheddar cheese.

Vary It! You can determine how tangy and hot you want this meal by the type of salsa you add: mild, medium, or hot. Or you can use taco sauce or enchilada sauce instead of the salsa if that's what you have left over in the fridge.

Vary It! If you don't have corn in the freezer, substitute another frozen vegetable (lima beans, cut green beans, or peas), or chop up leftover veggies that are hiding in the refrigerator.

Tip: A flavor packet is enclosed in the Ramen noodles package. You don't need it for this recipe, so put it aside to use in a stir-fry or when you make rice or soup.

Pasta with Lentils

Prep time: 2 min • **Cook time:** 8 min • **Yield:** 1 serving

Ingredients	Directions
4 cups water	*1* Bring the water to a boil in a medium saucepan over high heat.
2 ounces angel hair pasta	
⅔ cup canned, ready-to-serve lentil soup	*2* Add the pasta to the water and cook over high heat for 5 minutes, until tender. Drain the pasta and then return it to the saucepan.
2 dashes black pepper	
2 tablespoons grated Parmesan cheese	*3* Stir in the lentil soup and pepper and cook for 1 minute over medium-high heat, or until the mixture is hot.
	4 Spoon the pasta and sauce onto a platter and top with cheese.

Per serving: Calories 337 (From Fat 43); Fat 5g (Saturated 2g); Cholesterol 8mg; Sodium 486mg; Carbohydrate 56g (Dietary Fiber 6g); Protein 17g.

Note: Lentils are so good for you it's almost scary. They're very high in protein and soluble fiber, and they're loaded with vitamins.

Tip: To convert this recipe to vegan, use nondairy cheese in place of the Parmesan.

Pasta with Cottage Cheese and Spinach

Prep time: 4 min • **Cook time:** 6 min • **Yield:** 1 serving

Ingredients	Directions
4 cups water	*1* Bring the water to a boil in a medium saucepan over high heat.
2 ounces angel hair pasta	
3 cups baby spinach, chopped	*2* Add the pasta to the water and cook over medium-high heat for about 4 minutes. Drain the pasta and return it to the pan.
1 tablespoon butter	
Dash salt	
Dash black pepper	*3* While the pasta cooks, sauté the spinach in the butter in a medium skillet over medium-high heat, stirring occasionally, just until the spinach wilts, about 2 minutes. Add the salt, pepper, dill, and lemon juice.
¼ teaspoon dried dill	
1 tablespoon lemon juice	
½ cup low-fat cottage cheese	
2 tablespoons grated Parmesan cheese	*4* Add the spinach mixture, cottage cheese, and Parmesan cheese to the pasta and toss.

Per serving: Calories 468 (From Fat 147); Fat 16g (Saturated 10g); Cholesterol 43mg; Sodium 905mg; Carbohydrate 55g (Dietary Fiber 5g); Protein 28g.

Vary It! If you don't have angel hair pasta, you can use ramen noodles, or, if you have a few extra moments to spare, use most any kind of short macaroni (ziti, elbow, corkscrew, or small shells). In place of the cottage cheese, you can use crumbled feta cheese and a dash of Italian seasoning.

Creating a Stir with Rice and Polenta Dishes

Rice and polenta are filling, taste great, are easy to cook, don't cost much, and you can add just about anything to them to make a complete meal. Check out the rice and polenta recipes in this section for some great dinner ideas.

Rice comes in three basic kinds:

✔ Short grains are sticky and perfect for Asian dishes and puddings.

✔ Medium grains aren't quite as soft as short grains, and they're a bit chalky in texture, which makes them perfect for risotto (an Italian dish) and vegetarian paella (a Spanish dish).

✔ The long grain varieties are the firmest of the three; the grains remain separate from one another. Long grains are the best choice when cooking Thai and Indian foods.

Benefiting from brown rice

Brown rice is brown. (No surprise there!) But have you ever wondered why? It's brown because the bran layer is still on the rice, and the bran layer is the part that's so high in fiber. White rice is lower in fiber and has a lower nutritional value than brown rice. Moral of the story: Choose brown rice.

You can cook regular long grain brown rice two ways:

✔ Soak it for 25 to 30 minutes before cooking to soften the outside, and then cook 1 cup of rice in 2 cups of water or broth for about 15 minutes.

✔ Instead of soaking the rice first, cook the rice a little longer. To soften the outside layer, you need to add more liquid (1 cup of rice to 3 cups of water or broth) and cook for 25 minutes.

You also have the option of using instant brown rice. It, too, cooks in about 15 minutes, but you don't have to soak it first.

Stir-fry Sensation

Prep time: 2 min • **Cook time:** 3 min • **Yield:** 1 serving

Ingredients	Directions
2 teaspoons olive oil	*1* Heat the oil in a medium skillet, and then add the vegetables and stir-fry for 3 minutes, or just until they're thawed and slightly cooked but still crisp. Stir in the soy sauce and sesame seeds.
1½ cups frozen stir-fry vegetables	
2 teaspoons low-sodium soy sauce	
½ teaspoon sesame seeds	*2* Heat the rice in the microwave for 1 minute.
1 container (1 cup) instant, ready-to-serve brown rice	*3* Spoon the rice onto a dish and top with the vegetables.

Per serving: Calories 387 (From Fat 111); Fat 12g (Saturated 2g); Cholesterol 0mg; Sodium 492mg; Carbohydrate 59g (Dietary Fiber 9g); Protein 10g.

Tip: If you have more than a few minutes to prepare dinner, forget the frozen veggies and replace them with cut-up fresh vegetables that you have in your refrigerator (such as carrots, onions, green pepper, and broccoli).

Layered Dinner Salad

Prep time: 5 min • **Yield:** 1 serving

Ingredients	*Directions*
1½ **cups fresh spinach**	**1** Put the spinach on a plate (or into a plastic container if you're taking the salad to go).
1 **cup leftover rice or a 1-cup container of precooked rice**	
1 **tablespoon fat-free Italian dressing**	**2** Sprinkle the rice over the spinach.
¼ **avocado, peeled, pitted, and chopped**	**3** Drizzle the dressing over the rice.
½ **cup canned black beans, rinsed and drained**	**4** Sprinkle the avocado over the dressing and rice.
¼ **cup salsa**	
2 **tablespoons crumbled feta cheese**	**5** Sprinkle the beans over the avocado.
	6 Drizzle the salsa over the beans.
	7 Sprinkle the cheese over the salsa.

Per serving: Calories 485 (From Fat 107); Fat 12g (Saturated 4g); Cholesterol 17mg; Sodium 1,010mg; Carbohydrate 75g (Dietary Fiber 13g); Protein 18g.

Vary It! This is another one of those dishes where you can totally improvise the ingredients by substituting whatever leftovers you have in the refrigerator. Change the kind of beans, cheese, and veggies if you like. Instead of the salsa, try taco sauce. The rice on the tortilla can be cold (leftover and from the refrigerator) or warm (heat rice in the microwave for 30 seconds before adding it to the salad).

Tip: To convert the recipe to vegan, omit the cheese or use nondairy cheese.

Pronto Polenta

Prep time: 4 min • **Cook time:** 4 min • **Yield:** 1 serving

Ingredients	Directions
1 tablespoon spaghetti sauce plus 2 tablespoons spaghetti sauce	**1** Preheat the broiler.
2 slices polenta (from a prepared polenta log), each about ½-inch thick ¼ cup shredded low-fat mozzarella cheese ⅛ teaspoon Italian seasoning	**2** Spread 1 tablespoon of the spaghetti sauce in the bottom of a small baking dish. Lay the polenta slices side by side on top of the sauce. Top each slice with 1 tablespoon of the cheese, then 1 tablespoon of the sauce, then the Italian seasoning, and finally, 1 tablespoon of the cheese again.
	3 Broil for 4 minutes, or until hot and lightly browned.

Per serving: Calories 133 (From Fat 27); Fat 3g (Saturated 1g); Cholesterol 10mg; Sodium 641mg; Carbohydrate 21g (Dietary Fiber 3g); Protein 5g.

Tip: You can easily convert this recipe to vegan just by using nondairy mozzarella cheese instead of the milk-based mozzarella.

Vary It! If you feel like getting fancier, cook some mushrooms and onions slowly in 1 tablespoon of oil until the onions begin to caramelize, and then spoon them on top of the polenta before adding the cheese.

Tex-Mex Rice

Prep time: 4 min • **Cook time:** 4 min • **Yield:** 1 serving

Ingredients	Directions
1 teaspoon olive oil 1 cup meatless crumbles 1 container (1 cup) instant, ready-to-serve brown rice ⅔ cup tomato sauce ½ cup condensed cheddar cheese soup 1 tablespoon taco seasoning mix ⅓ cup salsa	***1*** In a medium skillet over medium-high heat, heat the oil for 20 seconds. Add the crumbles and cook, stirring constantly, for 40 seconds. ***2*** Stir in the rice, tomato sauce, soup, taco seasoning, and salsa. Simmer over medium heat for 3 minutes.

Per serving: Calories 661 (From Fat 147); Fat 16g (Saturated 4g); Cholesterol 15mg; Sodium 3,581mg; Carbohydrate 103g (Dietary Fiber 14g); Protein 47g.

Vary It! Use hot salsa if you really want to spice things up, medium salsa if you enjoy just a touch of excitement, and mild salsa if you have gentler tastes.

Keeping the Focus on Vegetables

There must be a million ways to serve veggies. In this section, you find recipes for vegetables that are served hot or cold, stuffed and unstuffed, smothered with sauce, mashed, cooked whole . . . but definitely not plain. If variety is the spice of life, then get ready to have some fun preparing these recipes, which will definitely add variety to your dinner table.

Picking through types of potatoes

The two basic kinds of potatoes are *baking potatoes* and *boiling potatoes*. The difference between them is based on the amount of starch each has. Baking potatoes are high in starch; boiling potatoes are low on the starch chart. But nothing in life is ever as simple as that; here are a few additional differences.

✔ Because of all their starch, baking potatoes are kind of dry and super solid inside until they're cooked, and then . . . abracadabra . . . they suddenly become light and fluffy. They're usually big and shaped like long ovals. They're perfect for making French fries and mashed potatoes, for frying in a skillet, and of course, for making that American staple, the baked potato. Some varieties of baking potatoes include russet and long whites.

✔ Boiling potatoes, on the other hand, come in all sorts of sizes and shapes — long, round, thin,

and fat. What they lack in starch they make up for in sugar. These potatoes, when boiled, hold together better than their baking cousins, so they're great for soups, stews, and potato salad. Red and yellow varieties of boiling potatoes are common.

Then there are the potatoes that are searching for their identity, a place to belong. They don't really fall into either of the preceding categories, so they're lumped together in the category of *all-purpose potatoes*. Yukon Gold is probably the most recognized name in this category. All-purpose potatoes are moister than the other two groups, so they do best in a roasting pan.

The final group of potatoes is an off-spring of all the preceding groups. Any potato from any group falls into this category if it's small enough. These are called *new potatoes*. As the name indicates, they're immature, small, and can be any variety of potato.

Caesar Salad Deluxe

Prep time: 5 min • **Yield:** 1 serving

Ingredients	*Directions*
2 cups romaine lettuce, torn into bite-sized pieces	*1* In a medium bowl, toss the romaine with the dressing until evenly coated.
3 tablespoons Caesar salad dressing (without anchovies or Worcestershire sauce)	*2* Add the artichoke hearts and croutons to the bowl and toss again.
2 canned artichoke hearts, drained and quartered	*3* Spoon the mixture onto a salad plate and lay the egg quarters on top. Sprinkle with the cheese.
½ cup croutons	
1 hardboiled egg, quartered	
1 tablespoon grated Parmesan cheese	

Per serving: Calories 311 (From Fat 198); Fat 22g (Saturated 3g); Cholesterol 216mg; Sodium 814mg; Carbohydrate 16g (Dietary Fiber 3g); Protein 13g.

Note: Anchovies weren't part of the recipe when Caesar salad was originally introduced. Somehow, through the years, the recipe morphed. Luckily, you can find several commercial brands of Caesar dressing that don't use anchovies or Worcestershire sauce in their ingredients, including Follow Your Heart brand and Annie's Caesar Dressing (both are available at Whole Foods stores).

Vary It! You can add all sorts of extras to this salad, like sliced beets, green olives, grape tomatoes, and/or thin slices of zucchini or cucumber.

Feta Stuffed Chili Peppers

Prep time: 5 min • **Cook time:** 45 sec • **Yield:** 1 serving

Ingredients	Directions
¼ cup crumbled feta cheese	**1** In a small bowl, mash the cheese with the back of a fork. Add the oil, garlic, pepper, and Italian seasoning; continue mashing until all the ingredients are blended. Stir in the roasted red pepper.
1 teaspoon olive oil	
¼ teaspoon chopped garlic	
⅛ teaspoon black pepper	
⅛ teaspoon Italian seasoning	**2** Using a small spoon, stuff the cheese mix into the chili peppers, being careful not to break or tear the peppers. Fold each pepper closed as best as possible. Break off a piece of bread and press it into each end of the peppers to keep the filling from melting out during cooking.
1 tablespoon jarred, chopped roasted red pepper	
1 can (4 ounces) whole green chili peppers	
1 slice whole-wheat bread	
Nonstick cooking spray	**3** Spray a microwave-safe dish with nonstick spray, and lay the peppers on it. Cover with wax paper and microwave on high for 45 seconds to melt the cheese.

Per serving: Calories 241 (From Fat 126); Fat 14g (Saturated 7g); Cholesterol 33mg; Sodium 1,924mg; Carbohydrate 22g (Dietary Fiber 4g); Protein 9g.

Note: Sometimes you just want something different for dinner. You're tired of eating the same thing all the time. This dish fits the bill. Add a side of brown rice or a baked potato and you have a complete meal. You can preassemble these peppers the day before, cover them, and keep them in the refrigerator until dinnertime.

Tip: Unless you're super ambitious and choose to roast your own red peppers, you can pick up a jar of roasted red peppers at the grocery store, either where the pickles and olives are sold or where the store displays all the Italian products (pastas, spaghetti sauces, and so on).

Smothered Potatoes

Prep time: 1 min • **Cook time:** 5 min • **Yield:** 1 serving

Ingredients	*Directions*
2 medium, unpeeled red potatoes, cut in half **1 can (15 ounces) vegetarian chili**	*1* Set the potato halves cut side down on a microwave-safe plate. Nuke on high for 5 minutes, or until the potatoes are cooked through. (Depending on the size of the potatoes, they may cook more quickly, so check them after 3 minutes.) Move them to a serving dish.
	2 While the potatoes cook, pour the chili into a small saucepan and heat, stirring occasionally, for about 2 minutes, or until hot. Spoon the chili over the potatoes.

Per serving: Calories 661 (From Fat 15); Fat 2g (Saturated 0g); Cholesterol 0mg; Sodium 1,367mg; Carbohydrate 133g (Dietary Fiber 23g); Protein 29g.

Vary It! Accessorize these potatoes by sprinkling grated cheddar cheese (if you eat dairy products) or minced green onion over the chili, or plunk down a dollop of sour cream on top. In addition, instead of the chili, try topping the potatoes with vegetarian baked beans or frozen (then microwaved) broccoli in cheese sauce.

Tip: For a vegan version of "loaded" baked potatoes, top the potatoes with nondairy cheese and nondairy sour cream.

Shepherd's Pie

Prep time: 4 min • **Cook time:** 2 min • **Yield:** 1 serving

Ingredients	*Directions*
1 meatless burger	*1* Spray both sides of the burger with nonstick spray. Put the burger on a dish and microwave for 40 seconds.
Nonstick cooking spray	
½ cup refrigerated, premade mashed potatoes	*2* Spray a 12-ounce, microwave-safe bowl well with nonstick spray. Spoon the mashed potatoes into the bottom of the bowl and smooth the top. Spread the green beans over the mashed potatoes. Spoon the gravy over the beans. Lay the burger on top.
1 can (8 ounces) French cut green beans, drained well	
3 tablespoons vegetarian gravy	
	3 Cover the cup with wax paper and microwave for 80 seconds.
	4 With a knife, cut around the inside of the bowl to loosen the contents. Place a dish over the bowl and invert the dish and bowl. Carefully remove the bowl.

Per serving: *Calories 411 (From Fat 154); Fat 17g (Saturated 3g); Cholesterol 2mg; Sodium 2,005mg; Carbohydrate 43g (Dietary Fiber 6g); Protein 20g.*

Vary It! Vegetarian gravy does indeed exist, but sometimes it's hard to find. Franco-American canned Mushroom Gravy is vegan. If you can't find the gravy, you can always use salsa or tomato sauce instead.

Tip: This dinner will unmold easier if you use a glass bowl or a large glass custard cup as the container.

Yamburger Casserole

Prep time: 4 min • **Cook time:** 2 min • **Yield:** 1 serving

Ingredients	Directions
1 can (7 ounces) sweet potatoes, drained	**1** In a small bowl, use a fork to mash the sweet potatoes with the cinnamon and brown sugar. Stir in the pecans.
¼ teaspoon cinnamon	
1 teaspoon brown sugar	**2** Spray a custard cup with nonstick spray, and then spoon the potatoes into the cup.
2 tablespoons chopped pecans	
Nonstick cooking spray	**3** Sprinkle the crumbles on top of the potatoes and sprinkle lightly with salt and pepper.
⅓ cup meatless beef-flavored crumbles	
Dash salt	**4** Drizzle the syrup on top of the crumbles.
Dash black pepper	
2 teaspoons pancake syrup	**5** Cover loosely with wax paper and microwave on high for 2 minutes.

Per serving: Calories 412 (From Fat 107); Fat 12g (Saturated 1g); Cholesterol 0mg; Sodium 467mg; Carbohydrate 69g (Dietary Fiber 10g); Protein 14g.

Tip: Sweet potatoes are mighty powerful in providing you with vitamins A and C, and the canned potatoes are so easy to use. You can put this dish together several hours ahead of time, cover and refrigerate it, and then quickly nuke it when your stomach sends you signals that it's dinnertime.

Note: Bruce's brand has 7-ounce cans of cut yams. If you can't find that small of a can, get the 15-ounce size and either double this recipe or use the other half of the can tomorrow to make mashed sweet potato patties or yams with dried cranberries as a side dish.

Note: With a name like Yamburger Casserole, I bet you thought the ingredients would include yams, but I list sweet potatoes instead, for two good reasons. First, though the two potatoes are very similar, they're not exactly the same, and yet in America they are. The yams in the United States aren't true yams; they're actually a type of sweet potato. Second, you can't find canned yams in 7-ounce cans to prepare an individual serving, but you can find canned sweet potatoes in that size.

Spinach à la Spaghetti Sauce

Prep time: 3 min • **Cook time:** 2½ min, plus 1 min rest time • **Yield:** 1 serving

Ingredients	Directions
⅓ cup spaghetti sauce	**1** Warm the spaghetti sauce in a medium saucepan over medium-high heat for 20 seconds.
2 cups fresh baby spinach	
¼ teaspoon Italian seasoning	
1 ounce or 1 tablespoon mozzarella string cheese, cut into thin rounds	**2** Stir in the spinach and seasoning. Cook, stirring frequently, about 2 minutes, or until the spinach has wilted.
	3 Remove the pan from the heat. Stir in the cheese, cover the pan, and let it sit for 1 minute to melt the cheese.

Per serving: Calories 148 (From Fat 71); Fat 8g (Saturated 4g); Cholesterol 22mg; Sodium 523mg; Carbohydrate 13g (Dietary Fiber 4g); Protein 8g.

Tip: To make this recipe vegan-friendly, use nondairy cheese in place of the mozzarella.

Athena's Potatoes

Prep time: 2 min • **Cook time:** 5½ min • **Yield:** 1 serving

Ingredients	*Directions*
3 small red potatoes, unpeeled Nonstick cooking spray 1½ tablespoons low-fat sour cream 3 tablespoons grated low-fat sharp cheddar cheese 1 tablespoon grated Parmesan cheese 2 dashes salt 2 dashes black pepper 2 tablespoons seasoned bread crumbs	**1** Cut each potato into four parallel, vertical slices. Set the slices on a microwave-safe dish, cover with wax paper, and nuke on high for 5 minutes, or until tender.
	2 While the potatoes are cooking, in a small bowl, stir together the sour cream, cheddar cheese, Parmesan cheese, salt, and pepper.
	3 Spoon some of the cheese mixture on top of each potato slice, and then sprinkle the tops with breadcrumbs.
	4 Microwave on high for 30 seconds, or until the cheese begins to melt.

Per serving: Calories 538 (From Fat 65); Fat 7g (Saturated 4g); Cholesterol 16mg; Sodium 823mg; Carbohydrate 97g (Dietary Fiber 8g); Protein 20g.

Tip: To veganize this recipe, use nondairy sour cream and nondairy cheddar and Parmesan cheeses.

Mashed Potato Combo

Prep time: 4 min • **Cook time:** 4 min • Yield: 1 serving

Ingredients	*Directions*
1½ cups refrigerated, ready-made mashed potatoes	**1** Spoon the mashed potatoes onto a microwave-safe plate. Heat in the microwave, covered with wax paper, for 1½ minutes, or as package directs.
2 teaspoons olive oil	
¼ teaspoon minced garlic	**2** In a large skillet, sauté the garlic in the oil for 30 seconds over medium-high heat, and then add the spinach and red pepper flakes. Continue to cook, stirring frequently, until the spinach has wilted (about 2 minutes).
2 cups fresh baby spinach	
Dash red pepper flakes	
¼ cup low-fat sour cream	
1 tablespoon grated Parmesan cheese	**3** Stir the sour cream and cheese into the spinach mixture.
	4 Spoon the spinach mixture over the mashed potatoes.

Per serving: Calories 564 (From Fat 207); Fat 23g (Saturated 8g); Cholesterol 31mg; Sodium 1,068mg; Carbohydrate 76g (Dietary Fiber 2g); Protein 16g.

Vary It! In the recipe, you spoon the spinach on top of the mashed potatoes. However, you can opt for a "combined" version; you can chop the spinach before sautéing it. After you add the sour cream and cheese, fold the mashed potatoes into the spinach mixture.

Chapter 12

30 Minutes till Mealtime: Suppers

In This Chapter

▶ Producing pasta dinners

▶ Developing dinners from grains

▶ Preparing veggies with flair

1 know you're super-busy, but every once in a while, you discover you have a free evening — right? On those nights, why not spend a little extra time cooking a delicious (and healthy!) vegetarian dinner? Most of the recipes in this chapter take 30 minutes or less from start to finish, but a few take just a tad longer. Don't worry — all you need is a few minutes of prep time while a slow cooker does the rest of the work. Enjoy!

If you want to get food on the table as quickly as possible, being organized helps. Set out all the ingredients before you start to cook so you know what you have on hand. In a lot of the recipes in this chapter, you can chop veggies while the grain or pasta is cooking (also known as multi-tasking).

Picking Pasta for Dinner

Think "thin" when making pasta — the thinner the pasta, the faster it cooks. Instant rice cooks faster than regular rice. Sauces from a can or jar take less time to prepare than making sauces from scratch. Take advantage of these shortcuts.

Convenient vegetarian dinners from around the world

You may want to cook, fully intend to cook, and even come home and start preparing to cook, but then something happens and you just don't have time to cook. That's when you need to depend on a few good standbys in the cupboard or freezer to come to the rescue. Some pretty good ethnic vegetarian dinners are available; here are a few:

- Many frozen Indian foods are meatless.

- Some frozen Asian stir-fries have no meat or seafood.

- Most grocery stores carry Japanese miso soup, tempura, edamame, and sushi. (Be careful with Japanese food though; it often includes fish or seafood sauce.)

- Spanish polenta and a lot of tapas are vegetarian.

- Mexican cuisine has rice and bean dishes.

- Italians give you ratatouille, pasta marinara, and eggplant parmigiana.

- Greeks have spinach-and-cheese-filled spanakopita (with the frozen foods) and rice-stuffed grape leaves (in the deli).

- Don't overlook the Slavic contribution of cheese pirogies.

- From the Middle East come falafel, hummus, tahini, and couscous.

- The Welsh offer Welsh rarebit (in the frozen food aisle).

Rice Noodle Caboodle

Prep time: 5 min • **Cook time:** 6 min • **Yield:** 1 serving

Ingredients	*Directions*
Water	*1* Fill a medium saucepan two-thirds full with water and bring it to a boil over high heat.
1 tablespoon olive oil	
1 cup shredded cabbage	
1 cup broccoli florets, coarsely chopped	*2* While the water gets hot, warm the oil in a medium skillet over medium-high heat for 20 seconds. Add the cabbage, broccoli, and green onion; cook for 3 minutes, stirring occasionally. Add the pea pods and stir-fry for 2 more minutes. Add the broth, soy sauce, and red pepper flakes. Remove the pan from the heat.
1 green onion, sliced	
4 pea pods	
½ cup vegetable broth	
1½ teaspoons low-sodium soy sauce	
⅛ teaspoon dry red pepper flakes	*3* Stir the noodles into the boiling water. Turn off the heat and let the noodles soak for 2 minutes, or just until tender, and then drain them. (Don't overcook them or they'll get mushy.)
1½ cups thin rice noodles	
	4 Remove the strainer from the saucepan, holding it above the pan for a minute to let all the water drain out.
	5 Stir the noodles into the skillet with the vegetables and spoon onto a dinner dish.

Per serving: Calories 389 (From Fat 134); Fat 15g (Saturated 2g); Cholesterol 0mg; Sodium 940mg; Carbohydrate 59g (Dietary Fiber 5g); Protein 7g.

Note: It's important that your saucepan be two-thirds full of water to cook the rice noodles properly, so the amount of water you use depends on the size of your pan. That's why this recipe doesn't list a specific water amount.

Tip: Get the broccoli florets from the fresh salad bar at the grocery so you don't have to spend time cutting them and you don't have to worry about what to do with all the broccoli that's left over. You can usually find peas at the salad bar, too.

Onion Soup Pasta

Prep time: 4 min • **Cook time:** 10–14 min • **Yield:** 1 serving

Ingredients	Directions
4 cups water plus 3 tablespoons water	*1* Bring 4 cups of water to a boil in a medium saucepan over high heat. Stir in the pasta and cook for 8 to 12 minutes (depending on what pasta is used), or until tender, stirring occasionally.
¾ cup rigatoni, ziti, or elbow macaroni pasta	
2 teaspoons olive oil	
½ cup meatless crumbles	*2* While the pasta cooks, heat the oil in a medium skillet over medium heat for 20 seconds. Add the crumbles and cook for 1 minute. Stir in the soup mix.
1½ tablespoons dry onion soup mix	
½ cup tomato sauce	
½ cup shredded sharp low-fat cheddar cheese	*3* Stir in the tomato sauce and 3 tablespoons of water and simmer on medium-low heat, covered, for 3 minutes.
	4 Drain the pasta. Stir the pasta and cheese into the soup mixture until the cheese has melted.

Per serving: Calories 515 (From Fat 191); Fat 21g (Saturated 6g); Cholesterol 13mg; Sodium 2,670mg; Carbohydrate 50g (Dietary Fiber 7g); Protein 33g.

Vary It! Rigatoni and ziti pastas are listed in this recipe, but use any pasta you have on hand (adjust the cooking time accordingly). If you have an open jar of spaghetti sauce, use that instead of the tomato sauce. For variety, leave out the cheddar cheese and use mozzarella or provolone cheese instead.

Tip: You may think that dry onion soup mix has beef broth in it, but it doesn't. That's cool, because you can use the soup mix to flavor casseroles, as a soup base, stirred into pasta sauce, and with veggie dishes. Hooray for convenience foods!

Tip: Convert this recipe to vegan by using nondairy cheese in place of the cheddar cheese.

Blue Cheese Fettuccine

Prep time: 5 min • **Cook time:** 11 min • **Yield:** 1 serving

Ingredients	*Directions*
4 cups water	*1* Bring the water to a boil in a medium saucepan over high heat. Add the fettuccine and cook about 8 minutes, or until the pasta is almost tender.
2 ounces fettuccine	
1½ cups broccoli florets, cut into bite-size pieces	
1 teaspoon olive oil	*2* Add the broccoli to the pasta and cook 1 minute more. Drain the pasta and broccoli and then return them to the pan.
¾ cup sliced fresh white mushrooms	
⅓ cup jarred Alfredo sauce	*3* While the pasta cooks, heat the oil in a small skillet over medium-high heat for 20 seconds. Add the mushrooms and sauté, stirring occasionally, about 4 minutes, or until the mushrooms are browned.
Dash salt	
Dash black pepper	
¼ cup crumbled blue cheese	
	4 Add the Alfredo sauce, salt, and pepper to the mushrooms. Bring to a simmer and simmer for 1 minute, or until heated through, stirring occasionally.
	5 Stir the mushroom mixture into the fettuccine and toss to coat evenly. Stir in the blue cheese.

Per serving: Calories 646 (From Fat 354); Fat 39g (Saturated 17g); Cholesterol 58mg; Sodium 1,436mg; Carbohydrate 55g (Dietary Fiber 6g); Protein 24g.

Tip: You can measure most ingredients in a measuring cup, but fettuccine are long strands of pasta that simply don't bend to fit into a cup. The easiest way to figure out how much pasta you need for 2 ounces is to grab a handful of fettuccine strands; when the bundle is 1-inch across in depth, you have about 2 ounces.

Note: Blue cheese is a love/hate relationship with most people. Even if you didn't like it as a child, try it again. With most recipes in this book, if you don't have one cheese on hand you can substitute another. But how do you create Blue Cheese Fettuccine without blue cheese?

Broccoli Couscous

Prep time: 6 min • **Cook time:** 6 min, plus 5 min rest time • **Yield:** 1 serving

Ingredients	Directions
1 teaspoon olive oil	**1** In a medium saucepan, heat the oil over medium-high heat for 20 seconds. Add the onion, garlic, and green pepper and sauté for 3 minutes, or until the onions are soft. Add the broccoli and continue to cook 2 more minutes, stirring occasionally. Add the broth, lemon juice, dill, salt, and pepper; bring the mixture to a boil.
¼ onion, diced	
½ teaspoon minced garlic	
¼ cup diced green pepper	
1 cup chopped broccoli florets	
⅔ cup vegetable broth	
2 teaspoons lemon juice	**2** Stir in the couscous, cover the pan, remove the pan from the heat, and set aside for 5 minutes (so the couscous can absorb the liquid and cook through).
¼ teaspoon dried dill	
¼ teaspoon salt	
⅛ teaspoon black pepper	**3** Stir in the Parmesan cheese and almonds with a fork, fluffing up the couscous.
⅓ cup plain couscous	
1 tablespoon grated Parmesan cheese	
2 tablespoons coarsely chopped almonds	

Per serving: Calories 409 (From Fat 121); Fat 13g (Saturated 2g); Cholesterol 4mg; Sodium 1,376mg; Carbohydrate 60g (Dietary Fiber 8g); Protein 16g.

Tip: For a vegan version of this recipe, either omit the Parmesan cheese or replace it with grated nondairy cheese.

Tip: Because this dish is also great served cold, save any leftovers to fill a pita pocket for lunch the next day.

Soy Sauce Pasta

Prep time: 7 min • **Cook time:** 11 min • **Yield:** 2 servings

Ingredients	Directions
4 cups water	*1* Bring the water to a boil in a medium saucepan over high heat. Add the ziti and cook just until tender, about 8 minutes or according to package directions. Drain, rinse under cold water, and drain again.
1 cup ziti or other small-shaped pasta	
Nonstick spray	
1 tablespoon sesame seeds	*2* Spray a small skillet with nonstick spray. Add the sesame seeds and cook them, stirring often, until they're light golden brown. Watch them closely so they don't burn. Remove from heat and set aside.
4 teaspoons low-sodium soy sauce	
1 tablespoon olive oil	
1 teaspoon lemon juice	
⅛ teaspoon salt	*3* While the pasta cooks, whisk together the soy sauce, oil, lemon juice, salt, pepper, ginger, and red pepper flakes in a small bowl.
⅛ teaspoon black pepper	
⅛ teaspoon dry ground ginger	
⅛ teaspoon crushed red pepper flakes	*4* In a medium, microwave-safe bowl, nuke the onion, snow peas, carrots, and red pepper for 30 seconds on high. Stir in the pasta and soy sauce mixture. Nuke for 1 minute more.
½ onion, sliced	
1 cup snow peas, trimmed and sliced diagonally	
3 baby carrots, cut diagonally	*5* Spoon onto a plate and sprinkle the sesame seeds on top.
¼ red bell pepper, cut in half crosswise and thinly sliced lengthwise	

Per serving: Calories 270 (From Fat 88); Fat 10g (Saturated 1g); Cholesterol 0mg; Sodium 559mg; Carbohydrate 38g (Dietary Fiber 4g); Protein 8g.

Vary It! Don't panic if you don't have all the right ingredients for this recipe. Substitutions are definitely okay as long as you don't tell anyone! No ziti? Use egg noodles, spaghetti, or even rice. No soy sauce? Use balsamic vinegar instead. You can add a few drops of hot pepper sauce in place of the crushed red pepper and use green pepper in place of the red bell pepper. If snow peas aren't in season (or you forgot to buy any), use broccoli florets or regular peas.

South of the Border Pasta Dinner

Prep time: 4 min • **Cook time:** 11 min, plus 4 min rest time • **Yield:** 2 servings

Ingredients	Directions
1 cup meatless beef-flavored crumbles	**1** Put the crumbles in a microwave-safe bowl, cover with wax paper, and microwave on high for 40 seconds.
¾ cup water	
⅓ cup low-fat milk	**2** Spoon the crumbles into a medium skillet. Add the water, milk, and butter to the skillet and bring to a boil over high heat.
1 tablespoon butter	
½ seasoning packet from a 6-ounce box of Pasta Roni Shells & White Cheddar	**3** Stir in the seasoning packet, chili powder, and pasta. Return to a boil over high heat. Reduce the heat to medium and simmer for 7 minutes, stirring occasionally.
½ teaspoon chili powder	
1¼ cups (half of a 6-ounce box) Pasta Roni Shells & White Cheddar	**4** Stir in the salsa, corn, and peas. Boil gently for 2 minutes over medium heat, or until the pasta is almost tender, stirring frequently. Remove the pan from the heat.
½ cup medium chunky salsa	
½ cup corn	**5** Stir in the pepper cheese and let the mixture set for 4 minutes, or until the sauce has thickened.
¼ cup peas	
¼ cup pepper jack cheese	

Per serving: Calories 464 (From Fat 184); Fat 21g (Saturated 9g); Cholesterol 33mg; Sodium 1,280mg; Carbohydrate 49g (Dietary Fiber 7g); Protein 24g.

Note: Quite a few of the Pasta Roni mixes are vegetarian, but you should read the ingredients label each time you pick up a box just to make sure.

Zucchini Alfredo

Prep time: 10 min • **Cook time:** 10 min • **Yield:** 1 serving

Ingredients	Directions
3 cups water	*1* Bring the water to a boil in a medium saucepan over high heat. Add the noodles and cook for 8 minutes, or until they're soft but not mushy, stirring occasionally. Drain.
2 ounces egg noodles	
2 teaspoons olive oil	
1 clove garlic, minced	
¼ onion, minced	*2* While the noodles cook, heat the oil in a small skillet over medium heat. Add the garlic, onion, and mushrooms and sauté about 1 minute, or until the garlic begins to brown, stirring frequently.
4 fresh white mushrooms, sliced	
½ cup thinly sliced, unpeeled zucchini	
¼ teaspoon Italian seasoning	*3* Add the zucchini, Italian seasoning, salt, and pepper and sauté over high heat for 3 minutes, or until the zucchini is tender crisp.
⅛ teaspoon salt	
⅛ teaspoon black pepper	
3 tablespoons whole milk	*4* Reduce the heat to medium. Add the milk and cream cheese and stir for about 1 minute, or until the cheese is melted. Add the noodles and toss everything together until the sauce and veggies are evenly distributed.
1½ tablespoons low-fat cream cheese, cubed	
2 teaspoons grated Parmesan cheese	
	5 Spoon the noodles onto a dish and top with Parmesan cheese.

Per serving: Calories 416 (From Fat 170); Fat 19g (Saturated 6g); Cholesterol 71mg; Sodium 477mg; Carbohydrate 49g (Dietary Fiber 5g); Protein 15g.

Note: Why add salt to the boiling water when cooking pasta? Glad you asked. Salt raises the temperature of the boiling water so the pasta cooks more quickly. When you drain the pasta, most of the salt goes down the drain with the water, so you don't actually consume most of the salt you added to the pot.

Tip: Most recipes in this book that use milk call for low-fat milk. For this Alfredo sauce, you need to use whole milk (or soymilk) to get the sauce thick enough.

Gearing Up for Dinner with Grains

You probably keep hearing how whole grains are supposed to be so good for you. That's because they are. Historically, they've been called the "staff of life" because they've fed people for centuries. What makes them so healthy is that their bran layer and germ haven't been removed through milling. Consequently, you get all the nutrition from the grain as well as all the fiber.

Having grains with every meal is super easy. For breakfast, have a bowl of whole-grain cereal. For lunch, make a sandwich on whole-grain bread. At dinner, cook up some brown rice or enjoy a dish of cooked whole-grain pasta topped with a fresh marinara sauce.

Snacking before dinner (if you must)

Like your mom always said, you shouldn't spoil your appetite for dinner, but for those times when dinner really is a long time away, you can keep commercial grab 'n' go foods on hand for snacking. Keep a supply of some of the following items to satisfy the urge to munch (and flip to Chapter 13 for snack recipes to whip up yourself):

✔ Natural fruit leathers

✔ Low-fat fruit and cereal bars or granola bars

✔ Trail mix (dried fruits with nuts and seeds)

✔ Rice cakes or flavored mini rice cakes

✔ Small containers of low-fat plain or fruit yogurt

✔ Individual containers of apple-sauce or fruit cups

✔ Naturally sweetened cereal (to eat dry or with milk)

✔ Graham crackers, bagel crisps, or sesame breadsticks

✔ Fruit-sweetened cookies

✔ Fresh fruit

Pilaf Florentine

Prep time: 8 min • **Cook time:** 7 min • **Yield:** 1 serving

Ingredients	*Directions*
2 teaspoons olive oil	*1* In a medium saucepan over medium heat, heat the oil for 20 seconds. Add the onion and garlic and sauté for about 4 minutes, or until tender, stirring frequently.
¼ cup chopped onion	
1 small garlic clove, minced	
½ teaspoon dried mint	*2* Stir in the mint, dill, salt, pepper, spinach, lemon juice, and rice. Lower the heat, cover the pot, and cook for 2 minutes, or until the spinach is limp and the rice is hot.
½ teaspoon dried dill	
Dash salt	
Dash black pepper	
2 cups chopped fresh spinach	
¾ teaspoon lemon juice	*3* Spoon the mixture onto a dinner plate and top with the feta cheese crumbles.
1 container (1 cup) instant, ready-to-serve brown rice	
2 tablespoons crumbled feta cheese	

Per serving: Calories 423 (From Fat 140); Fat 16g (Saturated 4g); Cholesterol 17mg; Sodium 415mg; Carbohydrate 60g (Dietary Fiber 6g); Protein 11g.

Tip: You can freeze leftovers or use them to fill a pita pocket for lunch the next day.

Reeling Rice and Beans

Prep time: 5 min • **Cook time:** 17 min • **Yield:** 4 servings

Ingredients	Directions
1 can (15.5 ounces) light red kidney beans, rinsed and drained	*1* In a medium saucepan, stir together the beans, tomatoes, water, rice, salt, pepper, and red pepper flakes. Bring to a boil over high heat. Reduce the heat to medium, cover, and simmer for 15 minutes, or until the rice is tender.
1 can (14.5 ounces) canned diced tomatoes, undrained	
1 cup water	
¾ cup instant brown rice	*2* Stir in the spinach.
¼ teaspoon salt	
¼ teaspoon black pepper	*3* Spoon the mixture into bowls and top with cheese.
¼ teaspoon red pepper flakes	
1 box (10 ounces) frozen chopped spinach, thawed and drained	
½ cup grated pepper jack cheese	

Per serving: Calories 235 (From Fat 51); Fat 6g (Saturated 3g); Cholesterol 13mg; Sodium 423mg; Carbohydrate 36g (Dietary Fiber 11g); Protein 13g.

Tip: You've probably tried rice and beans before, but you've never had them like this. This dish is delicious! This recipe makes quite a bit, but you can cover the leftovers and enjoy them for dinner the next day or quickly heat some in the microwave and spoon it into a pita pocket for a grab-'n'-go lunch. You can even add some cold rice-and-bean mixture to a tossed salad or tortilla.

Tip: To thaw spinach quickly, place the unwrapped frozen box on a dish and microwave on the defrost setting for 6 minutes.

Tip: This recipe is simple to convert to vegan; just use nondairy pepper jack cheese in place of the dairy cheese.

Taking Your Time with Veggie-Based Dinners

Veggies are jampacked with nutrition. Sure, you can make steamed broccoli for dinner, but there are so many more ingenious ways to serve up vegetables! The recipes included here are fun to make and delicious to eat because the veggies are hidden under cheese, or shredded or mashed to disguise their identity, or hidden under a sauce. Live dangerously and have fun trying something new.

Carnivores have an easy time thinking of a side dish to serve with meat, fish, or chicken — they can serve a vegetable. But when vegetables are the entrée — the main course for dinner — what do you serve with them? Maybe one of the following suggestions will go well with your dinner:

✔ Tossed salad (or any other kind of salad with greens)

✔ Veggie salad (like marinated asparagus or artichoke hearts with button mushrooms, sliced cucumbers with tzatziki sauce, or tomato slices with mozzarella balls)

✔ Coleslaw

✔ Bean or lentil salad

✔ Pasta or potato salad

✔ Fruit salad

✔ Broiled marinated tomatoes (or broiled zucchini fans, or broiled baby portobello mushrooms)

✔ Baked or mashed potatoes, rice, pasta, or sweet potato fries

✔ Potato pancakes or latkes

✔ A bed of sautéed spinach (just place the entrée on top)

✔ Garlic toast or rolls

✔ Cinnamon apples

Sweet Potato Special

Prep time: 4 min • **Cook time:** 7 min • **Yield:** 2 servings

Ingredients	Directions
1 tablespoon butter	**1** Melt the butter in a small skillet over medium-high heat; add the onion and pecans and sauté for about 4 minutes, or until the onion is soft.
½ small onion, sliced	
2 tablespoons chopped pecans	
Dash salt	**2** Stir in the salt, pepper, rice, sweet potatoes or yams, and broth. Cook over medium heat, stirring frequently, for 3 minutes, or until the potatoes and rice are warmed.
Dash black pepper	
1 container (1 cup) instant, ready-to-serve brown rice	
1 8-ounce can sweet potatoes or yams, drained and chopped	**3** Stir in the cheese.
¼ cup vegetable broth	
2 tablespoons grated Parmesan cheese	

Per serving: Calories 305 (From Fat 123); Fat 14g (Saturated 5g); Cholesterol 19mg; Sodium 321mg; Carbohydrate 41g (Dietary Fiber 5g); Protein 6g.

Tip: You can easily convert this recipe to vegan by using nondairy margarine in place of the butter and grated nondairy cheese in place of the Parmesan cheese.

Potato Broccoli Bake

Prep time: 5 min • **Cook time:** 6 min • **Yield:** 1 serving

Ingredients	*Directions*
1½ cups refrigerated pre-made mashed potatoes	*1* Preheat the oven to 375 degrees.
1½ tablespoons low-fat cream cheese, softened and cut into tiny pieces	*2* Spoon the potatoes into a bowl and stir in the cream cheese, milk, and fried onions.
2 tablespoons low-fat milk ¼ cup canned French fried onions Nonstick cooking spray	*3* Spray a glass custard cup with nonstick spray, and then spoon the potato mixture into the cup. Heat it in the oven for 4 minutes, or until the potatoes are warmed.
1½ cups broccoli florets, cut into bite-size pieces 1 cup water ½ cup shredded low-fat cheddar cheese	*4* While the potatoes bake, put the broccoli in a small, microwave-safe bowl and add the water. Microwave for 1 minute and 20 seconds, or until the broccoli is tender crisp. Drain.
	5 Lay the broccoli over the potatoes. Sprinkle cheese on top of the broccoli. Return the custard cup to the oven for 2 minutes to melt the cheese.

Per serving: Calories 585 (From Fat 257); Fat 29g (Saturated 15g); Cholesterol 59mg; Sodium 1,883mg; Carbohydrate 56g (Dietary Fiber 9g); Protein 27g.

Tip: What to do with the leftover mashed potatoes? Add some chopped onion and grated cheese, form them into patties, and then dust them with breadcrumbs so you have potato cakes to fry in the morning for breakfast.

Mediterranean Medley

Prep time: 8 min • **Cook time:** 7 min • **Yield:** 1 serving

Ingredients	Directions
Nonstick cooking spray	*1* Preheat the broiler to high. Set the broiler rack in the highest position (as close to the broiler heating element as possible).
1 small, unpeeled zucchini or yellow squash, cut lengthwise into ½-inch-thick slices	
	2 Spray a baking sheet with nonstick spray.
6 thin onion slices	
¼ green pepper, cut into ½-inch-thick strips	*3* Put the zucchini, onion, green pepper, and mushrooms in a medium bowl. Add the oil, vinegar, Italian seasoning, salt, and pepper. Blend ingredients so the vegetables are evenly coated. Spread the vegetables in the baking pan so they don't overlap.
6 white mushrooms, sliced	
2 tablespoons olive oil	
1 tablespoon balsamic vinegar	
½ teaspoon Italian seasoning	*4* Broil for 7 minutes, or until the veggies are browned. (You don't need to turn the vegetables.)
¼ teaspoon salt	
⅛ teaspoon black pepper	*5* While the veggies cook, in a small, microwave-safe bowl, stir together the hummus and feta cheese. Warm this mixture in the microwave for 30 seconds.
⅓ cup hummus	
¼ cup crumbled feta cheese	
	6 When you're ready to eat, lay the vegetables on a dish and spoon the hummus mixture over the top.

Per serving: Calories 537 (From Fat 387); Fat 43g (Saturated 10g); Cholesterol 33mg; Sodium 1,294mg; Carbohydrate 27g (Dietary Fiber 9g); Protein 17g.

Tip: To convert this recipe to vegan, omit the feta cheese.

Pseudo Zucchini Parm

Prep time: 10 min • **Cook time:** 7 min • **Yield:** 1 serving

Ingredients	Directions
Nonstick cooking spray	**1** Preheat the broiler. Spray a baking sheet (preferably dark-coated) with nonstick spray.
¼ cup seasoned breadcrumbs	
½ teaspoon Italian seasoning	
1 medium, unpeeled zucchini, cut into ½-inch slices	**2** On a sheet of wax paper, mix together the breadcrumbs and Italian seasoning.
½ cup spaghetti sauce	**3** Wash off the zucchini slices so they're wet, and then dip both sides of each slice into the crumb mixture. Set the slices on the baking sheet.
¼ cup shredded low-fat mozzarella cheese	
2 tablespoons grated Parmesan cheese	**4** Broil the zucchini for 6 minutes, or until both sides are browned, turning once.
	5 Spoon the spaghetti sauce over the zucchini, and then sprinkle with the mozzarella cheese and the Parmesan cheese.
	6 Return the pan to the hot oven for 1 minute, or until the cheese melts.

Per serving: Calories 308 (From Fat 80); Fat 9g (Saturated 4g); Cholesterol 18mg; Sodium 1,702mg; Carbohydrate 43g (Dietary Fiber 7g); Protein 16g.

Cabbage Hash Browns

Prep time: 9 min • **Cook time:** 13 min • **Yield:** 1 serving

Ingredients	Directions
2 tablespoons olive oil	*1* In a small skillet, heat 1 tablespoon oil for 20 seconds over medium-high heat. Add the cabbage and onion and sauté for 10 minutes, stirring frequently. Remove the pan from the heat and allow it to cool for 5 minutes.
2 cups shredded cabbage	
1 tablespoon minced onion	
1 egg	
⅛ teaspoon salt	*2* In a small bowl, whip the egg, salt, pepper, dill, and cheese with a fork. Stir in the cabbage and onion and 3 tablespoons breadcrumbs until well blended.
⅛ teaspoon black pepper	
¼ teaspoon dried dill	
1 tablespoon grated Parmesan cheese	*3* On a piece of wax paper, form the mixture into two patties. Coat the outside of the patties with the remaining 3 tablespoons breadcrumbs.
6 tablespoons seasoned breadcrumbs	
	4 Heat the remaining 1 tablespoon oil in a medium skillet over medium heat. Place the patties in the pan. Cook for about 2 minutes per side, until both sides are browned.

Per serving: Calories 541 (From Fat 316); Fat 35g (Saturated 7g); Cholesterol 217mg; Sodium 1,665mg; Carbohydrate 41g (Dietary Fiber 5g); Protein 17g.

Tip: Save time shredding the cabbage yourself by buying a bag of shredded cabbage or shredded coleslaw mix. Use the leftover cabbage in soups, on sandwiches, and in vegetable casseroles, or just boil the cabbage with some cut potatoes, drain, and then drizzle with butter, salt, and pepper for another dinner.

Ratatouille Stew

Prep time: 10 min • **Cook time:** 12 min • **Yield:** 2 servings

Ingredients	*Directions*
2 small new red potatoes, unpeeled, cut into ½-inch cubes	*1* Put the potatoes on a microwave-safe dish, cover with wax paper, and nuke for 2 minutes.
3 tablespoons olive oil	
1 peeled baby eggplant, cut into ½-inch cubes	*2* In a large skillet, warm the oil for 20 seconds. Add the eggplant, zucchini, carrots, green pepper, onion, garlic, and potatoes. Sauté for 8 minutes over medium-high heat, stirring occasionally, until the veggies are tender.
1 small, unpeeled zucchini, cut into ½-inch cubes	
4 baby carrots, sliced thin	
¼ green pepper, chopped	*3* Stir in the spaghetti sauce, parsley, Italian seasoning, salt, and pepper. Cook, stirring, for 1 minute more.
½ medium onion, chopped	
2 cloves garlic, minced	
1 cup spaghetti sauce	*4* Sprinkle the cheese on top of the veggies.
1 tablespoon dried parsley flakes	
½ teaspoon Italian seasoning	
¼ teaspoon salt	
¼ teaspoon black pepper	
2 tablespoons grated Parmesan cheese	

Per serving: Calories 455 (From Fat 225); Fat 25g (Saturated 4g); Cholesterol 4mg; Sodium 924mg; Carbohydrate 51g (Dietary Fiber 9g); Protein 10g.

Note: Ratatouille usually takes an hour to bake, but not this version. I've tailored this recipe for the microwave, so you'll be sitting down to dinner before you can jam all the eggplant peels down the garbage disposal.

Tip: Don't let the number of ingredients scare you off. This is one delicious meal! Serve it with some garlic bread and you've reached nirvana.

Tip: If you're vegan, either omit the cheese or use grated nondairy cheese.

Micro-broiled Veggies

Prep time: 9 min • **Cook time:** 14 min • **Yield:** 2 servings

Ingredients	Directions
Nonstick cooking spray	*1* Preheat the broiler. Spray a 5-x-7-inch, microwave-safe glass baking dish with nonstick spray.
2 baby carrots, cut lengthwise into quarters	
1 medium, unpeeled red potato, cut into ¾-inch cubes	*2* Mix all the ingredients together in a medium bowl until they're evenly coated. Spoon the veggies into the baking dish.
½ cup peeled sweet potato or yam, cut into ¾-inch cubes	
½ cup unpeeled chopped zucchini	*3* Microwave for 4 minutes, and then broil for 10 minutes, or until the potatoes are tender and golden brown.
⅛ green pepper, chopped	
½ small onion, chopped	
¼ portobello mushroom, chopped	
1½ tablespoons olive oil	
¼ teaspoon Italian seasoning	
⅛ teaspoon salt	
⅛ teaspoon black pepper	

Per serving: Calories 370 (From Fat 189); Fat 21g (Saturated 3g); Cholesterol 0mg; Sodium 316mg; Carbohydrate 41g (Dietary Fiber 5g); Protein 6g.

Undercover Veggie Pie

Prep time: 10 min • **Cook time:** 20 min • **Yield:** 1 serving

Ingredients	Directions
Nonstick cooking spray	*1* Preheat the oven to 400 degrees. Spray a 2½ cup baking pan with nonstick spray.
½ cup unpeeled zucchini, cut into ¼-inch cubes	
¼ cup unpeeled yellow squash, cut into ¼-inch cubes	*2* In a small bowl, stir together the zucchini, squash, tomato, onion, green pepper, dill, and cheese. Spoon this mixture into the baking pan.
¼ cup tomato, cut into ¼-inch cubes	
2 tablespoons minced onion	*3* In the same bowl, whisk together the biscuit mix, milk, egg, salt, and pepper until smooth. Pour this mixture over the vegetables to cover them completely.
2 tablespoons minced green pepper	
½ teaspoon dried dill	
3 tablespoons grated Parmesan cheese	*4* Bake for 20 minutes, or until a knife inserted in the center comes out clean.
⅔ cup biscuit-baking mix	
½ cup low-fat milk	
1 egg	
⅛ teaspoon salt	
¼ teaspoon black pepper	

Per serving: Calories 605 (From Fat 226); Fat 25g (Saturated 9g); Cholesterol 229mg; Sodium 1,837mg; Carbohydrate 72g (Dietary Fiber 5g); Protein 25g.

Vary It! If you don't have yellow squash, increase the amount of zucchini by ¼ cup (or you can use eggplant). If you're out of Parmesan cheese, use shredded pepper jack cheese. And if you're out of biscuit-baking mix, quickly run out and buy some!

Quick Vegetable Soup

Prep time: 3 min • **Cook time:** 30 min • **Yield:** 6 servings

Ingredients	Directions
8 cups water	**1** Bring the water to a boil in a medium saucepan over high heat. Stir in the soup mixes and the spaghetti sauce.
1 package (2.15 ounces) Knorr Vegetable Soup Mix	
1 package (1.9 ounces) Lipton Onion Soup Mix	**2** Lower the heat to medium and stir in the orzo, vegetables, pepper, and pepper sauce. Simmer, stirring occasionally, for 30 minutes, or until pasta is tender.
3 cups spaghetti sauce	
1 cup orzo or other small pasta	
1 bag (16 ounces) frozen mixed vegetables	
¼ teaspoon black pepper	
12 drops hot pepper sauce	

Per serving: Calories 278 (From Fat 37); Fat 4g (Saturated 1g); Cholesterol 0mg; Sodium 1,989mg; Carbohydrate 53g (Dietary Fiber 8g); Protein 10g.

Note: I list two specific soup mixes in this recipe because they're certified to be vegetarian. However, you still have to read labels for ingredients because food manufacturers change their recipes, their suppliers, and their production methods, which means that the ingredients on the label can also change.

Tip: This recipe makes more soup than you can eat in one sitting, but it keeps in the refrigerator for several days (you may have to add a little more water when you reheat the soup), or you can freeze what's left in single-serving containers to eat on the days when you don't have time to cook.

Slow Cooker Potatoes

Prep time: 7 min • **Cook time:** 4 hr • **Yield:** 1 serving

Ingredients	Directions
Nonstick cooking spray	*1* Spray the inside of a 2-quart slow cooker well with nonstick spray.
1 large, unpeeled russet potato, sliced ¼-inch thick	
½ onion, sliced thin	*2* Arrange the potato slices in the cooker in overlapping rows. Lay the onion slices on top, and then the tomato slices.
2 Roma or plum tomatoes, sliced thin	
½ teaspoon paprika	*3* Sprinkle the tomatoes with the paprika, pepper, and cheese. Spoon the soup over the cheese.
⅛ teaspoon black pepper	
⅓ cup shredded sharp low-fat cheddar cheese	*4* Cover the cooker and cook on high for 4 hours.
1 cup (10.75 ounces) condensed cream of mushroom soup	

Per serving: Calories 596 (From Fat 143); Fat 16g (Saturated 6g); Cholesterol 18mg; Sodium 2,012mg; Carbohydrate 95g (Dietary Fiber 11g); Protein 23g.

Note: Although you can't finish cooking in a crockpot in the 30-minute time frame of this chapter, the assembly time certainly qualifies. Take a few minutes to toss some chopped veggies into the pot, add the soup, and set the lid on top; then walk away until dinner time.

Note: Say this aloud three times: "I will NOT lift the lid and peek inside the pot during the first few hours of cooking." Every time you lift the lid on a slow cooker, especially during the first few hours, you make the cooking time longer because you let so much heat escape.

Tip: If you won't be around to eat in 4 hours, you can set the cooker on low (rather than high) and cook the dish for 7 hours.

Stewed Vegetable Dinner

Prep time: 8 min • **Cook time:** 8 hr • **Yield:** 2 servings

Ingredients	Directions
Nonstick cooking spray	**1** Spray the inside of a 2-quart slow cooker with nonstick spray.
3 medium, unpeeled red potatoes, cut into wedges	
1 small onion, diced	**2** Stir all the ingredients except the peas into the slow cooker, making sure the potato wedges are at the bottom (because they take a little longer to cook than the other vegetables).
6 baby carrots, sliced thin	
1 stalk celery, sliced thin	
1 box (10 ounces) frozen chopped spinach, thawed	
1 can (8 ounces) French cut green beans plus liquid	**3** Cover the pot and cook for 8 hours on low. Fifteen minutes before serving, stir in the peas.
1 can (8 ounces) garbanzo beans, rinsed and drained	
1 tablespoon olive oil	
1 can (8 ounces) tomato sauce	
½ teaspoon minced garlic (fresh or from a jar)	
¼ teaspoon cinnamon	
1 tablespoon dried parsley flakes	
¼ teaspoon Italian seasoning	
¼ teaspoon salt	
¼ teaspoon black pepper	
1 cup frozen peas	

Per serving: Calories 516 (From Fat 84); Fat 9g (Saturated 1g); Cholesterol 0mg; Sodium 1,553mg; Carbohydrate 93g (Dietary Fiber 20g); Protein 20g.

Note: Eight hours of cooking time definitely exceeds the 30-minute limit of this chapter, but follow the reasoning here. This dinner takes only about 8 minutes to assemble, and the slow cooker does the rest, so technically, it's not your time that's being monopolized. Right?

Part III
Beyond Three Squares

The 5th Wave

By Rich Tennant

©RICHTENNANT

"Let's see—maybe there's a better place for your vegetarian cookbook than on the butcher block between the steak knives and the A1 sauce?"

In this part . . .

*P*art II is filled with recipes for breakfast, lunch, and dinner, but people love to eat *so* many other things, like snacks, appetizers, and baked goods. I cover those dishes in this part, and I also include all kinds of quick yet decadent dessert recipes.

And no matter how well you plan your meals, sometimes you have leftovers. This part features hints for all sorts of innovative ways to use those little bits of veggies in your refrigerator, that small bowl of last night's pasta, and the remains of a jar of taco sauce (among other things!).

Chapter 13

Serving Up Snacks, Appetizers, and Baked Goodies

In This Chapter

▶ Snacking on munchable treats
▶ Pleasing the palate with vegetarian appetizers
▶ Makin' muffins and other doughy delights

Man does not live by meals alone. At times you probably crave snack foods, appetizers, and baked goods. This chapter has delicious vegetarian options for all three categories (some healthier than others).

Munching on Simple Snacks

Between school, homework, sports, maybe a part-time job, and hanging out with friends, finding time to cook at home can be hard . . . so you snack. Sometimes, hours have passed since your last meal . . . so you snack. And occasionally, you just want something to munch on in the evenings . . . so you snack.

Sure, snacks can be fattening, depending on what you choose to eat. Keep in mind that one not-so-healthy snack (say, a bag of potato chips) or one day of splurging (Thanksgiving, for example) isn't going to make or break your health. What counts is what you eat most of the time, on a daily basis. In this section, I provide recipes for some tasty vegetarian snacks that you can feel good about eating.

Homemade Microwave Popcorn

Prep time: 1 min • **Cook time:** 3 min, 20 sec • **Yield:** 1 serving

Ingredients	*Directions*
½ cup popcorn kernels 1 tablespoon butter ¼ teaspoon salt	*1* Pour the kernels into a brown paper lunch bag and fold the top down twice. Press down firmly on each fold. Each fold should be about a half inch deep to allow for expansion room inside the bag.
	2 Microwave (on a turntable) on high for 3 minutes, or until the pops are 2 to 3 seconds apart.
	3 Remove the bag and pour the contents into a bowl.
	4 Put the butter into a small, microwave-safe bowl, cover the bowl with wax paper, and nuke on high for 20 seconds, or until the butter has melted. Drizzle the butter over the popcorn and sprinkle with the salt.

Per serving: Calories 460 (From Fat 147); Fat 16g (Saturated 7g); Cholesterol 31mg; Sodium 583mg; Carbohydrate 72g (Dietary Fiber 12g); Protein 12g.

Tip: Vegans, you can enjoy this popcorn too, by substituting nondairy margarine for the butter.

Delectable Dates

Prep time: 5 min • **Yield:** 5 servings

Ingredients	*Directions*
10 walnut quarters	*1* Stuff a walnut piece inside of each date.
10 pitted dates	
2 teaspoons granulated sugar	*2* Spoon the sugar onto a small piece of wax paper. Roll the dates in the sugar to coat.

Per serving: Calories 89 (From Fat 34); Fat 4g (Saturated 0g); Cholesterol 0mg; Sodium 1mg; Carbohydrate 15g (Dietary Fiber 2g); Protein 1g.

Tip: Buy pitted dates. Pitting them yourself is the pits!

Note: If you're not going to eat the dates within two to three days, refrigerate them in a plastic container; they'll keep for three to four weeks.

Funky Fudge

Prep time: 5 min • **Cook time:** 3 min • **Yield:** 64 one-piece servings

Ingredients	*Directions*
⅓ **cup chopped dried apricots**	*1* In a small bowl, stir together the apricots, cranberries, and walnuts. Set aside.
⅓ **cup dried cranberries**	
⅓ **cup chopped walnuts**	*2* Place the chocolate pieces, butterscotch pieces, and milk in a microwave-safe bowl. Microwave at 50 percent power for 3 minutes, or until chips are almost melted, stopping once each minute to stir. (A few small, remaining chunks of chocolate or butterscotch just add to the flavor.)
1 bag (12 ounces) semisweet chocolate pieces	
⅓ **cup butterscotch pieces**	
1 (14-ounce) can sweetened condensed milk	
Nonstick cooking spray	*3* Stir the apricots, cranberries, and walnuts into the chocolate mixture.
	4 Spray a 9-inch square pan with nonstick spray, and pour the fudge into the pan, smoothing the top so it's level. When cool, use a wet knife to cut the fudge into 64 pieces (7 cuts down and 7 cuts across the pan).

Per serving: Calories 58 (From Fat 25); Fat 3g (Saturated 2g); Cholesterol 2mg; Sodium 9mg; Carbohydrate 8g (Dietary Fiber 0g); Protein 1g.

Note: You can cover and refrigerate this fudge; it will keep for up to a week without drying out.

Vary It! You can use almost any kind of nuts (pecans, hazelnuts, pistachios, peanuts, and so on) and almost any kind of dried fruits (blueberries or cherries), so have fun experimenting. If you don't like butterscotch, use milk chocolate pieces instead.

Tip: This fudge is like potato chips — you can't eat just one! Unless you've already decided that you're going to consume the entire pan, you'd better freeze the fudge to remove temptation, taking out one or two pieces as needed. Just place the fudge in a sealed plastic container and freeze it for up to two months. Remember to thaw the pieces first so you don't break a tooth biting into them!

Almond Balls

Prep time: 10 min • **Yield:** 6 servings

Ingredients	Directions
1 cup slivered almonds **1 cup raisins** **1 tablespoon honey** **1 teaspoon cinnamon** **½ teaspoon vanilla**	*1* Rinse the almonds and raisins with water. While they're still wet, put them in a blender. Add the honey, cinnamon, and vanilla.
	2 Mix on medium-high speed until thoroughly mixed (about 20 seconds) but not totally puréed, stopping several times to scrape down the sides.
	3 Spoon the mixture onto a sheet of wax paper and form the dough into 12 ¾-inch balls.

Per serving: Calories 199 (From Fat 83); Fat 9g (Saturated 1g); Cholesterol 0mg; Sodium 4mg; Carbohydrate 29g (Dietary Fiber 3g); Protein 5g.

Tip: To make this recipe suitable for vegans, use maple syrup or pancake syrup in place of the honey.

Tip: You don't need to refrigerate these rolls, but you do need to cover them. Store them in a sealed plastic container at room temperature; they'll keep for five days.

Snazzy Snack Mix

Prep time: 2 min • **Cook time:** 15 min • **Yield:** 4 servings

Ingredients	Directions
¾ cup olive oil	**1** Preheat the oven to 250 degrees.
1¼ tablespoons grated Parmesan cheese	**2** In a small bowl, stir together the oil, cheese, Italian seasoning, garlic powder, chili powder, and salt.
¼ teaspoon Italian seasoning	
⅛ teaspoon garlic powder	
⅛ teaspoon chili powder	**3** Put the crackers into a medium-sized bowl. Drizzle half of the oil mixture over the crackers. Using a rubber spatula, gently stir the crackers to distribute the oil evenly. Add the remaining oil mixture and continue to stir until the crackers are evenly coated.
⅛ teaspoon salt	
2 cups oyster crackers	
	4 Spread the crackers out on a baking sheet.
	5 Bake the crackers for 15 minutes, or until the crackers are crisp.

Per serving: Calories 570 (From Fat 456); Fat 51g (Saturated 11g); Cholesterol 20mg; Sodium 832mg; Carbohydrate 17g (Dietary Fiber 1g); Protein 13g.

Note: When the crackers cool, store them in an airtight container or a sealed plastic bag. They'll stay fresh for three to four days.

Tip: This is a great snack to have on hand for anytime. You can also toss these crackers on a salad like croutons, or drop a few into a bowl of soup. If they dry out, put them in a plastic bag, crush them, and sprinkle them on top of vegetables.

Baked Edamame

Prep time: 4 min • **Cook time:** 15 min • **Yield:** 2 servings

Ingredients	Directions
1 cup frozen edamame (soybeans in the pod)	**1** Preheat the oven to 400 degrees.
1 teaspoon olive oil ½ teaspoon salt ⅛ teaspoon cayenne pepper	**2** In a small bowl, toss the frozen beans with the oil, salt, and cayenne pepper until evenly coated.
	3 Spread the beans on a baking sheet and bake for 15 minutes, stirring occasionally.

Per serving: Calories 120 (From Fat 47); Fat 5g (Saturated 0g); Cholesterol 0mg; Sodium 611mg; Carbohydrate 9g (Dietary Fiber 4g); Protein 8g.

Vary It! This sure is a healthy snack! Experiment with the beans by adding different seasonings each time you make them, like chili powder and cumin, or low-sodium soy sauce and garlic powder, or paprika and grated Parmesan cheese, or honey and wasabi powder.

Great Granola

Prep time: 5 min, plus 15 min rest time • **Cook time:** 30–40 min • **Yield:** 4 (¾ cup) servings

Ingredients	Directions
2 cups of old-fashioned oats	*1* Preheat the oven to 300 degrees.
¾ cups chopped pecans	
¼ cup packed brown sugar	*2* In a large bowl, mix the oats, pecans, brown sugar, salt, and cinnamon; set aside.
¼ teaspoon salt	
¾ teaspoon ground cinnamon	*3* In a small saucepan, warm the oil, honey, and pancake syrup over medium-high heat; remove from the heat and stir in the vanilla.
2 tablespoons olive oil	
2 tablespoons honey	
2 tablespoons pancake syrup	*4* Slowly pour the liquid over the oat mixture. Stir with a rubber spatula until the mixture is evenly coated.
1 teaspoon vanilla	
Nonstick cooking spray	*5* Spray a large baking sheet with nonstick spray. Spread the granola onto the sheet and bake for 30 to 40 minutes, stirring every 10 minutes. Watch it closely so it doesn't burn.
½ cup dried cranberries	
	6 Remove the pan from the oven and let the granola cool completely (about 15 minutes). Stir in the dried cranberries.

Per serving: Calories 527 (From Fat 229); Fat 25g (Saturated 3g); Cholesterol 0mg; Sodium 154mg; Carbohydrate 72g (Dietary Fiber 7g); Protein 9g.

Tip: Vegans can use agave syrup in place of the honey in this recipe.

Note: You can store granola in an airtight container for up to one week at room temperature or up to three months in the freezer.

Tip: Granola is great for munching at night, for putting on cereal (hot or cold) or on top of grapefruit in the morning, for mixing into yogurt for an afternoon snack, or for sprinkling onto salad and on top of desserts.

Getting Fancy with Appetizers

What's the difference between an appetizer and a snack? An appetizer just looks a little fancier. For example, a bowl of cut-up veggies qualifies as a snack, but if you put a couple of spoonfuls of hummus or a sour cream dip in the bottom of a small juice glass and stand some sliced veggies in the glass, you've converted your snack into an appetizer.

In this section, I give you some recipes for great vegetarian appetizers. You can serve them to company or make them whenever you're in the mood for an extra special snack.

If someone comes over unexpectedly, you probably have plenty of appetizers right in your fridge. Arrange some foods in groups on a dish and serve with crackers. These foods can include things like sliced pickles, olives, cubed cheese, quartered hard-boiled eggs, roasted red peppers or sliced tomatoes, pepperoncini, and baby carrots. Add a handful of nuts and some fresh grapes and no one will go away hungry.

Goat Cheese Spread

Prep time: 4 min • **Cook time:** 20 sec • **Yield:** 4 servings

Ingredients	*Directions*
½ teaspoon olive oil	**1** In a small bowl, stir together the oil, lemon juice, and vinegar.
½ teaspoon lemon juice	
Dash balsamic vinegar	**2** On a piece of wax paper, stir together the pepper, Italian seasoning, and breadcrumbs.
Dash pepper	
¼ teaspoon Italian seasoning	
2 tablespoons seasoned breadcrumbs	**3** Roll the cheese in the oil mixture, coating all sides, and then roll it in the breadcrumb mixture, coating all sides.
1 package (4 ounces) soft goat cheese	
	4 Lay the coated roll on a microwave-safe dish and microwave on high for 20 seconds to soften the cheese.

Per serving: Calories 95 (From Fat 60); Fat 7g (Saturated 4g); Cholesterol 13mg; Sodium 204mg; Carbohydrate 3g (Dietary Fiber 0g); Protein 6g.

Note: Goat cheese is very popular. It's soft and rich (both in taste and cost) and is screaming to be put on a bagel. Or you can spread some prepared pesto on a cracker and top it with a slice of goat cheese, or use goat cheese instead of sour cream on top of your baked potato.

Tip: If you overbake this spread, that's okay — it will totally melt. In that event, scoop it into a bowl and call it a dip instead of a spread. Problem solved!

Pesto Rolls

Prep time: 5 min • **Yield:** 2 servings

Ingredients	*Directions*
1 tablespoon basil pesto 1 whole-wheat 8-inch tortilla 1 slice provolone cheese, cut in half ½ roasted red pepper, sliced thin 3 pitted kalamata olives, sliced thin	*1* Spread the pesto on one half of the tortilla, almost to the edges. Lay the cheese, red pepper, and olive slices on top of the pesto.
	2 Starting on the side with the pesto and cheese, roll up the tortilla tightly.
	3 Cut the tortilla into ¾-inch slices. Lay the slices, cut-side up, on a dish.

Per serving: Calories 161 (From Fat 88); Fat 10g (Saturated 4g); Cholesterol 12mg; Sodium 350mg; Carbohydrate 13g (Dietary Fiber 1g); Protein 7g.

Tip: Use nondairy cheese in place of the provolone cheese if you're vegan.

Tip: You can find jars of pesto and roasted red peppers at the grocery store — no need to make your own pesto and roast your own peppers!

Vary It! If you're out of provolone cheese, you can use mozzarella, pepper jack, or feta cheese in its place.

Super Spaghetti Sauce Spread

Prep time: 5 min • **Cook time:** 1½ min • **Yield:** 4 servings

Ingredients	Directions
Nonstick spray	**1** Spray a 2-cup baking dish with nonstick spray and set aside.
1 package (3 ounces) low-fat cream cheese, softened	
¼ cup low-fat sour cream	**2** Put the cream cheese, sour cream, onion, Italian seasoning, and red pepper flakes in a bowl and blend together with the back of a fork. With a rubber spatula, spread the mixture into the baking dish, smoothing the top.
1 green onion, chopped	
½ teaspoon Italian seasoning	
½ teaspoon red pepper flakes	
⅓ cup spaghetti sauce	**3** Spread the spaghetti sauce evenly over the top of the cheese mixture, and then sprinkle with Parmesan cheese.
2 tablespoons grated Parmesan cheese	
	4 Microwave on high for 1½ minutes, or until the spread is warmed through and the sauce on top is bubbly.

Per serving: Calories 117 (From Fat 75); Fat 8g (Saturated 5g); Cholesterol 23mg; Sodium 237mg; Carbohydrate 6g (Dietary Fiber 1g); Protein 5g.

Tip: This is one spread that everyone loves. Serve it with breadsticks, pita bread wedges, or crackers. Don't tell people how simple it is to make — make them think you slaved over it!

Greek Bruschetta

Prep time: 10 min • **Yield:** 4 servings

Ingredients	Directions
1 large tomato, chopped	**1** Stir all the ingredients together in a small bowl. Serve with pita bread wedges.
½ cup crumbled feta cheese	
1 green onion, minced	
2 tablespoons minced green pepper	
¼ teaspoon Italian seasoning	
3 tablespoons olive oil	
¼ cup pitted, chopped kalamata olives (optional)	
2 slices pita bread, each cut into 6 wedges	

Per serving: Calories 234 (From Fat 132); Fat 15g (Saturated 4g); Cholesterol 17mg; Sodium 375mg; Carbohydrate 20g (Dietary Fiber 1g); Protein 6g.

Vary It! If you don't have kalamata olives, just omit them or substitute pitted, chopped, ripe black or green olives.

Tip: If you're the kind of person who plans ahead, prepare this ahead of time, cover it, and then refrigerate it for an hour so the flavors can blend.

Tip: If you have any bruschetta mix left over (which you won't), put it in a pita pocket for lunch or use it as a salsa over steamed asparagus.

Cranberry Cups

Prep time: 5 min • **Cook time:** 10 min • **Yield:** 6 servings

Ingredients	Directions
6 mini phyllo shells, thawed 3 ounces low-fat cream cheese, softened	**1** Preheat the oven to 350 degrees. Bake the phyllo shells for 10 minutes, or according to package directions. Let the shells cool.
1 tablespoon grated onion 3 tablespoons whole berry cranberry sauce	**2** In a small bowl, stir together the cream cheese and onion.
	3 Spoon the cheese mixture into the phyllo shells, dividing evenly.
	4 Spoon ½ tablespoon cranberry sauce on top of each phyllo shell.

Per serving: Calories 68 (From Fat 39); Fat 4g (Saturated 2g); Cholesterol 11mg; Sodium 71mg; Carbohydrate 6g (Dietary Fiber 0g); Protein 1g.

Tip: Convert this to a vegan recipe by using nondairy cream cheese in place of the low-fat cream cheese.

Tip: Soften cream cheese quickly by cutting it into several slices, laying the slices on a dish, and microwaving for 15 seconds.

Note: If you're not going to serve these cups immediately, cover and refrigerate the cheese-filled cups for up to 4 hours, spooning the cranberry sauce on top just before serving.

Hot Artichoke Parmesan Spread

Prep time: 8 min • **Cook time:** 15 min • **Yield:** 3 servings

Ingredients	Directions
1 cup canned artichoke hearts, well drained and finely chopped	*1* Preheat the oven to 350 degrees.
½ cup grated Parmesan cheese plus another 1½ teaspoons grated Parmesan cheese	*2* In a small bowl, combine the artichoke hearts, ½ cup of the Parmesan cheese, mayonnaise, garlic, lemon juice, cayenne pepper, salt, and black pepper until well blended.
2 tablespoons mayonnaise	
⅛ teaspoon minced garlic	
¼ teaspoon lemon juice	*3* Spray a 2- or 3-cup baking dish with nonstick spray, and spread the mixture in an even layer in the dish. Sprinkle 1½ teaspoons Parmesan cheese over the top.
Dash cayenne pepper	
Dash salt	
Dash black pepper	*4* Bake for 15 minutes, or until the top is golden.
Nonstick cooking spray	

Per serving: Calories 157 (From Fat 105); Fat 12g (Saturated 4g); Cholesterol 17mg; Sodium 529mg; Carbohydrate 5g (Dietary Fiber 0g); Protein 8g.

Tip: For a vegan version of this recipe, use nondairy grated cheese in place of the Parmesan and egg-free vegan mayonnaise.

Vary It! If you want to get fancy, add some diced roasted red peppers, finely minced green onion, or chopped almonds to the mix.

Tip: In a time crunch, you can cook this spread in the microwave on high for 2 minutes instead of baking it in the oven.

Tip: Serve this with dark brown bread cubes or wedges of pita bread. Crackers work but breads are better.

Mushroom Squares

Prep time: 12 min, plus 5 min rest time • **Cook time:** 30–35 min • **Yield:** 12 two-piece servings

Ingredients	Directions
2 tablespoons butter	**1** Preheat the oven to 350 degrees.
3 cups finely chopped fresh mushrooms	**2** Melt the butter in a large skillet. Add the mushrooms and onions and cook over medium-high heat, stirring frequently, for 4 minutes.
2 tablespoons finely minced onion	
½ teaspoon garlic powder	
⅛ teaspoon salt	**3** Stir in the garlic powder, salt, lemon juice, and soy sauce. Cook about 6 minutes, or until all the liquid evaporates.
1 teaspoon lemon juice	
1 teaspoon low-sodium soy sauce	
1 can (8 ounces) refrigerated crescent rolls	**4** Unroll the dough (without separating it at the perforations) and lay it in an ungreased, 9-x-13-inch baking pan. The dough will be larger than the pan, so push the dough together to fit, to seal the perforations, and to cover the bottom of the pan.
1 package (3 ounces) low-fat cream cheese, softened and cut into small pieces	
¼ cup grated Parmesan cheese	**5** Sprinkle the pieces of cream cheese over the dough. Using the back of a spoon, evenly cover the dough. Top with the mushroom mixture, and then sprinkle with the Parmesan cheese.
	6 Bake for 20 to 25 minutes, or until golden brown. Cool 5 minutes before cutting into squares.

Per serving: Calories 116 (From Fat 64); Fat 7g (Saturated 3g); Cholesterol 12mg; Sodium 257mg; Carbohydrate 9g (Dietary Fiber 0g); Protein 3g.

Tip: Don't wash mushrooms under running tap water because they'll absorb water and become mushy. Instead, rub the dirt off with a damp paper towel.

Tip: If you don't have fresh mushrooms on hand, you can substitute an 8-ounce can of mushrooms, drained and chopped.

Vary It! In place of the fresh minced onions, you can use ½ teaspoon instant minced onion; add it when you add the garlic powder and other seasonings.

Treating Yourself to Baked Goods

Man may not live by bread alone, but bready stuff sure does taste good! A couple of things to keep in mind: When making muffin batter, mix ingredients lightly, only until all the dry ingredients are moistened. If you mix the batter too much, the muffins get a denser texture and form a peaked shape at the top. If you like warm muffins and sweet rolls, you can reheat them briefly in the microwave.

 Microwave breads are quick and easy, but they have one drawback — they stick to the bottom of the mug or casserole dish or whatever container you use to cook them. You can spray the bottom of the container with nonstick cooking spray or use butter or oil or any other lubricant, and that helps somewhat, but you'll still encounter a sticking issue if you let the bread cool in the baking container. Avoid this by inverting the muffin or bread onto a dish while it's still piping hot.

 Bread and other baked goods stay fresher longer when you wrap them well and keep them in the refrigerator. And make sure to get rid of a whole loaf of moldy bread even if only one slice is moldy. The rest of the loaf can have mold that's too small to see.

Microwave Cornbread

Prep time: 2 min • **Cook time:** 2–3 min • **Yield:** 2 servings

Ingredients	Directions
½ **cup cornmeal**	*1* In a medium, microwave-safe bowl, whisk together the cornmeal, baking mix, sugar, and salt.
½ **cup baking mix**	
2 tablespoons granulated sugar	*2* Make a well in the center of the cornmeal mixture and add the oil and milk. Use a rubber spatula to mix the ingredients together until thoroughly blended.
¼ **teaspoon salt**	
⅓ **cup olive oil**	
⅓ **cup low-fat milk**	*3* Spray a large, microwave-safe, 2-cup mug or bowl well with nonstick spray. Spoon in the batter and microwave on high for 2 to 3 minutes, or until the top stops bubbling and looks dry. Remove from microwave as soon as a toothpick inserted in the center comes out dry.
Nonstick cooking spray	
	4 To remove the bread, use a knife to cut around the outside edges as soon as it's done baking. Invert the mug or bowl onto a plate and tap the bottom of the mug or bowl with the palm of your hand to loosen the bottom. Remove the baking container and start eating!

Per serving: Calories 608 (From Fat 376); Fat 42g (Saturated 7g); Cholesterol 2mg; Sodium 691mg; Carbohydrate 55g (Dietary Fiber 3g); Protein 6g.

Tip: Use soy or rice milk in place of the low-fat milk for a vegan version of this recipe.

Note: If you peek through the microwave window as your bread cooks, you may become just a tad alarmed to see the bread rising almost to the microwave's roof. Don't panic — when it's done being nuked, the bread will quietly sink back into the mug or bowl where it belongs.

Tip: This may look like just a cornbread recipe to you (and a darn good one at that!), but it's actually a dinner-in-the-making. Cut the bread in half and lay one half on a dish; spoon vegetarian baked beans or hot vegetarian chili over the bread for a complete meal.

Cranberry Muffin

Prep time: 4 min • **Cook time:** 1½ min • **Yield:** 1 serving

Ingredients	Directions
1 egg white	*1* In a small bowl, whisk together the egg white, maple syrup, oil, and vanilla.
2 tablespoons maple syrup	
1 tablespoon olive oil	*2* In another small bowl, stir together the baking mix and cinnamon, and then stir in the cranberries.
½ teaspoon vanilla	
¼ cup baking mix	
½ teaspoon cinnamon	*3* Stir the dry mix into the liquids until completely combined.
2 tablespoons dried cranberries	
Nonstick cooking spray	*4* Spray a large, oversized mug (one that holds 1⅔ cups liquid) well with nonstick spray; pour the batter into the mug. Sprinkle the sugar on top.
¼ teaspoon granulated sugar	
	5 Microwave for 90 seconds.
	6 As soon as you remove the mug from the microwave, run a knife around the muffin, invert the mug onto a dish, and then remove the mug.

Per serving: Calories 422 (From Fat 165); Fat 18g (Saturated 3g); Cholesterol 0mg; Sodium 437mg; Carbohydrate 60g (Dietary Fiber 2g); Protein 6g.

Vary It! If you don't have maple syrup on hand, feel free to substitute regular ol' pancake syrup. You can also use fresh or frozen (and thawed) blueberries rather than dried cranberries.

Tip: The reason you add the cranberries to the dry baking mix is so they get coated with the flour, which helps prevent them from sinking to the bottom of the cup during baking. (They'll still sink a little.)

Chocolate Muffin

Prep time: 4 min • **Cook time:** 2½ min • **Yield:** 1 serving

Ingredients	Directions
¼ cup baking mix	**1** In a medium bowl, whisk together the baking mix, sugar, and cocoa.
¼ cup granulated sugar	
2 tablespoons unsweetened cocoa	**2** Whisk in the egg, milk, oil, and vanilla just until blended.
1 egg	
3 tablespoons low-fat milk	**3** Spray a mug (2-cup capacity) with nonstick spray. Spoon the dough into the cup. Sprinkle the chocolate on top.
2 tablespoons vegetable oil	
½ teaspoon vanilla	
Nonstick cooking spray	**4** Microwave on high for 2½ minutes. Run a knife around the inside edge, and then invert the muffin onto a plate.
1 tablespoon chopped dark chocolate	

Per serving: Calories 745 (From Fat 389); Fat 43g (Saturated 8g); Cholesterol 215mg; Sodium 468mg; Carbohydrate 84g (Dietary Fiber 5g); Protein 13g.

Yellow Squash Muffin

Prep time: 4 min • **Cook time:** 2½ min • **Yield:** 4 servings

Ingredients	Directions
1 egg	*1* In a medium bowl, whisk together the egg, sugar, vanilla, and oil. Stir in the squash.
⅓ cup granulated sugar	
½ teaspoon vanilla	*2* Add the baking mix, salt, and cinnamon, stirring until well combined. Stir in the walnuts.
¼ cup olive oil	
⅓ cup grated yellow squash, squeezed dry	*3* Spray a 3-cup, microwave-safe bowl well with nonstick spray; pour in the batter.
½ cup baking mix	
2 dashes salt	*4* Microwave on high for 2½ minutes, or until the top looks dry and the sides begin to pull away from the edge of the dish.
¾ teaspoon cinnamon	
2 tablespoons chopped walnuts	*5* Invert the bread onto a dish to cool.
Nonstick cooking spray	

Per serving: Calories 292 (From Fat 176); Fat 20g (Saturated 3g); Cholesterol 53mg; Sodium 240mg; Carbohydrate 27g (Dietary Fiber 1g); Protein 3g.

Sweet Potato Muffin

Prep time: 5 min • **Cook time:** 3 min • **Yield:** 1 serving

Ingredients	*Directions*
¼ cup canned sweet potato, drained	**1** In a medium bowl, mash the potatoes with the back of a fork. Add the egg and whisk the two together. Add the brown sugar, milk, oil, and vanilla and blend well.
1 egg	
¼ cup brown sugar	
2 tablespoons low-fat milk	**2** Add the baking mix and cinnamon and whisk until thoroughly blended. Stir in the pecans.
2 tablespoons olive oil	
¼ teaspoon vanilla	
½ cup baking mix	**3** Spray a 2-cup, microwave-safe baking dish or wide bowl generously with nonstick spray; pour in the batter.
½ teaspoon cinnamon	
¼ cup finely chopped pecans	
Nonstick cooking spray	**4** Microwave on high for 3 minutes, or until the top is dry to the touch and the sides are just starting to pull away from the pan.
	5 Run a knife around the side of the muffin, and then invert the muffin onto a dish.

Per serving: Calories 967 (From Fat 524); Fat 58g (Saturated 8g); Cholesterol 1mg; Sodium 818mg; Carbohydrate 109g (Dietary Fiber 6g); Protein 9g.

Note: If you look through the microwave window as the muffin bakes, you'll see it ballooning way above the top of the baking dish. No, it won't explode, and yes, it will shrink again. Actually, it's kind of cool to watch.

Tip: Microwaves cook at different rates. Your muffin may take a little longer to bake or perhaps a little less time. Begin checking it 15 seconds before the stated time. When the muffin begins to pull away from the sides of the baking container and the top looks dry, it's baked through.

Cheese Biscuits

Prep time: 4 min • **Cook time:** 6–8 min • **Yield:** 5 servings of three small biscuits each

Ingredients	*Directions*
Nonstick spray	*1* Preheat the oven to 325 degrees. Spray a baking sheet lightly with nonstick cooking spray.
¾ cup baking mix	
¼ teaspoon Italian seasoning	
⅓ cup low-fat milk	*2* In a small bowl, stir together the baking mix, Italian seasoning, milk, and cheese.
⅓ cup shredded low-fat sharp cheddar cheese	
4 teaspoons butter, melted	*3* Drop the dough by rounded teaspoonfuls onto the baking sheet.
⅓ teaspoon garlic powder	
	4 Bake for 6 to 8 minutes, or until the tops are very lightly browned.
	5 Put the butter in a small, microwave-safe bowl, cover with wax paper, and nuke it for 20 seconds, or until it has melted. Stir in the garlic powder. As soon as the biscuits come out of the oven, brush them with the butter mixture. Serve warm.

Per serving: Calories 150 (From Fat 59); Fat 7g (Saturated 3g); Cholesterol 10mg; Sodium 283mg; Carbohydrate 19g (Dietary Fiber 1g); Protein 5g.

Tip: If you're vegan, use soy or rice milk and nondairy vegan cheddar cheese in this recipe.

Note: Don't use a dark-coated baking pan to bake these biscuits, unless of course you're into that crunchy-burnt-on-the-bottom kind of thing.

Caramel Rolls

Prep time: 5 min • **Cook time:** 24–27 min • **Yield:** 5 servings

Ingredients	Directions
2 tablespoons butter	**1** Preheat the oven to 375 degrees.
¼ cup chopped walnuts	**2** Place the butter in a 9-inch square baking dish. Heat the dish in the oven until the butter melts, about 2 minutes.
½ cup caramel or butterscotch ice cream topping	
1 can (8 ounces) refrigerated crescent rolls	**3** Sprinkle the walnuts over the butter, and then pour the ice cream topping over the nuts, spreading the sauce evenly over the bottom of the pan.
	4 Remove the crescent rolls from the can but don't unroll them. Cut each section into 5 slices. Arrange the rolled slices in the pan.
	5 Bake the rolls for 22 to 25 minutes, or until they're golden brown.
	6 Immediately invert the pan and turn the rolls onto a serving platter or wax paper, scraping up any topping left in the pan and spreading it on the rolls. Yum!

Per serving: Calories 340 (From Fat 164); Fat 18g (Saturated 6g); Cholesterol 13mg; Sodium 472mg; Carbohydrate 40g (Dietary Fiber 1g); Protein 5g.

Note: Okay, so these rolls aren't high on the healthy foods list. Actually, they don't make the list at all. But they do have a few walnuts — that has to count for something, doesn't it? They're simple to make, and everyone loves them served hot out of the oven.

Chapter 14

Dishing Up Decadent Desserts

In This Chapter

▶ Putting great desserts together in a snap
▶ Whipping up some special desserts

Admit it: When you think of the word *dessert,* your lips unknowingly, uncontrollably form a smile. Sweets make you (and most everyone else) happy; they're the ultimate comfort food. In this chapter, all those feelings of digestive euphoria have been harnessed into vegetarian dessert recipes that taste amazing (some of them are vegan-friendly, too!).

Assembling Desserts in a Few Minutes Flat

Are you looking for vegetarian desserts that you can put together in only a few minutes? Luckily for you, this section contains a number of quick-to-throw-together desserts you can make.

Keep a few ready-to-consume desserts handy at home, but note that some are healthier than others. The healthier options are out there if you look for them. For example:

- ✔ Sponge cake topped with fresh strawberries is healthier than a large strawberry sundae.

- ✔ An all-fruit Popsicle is a better choice than an ice cream bar.

- ✔ You can have peach pie with a fattening crust, or you can buy a small container of canned peaches, drizzle a little apricot preserves over the fruit, and sprinkle with chopped nuts or coconut for something that will satisfy your sweet tooth.

Almost Instant Ice Cream Sandwich

Prep time: 2 min • **Yield:** 1 serving

Ingredients	*Directions*
2 store-bought or homemade cookies (about 2 to 2½ inches in diameter) **1 small scoop ice cream (about ¼ cup)**	*1* Scoop the ice cream onto one of the cookies; cover it with the second cookie and squish it down a bit to create a sandwich.

Per serving: Calories 163 (From Fat 73); Fat 8g (Saturated 4g); Cholesterol 15mg; Sodium 89mg; Carbohydrate 21g (Dietary Fiber 1g); Protein 2g.

Vary It! This recipe is ridiculously easy, but it needn't be. You can do so many different things to this sandwich to make it more involved and tempting. For starters, you can fold something into the ice cream (like bits of dried fruit, coconut, mini chocolate chips, orange zest, or Nutella) before scooping it onto the cookie. After you put the cookie sandwich together, roll the ice cream edges in something fun (like chopped nuts, coconut, sprinkles, crushed chocolate-covered coffee beans, or miniature candies). But don't stop there — set the filled cookie on a dish and drizzle it with a sauce (chocolate, fudge, caramel, butterscotch, strawberry, melted peanut butter, toffee, or maple syrup). Or you can melt some chocolate in a pan, dip half the cookie sandwich into the chocolate, and then set it on wax paper and put it in the freezer for a few minutes to set. Be creative and invent your own adaptation.

Tip: This recipe is definitely a make-it-and-eat-it-now dessert, but you can make several extra to freeze for later.

Tip: If you use vegan cookies and nondairy ice cream, this becomes a vegan recipe.

Walnut Honey Sundae

Prep time: 2 min • **Yield:** 1 serving

Ingredients	Directions
½ teaspoon vanilla	**1** Stir the vanilla into the yogurt.
1 container (6 ounces) Greek yogurt	**2** Spoon half of the yogurt into a small bowl, and then top it with half of the walnuts and half of the honey. Repeat the layers one more time.
¾ cup chopped walnuts	
¼ cup honey	

Per serving: Calories 957 (From Fat 557); Fat 62g (Saturated 8g); Cholesterol 11mg; Sodium 51mg; Carbohydrate 89g (Dietary Fiber 6g); Protein 28g.

Tip: Using Greek yogurt makes a huge difference in this sundae's taste, so searching for it is worth the trouble. Fage brand is especially good.

Tip: Toasting the nuts before sprinkling them on this dessert adds another dimension of taste. To toast the nuts, place them in a small baking dish and bake for about 5 minutes in a 350 degree oven. Watch them closely, because once they start to toast, they can burn quickly.

Tip: You can easily make this recipe vegan by using nondairy yogurt in place of the Greek yogurt and substituting maple syrup for the honey.

Tip: Before you measure honey (or molasses, or anything sticky), spray the measuring cup or spoon with nonstick spray so that the sticky stuff glides out easily.

Lickety-Split Lemony Tart

Prep time: 4 min • **Yield:** 8 servings

Ingredients	*Directions*
8 tablespoons lemon curd **8 mini phyllo shells, thawed** **2 teaspoons raspberry preserves**	***1*** Spoon 1 tablespoon lemon curd into each phyllo cup. Top each with ¼ teaspoon preserves.

Per serving: Calories 82 (From Fat 18); Fat 2g (Saturated 1g); Cholesterol 0mg; Sodium 23mg; Carbohydrate 14g (Dietary Fiber 0g); Protein 0g.

Note: Phyllo cups are stored in the freezer, so you have to take out as many cups as you plan to use and let them sit on the counter for about 15 minutes to come to room temperature. For crispier shells, warm them in a 350 degree oven for 3 minutes before filling them.

Tip: You can get lemon curd in cans where pie fillings or puddings are sold.

Banana Berry Wrap

Prep time: 4 min • **Yield:** 1 serving

Ingredients	*Directions*
1 tablespoon softened low-fat cream cheese	*1* Spread the cream cheese on the tortilla.
1 whole-wheat 8-inch tortilla	*2* Lay the banana, raspberries, and blueberries down the center of the tortilla about two-thirds of the way down. Drizzle with honey.
½ medium banana, sliced	
¼ cup raspberries	
2 tablespoons blueberries	*3* Fold up the bottom third of the tortilla so the filling won't ooze out, and then bring in the sides to make a wrap (see Chapter 7 for pointers on wrapping a tortilla).
1 teaspoon honey	

Per serving: Calories 246 (From Fat 44); Fat 5g (Saturated 2g); Cholesterol 8mg; Sodium 181mg; Carbohydrate 51g (Dietary Fiber 7g); Protein 6g.

Tip: Vegans can enjoy this dessert by substituting nondairy cream cheese for the cream cheese and using agave syrup instead of the honey.

Vary It! You can use almost any nut butter and almost any sliced or cut-up fruit in this wrap, so have fun experimenting. If you don't have honey, use pancake syrup. And if you're into the I-need-more-sugar-than-this mode, lose the honey and drizzle chocolate syrup or caramel ice cream topping over the fruit instead.

Peanut Butter Quesadilla

Prep time: 2 min • **Cook time:** 2 min, 10 sec • **Yield:** 2 servings

Ingredients	*Directions*
2 tablespoons low-fat peanut butter	*1* Spread the peanut butter over one side of the tortilla, and then drizzle the honey over the peanut butter.
1 whole-wheat 8-inch tortilla	
2 teaspoons honey	*2* Lay the banana halves on one half of the tortilla, and then fold the other half of the tortilla over the bananas.
½ banana, sliced in half lengthwise	
Nonstick cooking spray	*3* Spray a large skillet with nonstick spray. Heat the pan over medium-high heat for 10 seconds.
	4 Cook the tortilla 1 minute on one side; turn it over and cook it for another minute, or until the quesadilla is warm and lightly browned on both sides. Cut it in half to serve.

Per serving: Calories 186 (From Fat 58); Fat 7g (Saturated 1g); Cholesterol 0mg; Sodium 157mg; Carbohydrate 30g (Dietary Fiber 3g); Protein 6g.

Vary It! If you make this as is, it tastes great, but you can slip in semisweet chocolate chips, butterscotch chips, chopped walnuts, some shredded coconut, or even cut-up vegan marshmallows . . . or add all these things together! Yum.

Tip: It's super simple to convert this to a vegan recipe — just use maple syrup in place of the honey.

Fruited Parfait

Prep time: 4 min • **Cook time:** 15 sec • **Yield:** 1 serving

Ingredients	Directions
2 tablespoons all-fruit raspberry preserves	*1* Put the preserves in a small, microwave-safe bowl and nuke them for 15 seconds.
1 cup low-fat vanilla frozen yogurt	
½ banana, peeled and sliced	*2* Spoon half of the yogurt into a parfait glass or bowl. Top with half of the banana slices. Drizzle half of the preserves over the bananas, and then drizzle with half of the chocolate syrup.
2 tablespoons low-fat chocolate syrup	
	3 Repeat the layers.

Per serving: Calories 393 (From Fat 25); Fat 3g (Saturated 2g); Cholesterol 10mg; Sodium 160mg; Carbohydrate 84g (Dietary Fiber 2g); Protein 10g.

Vary It! You can use almost any flavor of yogurt with a variety of fruits and an assortment of jams. For example, instead of the banana, use very ripe peaches sliced thin or chopped canned peaches. (Peaches blend really well with the raspberry preserves.) If you're not a fan of raspberry preserves, you can easily use strawberry instead. You can also leave off the chocolate syrup if you want to, or use honey instead of the syrup.

Tip: If you're vegan, substitute nondairy ice cream for the frozen yogurt, and be sure to use Hershey's Special Dark Chocolate Syrup.

Honey Bars

Prep time: 3 min • **Cook time:** 2 min • **Yield:** 4 servings

Ingredients	Directions
Nonstick cooking spray	*1* Spray a 5-x-7-inch baking dish with nonstick spray.
2 tablespoons honey	
2 tablespoons brown sugar	*2* Stir the honey and brown sugar together in a medium saucepan. Over medium heat, bring the mixture to a boil, stirring occasionally (about 2 minutes). Remove from heat and stir in the peanut butter until it's melted.
3 tablespoons low-fat peanut butter	
1 cup honey nut cereal	
	3 Stir in the cereal until all the pieces are evenly coated.
	4 Press the mixture evenly into the pan.
	5 Using a knife that's been dipped in hot water, cut the bars into 3½-x-2½-inch pieces (make two cuts — cut the 5-inch side in half and cut the 7-inch side in half).

Per serving: Calories 155 (From Fat 40); Fat 4g (Saturated 1g); Cholesterol 0mg; Sodium 145mg; Carbohydrate 27g (Dietary Fiber 1g); Protein 4g.

Vary It! These bars aren't super healthy, but they're also not too disastrous on the nutrition scale, at least as far as desserts go. You can leave it at that or you can opt to be really decadent and sprinkle semisweet chocolate chips over the warm bars in the pan, let them set a minute to soften, and then, with the back of a spoon, press down on them and spread the chocolate over the top of the bars to form a frosting.

Note: Store the bars at room temperature in a plastic container with a tight-fitting lid. They'll stay fresh for about five days.

Fruity S'mores

Prep time: 5 min • **Cook time:** 15 sec • **Yield:** 1 serving

Ingredients	Directions
1 cinnamon graham cracker broken into 2 halves along the perforation	**1** Put 1 graham square on a piece of wax paper. Put the chocolate, and then the marshmallow, on top of the cracker.
⅓ ounce dark chocolate candy bar (about 3 squares of a 1.45-ounce bar)	**2** Place the cracker with the toppings, still on the wax paper, in the microwave and nuke on high for 15 seconds, or until the marshmallow has puffed up.
1 large vegan marshmallow	
1 large strawberry, sliced	
2 slices banana	**3** Lay the strawberry on top of the marshmallow, squishing the marshmallow down. Top with the banana slices and the kiwi.
2 slices kiwi	
1 teaspoon strawberry jam	
	4 Spread the jam on one side of the second graham cracker, and then place it, jam-side down, on top of the kiwi. Press down gently.

Per serving: Calories 177 (From Fat 42); Fat 5g (Saturated 2g); Cholesterol 1mg; Sodium 86mg; Carbohydrate 33g (Dietary Fiber 2g); Protein 2g.

Note: You can find vegan marshmallows at health food stores.

Tip: If you cut the banana slices without peeling the banana first, you can peel the skin off the two slices you're using now and then put plastic wrap around the unused portion to keep the rest of the banana fresh to slice over cereal in the morning.

Tip: You're going to have a lot of marshmallows left over. Cut them up and sprinkle them on your cereal in the morning, add them to fruit salads, or heat them up with preserves or caramel to spoon over ice cream. Just be sure to store them in a tightly-covered container or in a self-seal plastic bag so they don't dry out.

Vary It! You can use strawberry preserves in place of the strawberry jam; if you don't like the taste of strawberries, use raspberry jam or preserves.

Graham Apples

Prep time: 4 min • **Cook time:** 2 min • **Yield:** 1 serving

Ingredients	Directions
½ apple, peeled and diced	*1* Put the apples into a custard cup and sprinkle them with the water. Microwave on high for 1 minute.
1 teaspoon water	
½ cup cinnamon applesauce	*2* Stir in the applesauce and microwave for 1 more minute.
3 squares cinnamon graham crackers, crushed	
	3 Sprinkle the crushed crackers on top and enjoy.

Per serving: Calories 222 (From Fat 23); Fat 3g (Saturated 0g); Cholesterol 0mg; Sodium 131mg; Carbohydrate 51g (Dietary Fiber 3g); Protein 2g.

Tip: Dessert simply doesn't get any easier than this . . . oh wait, yes it does! Instead of cutting up a fresh apple, you can get already-diced apples in individual 1-serving containers at the grocery store where the canned fruit is sold. If you use the pre-diced apples, drain them well and skip Step 1.

Tip: If you don't have a rolling pin to crush the crackers, you can use a food processor or, if all else fails, crush them with the back of a spoon or the palm of your hand. (Ouch!)

Putting Some Time into Special Desserts

There's probably some significant historical reason for serving something sweet after dinner, but to my way of reasoning, dessert is the only food that people can eat even when they're no longer hungry. A really good dessert leaves you feeling happy. You need a little bit more than 5 or 10 minutes to make the desserts in this section, but the extra time it takes to create these delectable masterpieces is well worth the effort.

A few handy hints for baking cookies

If you want cookies to turn out really great (and why wouldn't you?), here are a few tips:

✔ If the dough sticks to the spoon as you form the cookies, dip the spoon into warm water and shake off the excess, or you can spray the spoon with nonstick spray.

✔ Don't bake cookies on a dark-coated pan or the bottom will burn before the inside is baked.

✔ After the dough is on the cookie sheet, pop the cookie sheet into the freezer for 5 minutes or in the refrigerator for 10 minutes to chill the dough. This keeps the cookies from spreading too much.

✔ Even when recipes specify that you shouldn't grease the cookie sheet, spraying the baking sheet very lightly with nonstick spray makes it easier to remove the hot cookies from the sheet without breaking them.

✔ After the cookies come out of the oven, let them sit for about 2 minutes, and then move them to a cooling rack (unless a recipe tells you to do otherwise). This gives the cookies time to hold together better so they don't fall apart on the cooling rack.

Chocolate Croissant

Prep time: 3 min • **Cook time:** 6 min • **Yield:** 1 serving

Ingredients	Directions
1 teaspoon butter	*1* Preheat the oven to 425 degrees.
1 tablespoon brown sugar	
1 teaspoon maple syrup	*2* Melt the butter in a small saucepan, and then stir in the brown sugar and maple syrup. Heat over medium heat, stirring constantly, until the sugar melts (about 1 minute). Remove the pan from the heat. Stir in the milk and walnuts.
1 tablespoon low-fat milk	
1 tablespoon chopped walnuts	
Nonstick cooking spray	
1 croissant, cut in half horizontally	*3* Spray a small baking dish with nonstick spray and put the bottom half of the croissant in the dish. Sprinkle the chips on the bottom half and cover with the top half of the croissant. Drizzle the sugar mixture over the top.
2 tablespoons chocolate chips	
	4 Bake for 5 minutes.

Per serving: Calories 490 (From Fat 244); Fat 27g (Saturated 13g); Cholesterol 49mg; Sodium 441mg; Carbohydrate 59g (Dietary Fiber 3g); Protein 7g.

Vary It! If you don't have maple syrup, use pancake syrup. If you don't have walnuts, use pecans or peanuts. If you don't have chocolate chips, either omit them or use butterscotch chips. If you don't have a croissant, put on a pair of shoes and go get one!

No-Bake Cookies

Prep time: 10 min • **Yield:** 8 cookies (8 servings)

Ingredients	*Directions*
8 squares cinnamon graham crackers (4 whole crackers broken into 2 pieces each), crushed	*1* Put the crushed crackers in a small bowl and add the raisins, cinnamon, peanut butter, and honey. Mix everything together with a rubber spatula until totally blended.
¼ cup raisins	
⅛ teaspoon cinnamon	*2* Divide the mixture into 8 parts. Roll each part into a ball, and then roll in the coconut to coat.
¼ cup smooth low-fat peanut butter	
2 tablespoons honey, plus 2 more teaspoons honey	
2 tablespoons shredded sweetened coconut	

Per serving: *Calories 85 (From Fat 27); Fat 3g (Saturated 1g); Cholesterol 3mg; Sodium 76mg; Carbohydrate 13g (Dietary Fiber 1g); Protein 3g.*

Apple Tarts

Prep time: 3 min, plus 5 min rest time • **Cook time:** 7½ min • **Yield:** 5 servings

Ingredients	Directions
5 mini phyllo shells, thawed	*1* Preheat the oven to 375 degrees. Place the tart shells on a baking tray.
1 Golden Delicious apple, peeled, cored, and minced into tiny pieces	
Juice from ¼ lemon	*2* Stir the apple and lemon juice together in a small bowl.
2 teaspoons butter	*3* In a small skillet, heat the butter until frothy (about 30 seconds). Add the brown sugar and cook until the sugar melts, about 1 minute. Stir in the apples, and then spoon the mixture into the tart shells.
4 teaspoons brown sugar	
2 tablespoons caramel ice cream topping	
	4 Bake for 6 minutes. Cool for 5 minutes, and then drizzle caramel topping over each tart.

Per serving: Calories 81 (From Fat 23); Fat 3g (Saturated 1g); Cholesterol 4mg; Sodium 43mg; Carbohydrate 15g (Dietary Fiber 1g); Protein 0g.

Molasses Bars

Prep time: 5 min, plus 10 min rest time • **Cook time:** 1 min • **Yield:** 16 servings

Ingredients	Directions
¼ cup molasses	*1* Stir together the molasses, honey, and brown sugar in a medium saucepan. Bring to a boil over medium-high heat, stirring frequently (about 1 minute).
¼ cup honey	
½ cup brown sugar	
½ cup low-fat peanut butter	*2* Remove the pan from the heat and add the peanut butter; stir until smooth.
2 cups quick cooking oats	
1 cup cereal	*3* Add the oats, cereal, almonds, chocolate chips, and cranberries; stir until everything is evenly coated.
½ cup chopped slivered almonds	
¼ cup semisweet chocolate chips	*4* Spray a 9-inch square pan with nonstick spray; press the mixture into the pan. Cool for 10 minutes before serving. Cut three equally-spaced slices on each side to give you four rows in each direction.
⅔ cup dried cranberries	
Nonstick cooking spray	

Per serving: Calories 189 (From Fat 53); Fat 6g (Saturated 1g); Cholesterol 0mg; Sodium 67mg; Carbohydrate 32g (Dietary Fiber 3g); Protein 5g.

Tip: You can use most any type of cereal to make these bars (flaked, puffed rice, o's, and so on), but cubed cereals don't work (Chex for example).

Tip: Vegans can use agave syrup in place of the honey and chopped nondairy dark chocolate in place of the semisweet chocolate chips.

Note: Store these bars at room temperature in a plastic container with a tight-fitting lid. They'll stay fresh for about four days.

Fruit Salsa with Cinnamon Chips

Prep time: 10 min, plus 5 min rest time • **Cook time:** 8 min • **Yield:** 6 servings

Ingredients	*Directions*
1 kiwi, peeled and diced	*1* Preheat the oven to 350 degrees.
1 apple, peeled, cored, and diced	*2* In a large bowl, toss together the kiwi, apple, plum, strawberries, raspberries, 2 teaspoons granulated sugar, brown sugar, and preserves. Cover and refrigerate while making the chips.
1 plum, peeled and diced	
3 cups (6 ounces) strawberries, diced	
½ cup raspberries	
2 teaspoons granulated sugar, plus another ¾ cup granulated sugar	*3* In a small bowl, stir together ¾ cup granulated sugar and the cinnamon.
1½ teaspoons brown sugar	*4* Cut each tortilla into six wedges and place them in a single layer on a baking sheet. Spray the wedges with nonstick spray, and then sprinkle them with the cinnamon sugar. Spray the tops again with nonstick spray (to help the cinnamon sugar stick).
4 teaspoons all-fruit raspberry preserves	
3 teaspoons cinnamon	
5 whole-wheat 8-inch tortillas	
Nonstick cooking spray	*5* Bake the tortilla wedges for 8 minutes, or until toasted and crispy but not hard. Cool the wedges for 5 minutes, and then serve with the salsa.

Per serving: Calories 140 (From Fat 9); Fat 1g (Saturated 0g); Cholesterol 0mg; Sodium 145mg; Carbohydrate 36g (Dietary Fiber 6g); Protein 3g.

Tip: If any of the raspberries are large, just cut them in half to keep all the pieces of the salsa small.

Vary It! If raspberries are out of your budget, just eliminate them from the recipe or replace them with a ripe, diced peach or nectarine.

Tip: If you have leftover fruit salsa, spread some cream cheese on a tortilla, add a little of the salsa, and create a wrap. If you have leftover tortilla wedges, put them in a small, self-seal bag and take them for a mid-afternoon snack.

Tip: To convert this recipe to vegan, use 1 teaspoon agave syrup in place of the brown sugar.

Nectarine Crisp

Prep time: 7 min • **Cook time:** 17 min • **Yield:** 1 serving

Ingredients	Directions
Nonstick cooking spray	**1** Preheat the oven to 350 degrees. Spray a 2-cup baking dish with nonstick spray.
4 teaspoons butter, melted	
1 tablespoon brown sugar	**2** In a small bowl, use a fork to blend the butter, brown sugar, baking mix, pecans, and cinnamon until the mixture is crumbly.
2 tablespoons baking mix	
1½ tablespoons chopped pecans	
⅛ teaspoon cinnamon	**3** Mix the nectarine pieces and vanilla in the baking dish. Spoon the nut topping evenly over the nectarines.
1 large, very ripe nectarine, peeled and chopped into ½-inch pieces	
¼ teaspoon vanilla	**4** Bake for 17 minutes.

Per serving: Calories 396 (From Fat 237); Fat 26g (Saturated 11g); Cholesterol 41mg; Sodium 196mg; Carbohydrate 41g (Dietary Fiber 4g); Protein 4g.

Vary It! If you're out of nectarines, substitute a peach, apple, or pear. You can also use walnuts in place of the pecans. And if you're feeling decadent, add a scoop of ice cream on top of the crisp!

Tip: Baking mix is a flour mixture that already has the baking powder added. Two of the most familiar brands are Bisquick and Jiffy Baking Mix.

Tip: You can convert this recipe to vegan by using nondairy margarine in place of the butter and white sugar in place of the brown sugar.

Raisin Bread Pudding

Prep time: 5 min, plus 5 min rest time • **Cook time:** 20 min • **Yield:** 2 servings

Ingredients	Directions
Nonstick cooking spray	*1* Preheat the oven to 350 degrees. Spray 2 custard cups with nonstick spray.
1 cup bread cubes	
3 tablespoons raisins	*2* Place ½ cup bread cubes in each custard cup. Sprinkle 1½ tablespoons raisins over the bread in each cup.
1 egg	
½ cup low-fat milk	
2 tablespoons brown sugar	*3* In a small bowl, whisk together the egg, milk, brown sugar, vanilla, cinnamon, and salt. Pour half of this mixture over each dish with the raisins.
½ teaspoon vanilla	
¾ teaspoon cinnamon	
Dash salt	*4* Put the butter in a small, microwave-safe bowl and nuke for 15 seconds on high, or until the butter has melted. Drizzle half the melted butter over each of the custard cups. Let the cups sit for 5 minutes to allow the bread to absorb some of the liquid.
1 tablespoon butter	
	5 Bake for 20 minutes, or until a knife inserted near the center comes out clean. Serve warm.

Per serving: Calories 430 (From Fat 108); Fat 12g (Saturated 5g); Cholesterol 124mg; Sodium 606mg; Carbohydrate 69g (Dietary Fiber 2g); Protein 13g.

Tip: Half of a hoagie or sub roll cut into ½-inch cubes works great for this recipe.

Tip: Make this into a vegan dessert by using vanilla soymilk in place of the low-fat milk, nondairy margarine in place of the butter, and white sugar in place of the brown sugar.

Vary It! Make this pudding just about any way you want to by adding or changing the ingredients to your liking. For example, use only half the milk and substitute a mashed banana or orange juice for the other half of the liquid. Use chopped, pitted dates or dried cranberries instead of or in addition to the raisins. You can add chopped nuts or diced, well-drained peaches, too.

White Chocolate Cookies

Prep time: 7 min, plus 12 min rest time • **Cook time:** 11–12 min • **Yield:** 12 servings

Ingredients	Directions
1 egg	*1* Preheat the oven to 375 degrees.
⅓ cup brown sugar	
2 tablespoons vegetable oil	*2* In a medium bowl, whisk together the egg, brown sugar, oil, and vanilla.
½ teaspoon vanilla	
¾ cup baking mix	*3* Using a rubber spatula, stir in the baking mix, salt, and cinnamon until everything is combined.
¼ teaspoon salt	
¼ teaspoon cinnamon	
¼ cup oats	*4* Stir in the oats, white chocolate, and walnuts.
⅓ cup white chocolate pieces	
⅓ cup chopped walnuts	*5* Drop the dough by rounded tablespoons, 2 inches apart, onto an ungreased baking sheet.
	6 Bake for 11 to 12 minutes, or until the cookies are puffed and just beginning to turn golden around the edges.
	7 Let the cookies cool on the pan for 2 minutes before transferring them to a cooling rack to cool completely (about 10 more minutes).

Per serving: Calories 134 (From Fat 69); Fat 8g (Saturated 2g); Cholesterol 19mg; Sodium 155mg; Carbohydrate 15g (Dietary Fiber 1g); Protein 2g.

Vary It! In place of the walnuts, you can add almost any dried fruit (raisins, cranberries, blueberries, chopped apricots, or dates). Chopped macadamia nuts are delicious to use instead of the walnuts, but they're oh so expensive. You can replace the white chocolate pieces with chocolate chips, but then you'd have to change the recipe name!

Tip: This recipe is really convenient because you can make the dough, put it in a plastic container, and refrigerate it for up to three days or freeze it for up to one month. Then just bake the dough when you're ready!

Apple Crescent Rolls

Prep time: 8 min • **Cook time:** 30 min • **Yield:** 8 servings

Ingredients	*Directions*
Nonstick cooking spray	*1* Preheat the oven to 375 degrees. Spray a 9-inch round cake pan or pie plate with nonstick spray.
2 tablespoons granulated sugar, plus another ½ cup granulated sugar	*2* In a small bowl, stir together 2 tablespoons of the sugar and the cinnamon. Set it aside.
1 teaspoon cinnamon	
1 can (8 ounces) refrigerated crescent rolls	*3* Separate the dough into eight triangles. Sprinkle each triangle with the cinnamon-sugar mixture and gently press so that the sugar adheres and flattens the dough slightly.
1 apple, peeled and cored, cut into 8 slices	
½ cup whipping cream	*4* Put an apple slice on the wide end of each triangle. Bring up the sides of the dough to cover the apple completely, sealing all the seams. Place the dough package, sealed side down, in the cake pan or pie plate.
1 tablespoon almond extract	
1 egg	
½ cup sliced almonds	
	5 Repeat Step 4 for the remaining seven rolls; place one roll in the center of the pan and the others surrounding it.
	6 Bake for 15 minutes, or until very lightly browned.
	7 In a small bowl, whisk together the remaining ½ cup of sugar, the whipping cream, the almond extract, and an egg until well blended. Spoon the sauce over the partially-baked rolls. Sprinkle the top with almonds.
	8 Bake an additional 15 minutes, or until the rolls are a deep golden brown. Serve warm.

Per serving: Calories 280 (From Fat 138); Fat 15g (Saturated 5g); Cholesterol 47mg; Sodium 237mg; Carbohydrate 31g (Dietary Fiber 1g); Protein 4g.

Decadent Peanut Butter Squares

Prep time: 10 min, plus 30 min rest time • **Cook time:** 21 min • **Yield:** 18 servings

Ingredients	Directions
1 can (4 ounces) refrigerated crescent rolls	*1* Preheat the oven to 375 degrees.
½ cup low-fat peanut butter	*2* Unroll the crescent dough and press it onto the bottom of an ungreased, 9-inch square baking pan, sealing all perforations.
¼ cup honey	
½ cup semisweet chocolate chips	*3* In a small bowl, stir together the peanut butter and honey and spread the mixture over the dough. Sprinkle the chocolate chips evenly over the top.
¼ cup (½ stick) butter	
1 cup rolled oats	
⅓ cup brown sugar	*4* Put the butter in a medium, microwave-safe bowl, cover with wax paper, and microwave for 40 seconds, or until it's melted.
	5 Stir the oats and brown sugar into the butter until crumbly. Sprinkle the crumbs over the chocolate pieces.
	6 Bake for 20 minutes, or until golden brown. Cool completely before cutting into bars (about 30 minutes). Cut the cooled bars into 18 pieces (five cuts in one direction and two cuts in the other direction).

Per serving: Calories 158 (From Fat 72); Fat 8g (Saturated 3g); Cholesterol 7mg; Sodium 78mg; Carbohydrate 19g (Dietary Fiber 1g); Protein 4g.

Tip: Some groceries don't carry the 4-ounce size of crescent rolls. If you have to buy the 8-ounce can, you're going to use only half the rolls. You can make a double batch of squares, or you can cover and refrigerate the leftover rolls to make another dessert. If you choose the second option, roll the remaining dough into small balls and fry them in vegetable oil over medium-high heat on the stove. When the dough is golden and cooked through, roll the balls in cinnamon sugar or powdered sugar and enjoy your donut holes!

Vegan Peanut Butter Praline Pie

Prep time: 8 min, plus 3½ hrs rest time • **Cook time:** 10 min • **Yield:** 2 servings

Ingredients	Directions
Nonstick cooking spray	*1* Preheat the oven to 350 degrees. Spray a 3-cup shallow baking dish with nonstick spray.
5½ tablespoons finely crushed crisp vegan cookies (about 5 cookies)	
2½ tablespoons nondairy margarine, plus 2 more tablespoons nondairy margarine, melted	*2* In a small bowl, use a fork to stir together the cookie crumbs and 2½ tablespoons of the margarine until evenly moistened. Press the mixture onto the bottom of the baking dish and bake for 7 minutes.
5 tablespoons brown sugar	
2 tablespoons chopped peanuts	*3* Raise the oven temperature to 450 degrees.
½ cup (4 ounces) silken tofu	*4* Put the remaining 2 tablespoons of melted margarine in a small saucepan. Stir in the brown sugar and peanuts. Cook over medium heat, stirring constantly, just until the sugar is completely melted, about 1 minute.
3 tablespoons smooth, natural peanut butter	
2 tablespoons soymilk	
2 tablespoons granulated sugar	
1 teaspoon vanilla	*5* Spread the brown sugar mixture on top of the cookie crust, being careful not to break up the crust. Bake for 2 minutes. Cool completely (about 30 minutes).
	6 Put the tofu, peanut butter, soymilk, granulated sugar, and vanilla into a food processor or blender. Blend until smooth. Spoon this into the cooled crust. Refrigerate at least 3 hours.

Per serving: Calories 709 (From Fat 424); Fat 47g (Saturated 8g); Cholesterol 0mg; Sodium 443mg; Carbohydrate 62g (Dietary Fiber 3g); Protein 11g.

Tip: You can use many different kinds of vegan cookies for this recipe, including vanilla wafers, chocolate cookies, or peanut butter cookies.

Chapter 15

Changing Recipes and Resurrecting Leftovers

· ·

In This Chapter

▶ Switching up ingredients in a recipe

▶ Using up food before it goes bad

· ·

Chances are pretty good that from time to time, you'll look in your fridge and see containers of food hiding undercover (known, of course, as leftovers). It's actually fun to reconfigure leftovers into something totally new. (Oh sure, you can just reheat some things, but where's the fun in that?) By the time you finish reading this chapter, you'll have a whole new outlook on the things hiding in your cupboards and fridge. I explain how to tweak recipes to fit what you already have in your kitchen, and I describe innovative ways to use up a variety of ingredients before they go bad. (And don't forget: Many recipes in this book tell you how to use up leftover ingredients or reinvent entire dishes.)

 If a leftover lunch or dinner dish is more than four days old, just toss it and kick yourself for not doing something with it sooner. Using up old food isn't worth the risk of getting sick.

 Almost everything can be recycled — the key word here is *almost.* But occasionally, sticking with the original is better. For example, if you went out to dinner last night and had eggplant parmigiana that was to die for, and you have enough left over for another meal, reheat it. Don't spoil something that's almost perfect just for the sake of saying you changed it.

Substituting Ingredients in a Recipe

It's happened to everyone: You're ready to start cooking dinner but discover that you're missing a single ingredient, and you don't have time to go to the grocery store. What to do? The easy solution is to change the recipe on the fly — yes, you're allowed! The following sections describe the types of ingredients that you can (and can't) substitute.

Knowing which ingredients you can change

Starches are pretty easy to exchange for one another. All you need to do is substitute equal amounts. For example, if you cook some veggies to put over 1 cup of cooked spaghetti but discover that you're out of spaghetti, go with the flow — use 1 cup of cooked noodles, macaroni, or rice in place of the spaghetti. No rule exists that says you have to use spaghetti. For that matter, you can put the veggies over mashed potatoes or even fried potatoes.

Substituting veggies is just as easy. If you're out of a particular vegetable, take a look to see what you have on hand and use an equal amount of what's called for in the recipe. For example: If you have a recipe for a stir-fry that calls for 1 cup of broccoli but you have only carrots, onions, and cauliflower, slice ⅓ cup of carrots, ⅓ cup of cauliflower, and ⅓ cup of diced onions; you won't miss the broccoli at all.

Zucchini makes an especially good substitution for eggplant; likewise, baby lima beans are great to use in place of peas.

Here are some other easy substitutions you can make when you don't have a certain ingredient for a recipe on hand. Just use equal amounts; for example, if the recipe calls for 1 cup of an ingredient, use 1 cup of the substitute ingredient.

- Black beans, kidney beans, garbanzo beans, northern beans, and navy beans are usually interchangeable.
- You can often use salsa rather than spaghetti sauce.
- In baking, a mashed banana can replace applesauce.
- Tofu can take the place of eggs.
- You can substitute a hoagie roll for French bread.

Noting that change isn't always a good thing

Some flavors just don't taste very good together. After you've been experimenting for a while, you'll get the hang of what flavors do and don't blend. For example, if you're making a veggie wrap for lunch and the recipe calls for salsa, you can add leftover spaghetti sauce instead, and it'll taste great. But if you also have a little bit of leftover guacamole and decide to add that to the wrap, scratch the spaghetti sauce and stick with the guacamole only. (The flavors in spaghetti sauce and guacamole don't complement each other.)

Here are a few food combinations that shouldn't be mixed:

- ✔ Potatoes and mayonnaise make a great potato salad. Cabbage and mayonnaise are a good base for coleslaw. Boiled cabbage and potatoes work together. But potatoes, cabbage, and mayonnaise simply don't go together.

- ✔ Cinnamon on peas, asparagus, or broccoli doesn't work, even though cinnamon on other vegetables, like carrots and yams, tastes great.

- ✔ Baked beans taste great and so does sauerkraut — but don't ever try mixing the sweet and the sour tastes of the two together.

- ✔ You can add apple cider to a lot of drinks to enhance the taste; the same holds true for orange juice. But orange juice and apple cider mixed together is a taste disaster.

- ✔ Yogurt is used in some salad dressings, as is balsamic vinegar, but balsamic vinegar mixed with yogurt just doesn't work.

Using Up Leftover Ingredients in Creative Ways

With all the cooking you've been doing, you're bound to have a number of ingredients left over in your fridge and pantry . . . and a limited amount of time in which to use them before they go bad. What to do? In the following sections, I provide a number of fun ideas for using up common ingredients in a vegetarian kitchen. Look at this whole food recycling stuff as an exciting challenge.

Are you truly stumped about what to do with some leftovers? Help is just a few keystrokes away. At BigOven.com (`www.bigoven.com/recipes/leftovers`), you find three drop-down boxes. From each box, choose one food that you have left over. After you enter all three foods, click the *BigOven, what can I make?* button, and easy recipes that use those three ingredients magically appear.

Partially used cans and jars of sauces and other stuff

Don't you hate it when you open a jar that's been in the refrigerator for who knows how long and the inside of the lid is all dark and crusty? Then you look inside the jar and see a healthy growth of something white and spongy sitting on top of the food? It's too late to reuse that food now, that's for sure. What a shame that you have to throw it out when, just a few weeks ago, you could have used it up as part of the sauce for a meal.

Now go open your refrigerator door. What partially used cans and jars are in there? Figure out a way to use them up at your next meal. Your choices are limited only by your imagination. The following sections describe some fun ideas for using a variety of canned and jarred sauces, veggies, and more.

If a food comes packaged in a metal can (like tomato sauce), transfer it to a plastic container and cover it with a lid or plastic wrap before storing the leftover part in the refrigerator. Most aluminum or tin cans today are treated with a plastic lining to help prevent corrosion, but it still isn't wise to keep an acidic food in an opened metal can where the acid and air can combine to spoil the contents.

Artichoke hearts

Artichoke hearts are delicious, but who can use up a whole jar at one meal? Try the following ideas:

- Slice some onto a pizza or into a salad.
- Make a veggie salad of artichoke hearts marinated in olive oil, a hint of balsamic vinegar, and a dash of salt, pepper, and Italian seasoning, along with grape tomatoes, mozzarella cubes, and baby mushrooms.
- Place them on a dish, drizzle them with olive oil, sprinkle them with dried dill, and microwave them for 1 minute or until warmed for a side dish.

- Add them to a quiche or frittata.

- Chop them and mix them with a little mayonnaise and Parmesan cheese for a luscious artichoke dip. You can eat this dip cold or microwave it for 45 seconds to enjoy it warm with wedges of pita bread.

Enchilada sauce, salsa, and taco sauce

If you have enchilada sauce, salsa, or taco sauce left over, try the following suggestions:

- For an easy version of Spanish rice, use half the amount of water you normally use to cook rice, and use the leftover sauce for the other half of the liquid.

- Pour a little sauce over scrambled eggs or stir some into frittatas.

- When you make a wrap, drizzle some sauce on top of the filling before rolling.

- Put a few spoonfuls on hot grits, along with some shredded sharp cheddar cheese.

- Put cheddar cheese on some tortilla chips, melt the cheese in the microwave, and then drizzle generously with sauce.

- Add a few spoonfuls to a grilled cheese sandwich or to macaroni and cheese.

- Stir some into soups or stews.

- Stir chopped green onions and feta cheese crumbles into the sauce to use as a salsa over zucchini.

- Pour the sauce over cream cheese for an easy dip with crackers.

- Add chopped cucumbers, jalapeños, tomatoes, and vegetable broth to the sauce, and then purée the mixture into gazpacho.

- Stir a little sauce into potato salad for added zing.

Spaghetti sauce

You probably don't use a whole jar of spaghetti sauce when you cook pasta. Why not give one (or more) of the following ideas a whirl?

- Use the leftover sauce with cheese to make a quick pita pizza.

- Warm up some sauce to use as a dip for garlic bread. Yummy!

- Spoon some sauce over fried rounds of polenta and top with Parmesan cheese.

- Add some sauce to soups or stews and use it as a base for ratatouille (a mixture of sliced or cubed zucchini, yellow squash, eggplant, bell peppers, tomatoes, onions, and garlic all smothered in a tomato-based sauce and topped with shredded cheese).

- Broil eggplant or zucchini slices, place them on a bun, and top with a few dollops of spaghetti sauce, ricotta cheese, and mozzarella cheese.

- Use some as a sauce for stuffed peppers.

- Stir some into cream of tomato soup.

- Fry eggs in pasta sauce (don't knock it if you haven't tried it!).

- Pour some over a 3-ounce piece of cream cheese, sprinkle on some seasoned breadcrumbs, and bake for 15 minutes for a spread with crackers.

Vegetarian baked beans and vegetarian chili

Vegetarian baked beans and vegetarian chili are great staples, but you probably won't eat an entire can. Here's what you can do with the leftovers:

- Spoon either one onto a baked potato half, over cornbread, or even over spaghetti squash, and then top with shredded cheddar cheese.

- Heat some meatless sausage, put it in a hot dog bun, and top it off with the chili or baked beans.

- Serve either one over rice with a sprinkling of sharp cheddar cheese, or boil some elbow macaroni to make your own chili mac.

- Spoon the beans/chili over a taco salad.

- Put some on a hamburger bun and eat it like a sloppy Joe.

- Put the beans inside a tortilla along with some chopped onions, lettuce, and sour cream for a quick burrito.

- Believe it or not, either the baked beans or the chili make a great filling for an omelet.

Wilting vegetables

In general, vegetables spoil fairly quickly, so you should use them up as fast as you can. The following sections provide pointers on how to use up several common vegetables.

If you see vegetables just beginning to wilt, add a few drops of white vinegar to cold water, soak the veggies, and then pat them dry. They will come back to life.

 Do you have veggies other than the ones in the following sections lying around? You can chop whatever else you have in the vegetable bin into tiny pieces, brown them in a little butter on the stove, and add them to couscous, rice, or scrambled eggs.

Carrots

 When you bring home carrots from the grocery store, wash and then dry them with paper towels. Place them in a self-seal plastic bag, and they'll stay fresh and crisp for two weeks.

You can tell when a carrot is getting old because the skin starts to turn chalky white. If you use a potato peeler to peel off the outer layer, though, the inside is still fresh. Try the following tips for using up carrots:

- Cut large carrots into rounds, boil them, and then drizzle them with pancake syrup, a sprinkling of pecans or walnuts, and dried cranberries.

- Boil the carrots, mash them, and add them to mashed potatoes.

- Julienne them (fancy lingo for cutting them into thin strips about 3 inches long) and use them in stir-fries.

- Toss julienned carrots with a little olive oil and chili powder and bake at 400 degrees for 15–20 minutes for carrot fries; they're good that way.

- Shred carrots onto salads and wraps and into soups and casseroles.

- Dip carrot sticks into hummus when you're hungry for a snack.

Potatoes

What's that you say? You have a potato that's starting to sprout? Never fear, a solution's here. Carve out any dark spots, and then use the potato in one of the following ways:

- Slice the potato and pan-fry it with onions and green pepper to make home fries, or shred it to make hash browns.

- Chop the potato and plop it into some soup.

- Cut the potato into cubes, fry them, and then scramble them with an egg or two for a real farmer's breakfast.

✔ Boil the potato with some cabbage, add a little butter, and voilà! You've got cabbage and potatoes for dinner.

✔ Slice the potato into thin strips and bake at 400 degrees for 20 minutes, stirring once after 10 minutes, to make French fries.

✔ Boil the potato and add some celery, green pepper, and onion. Slather with mayo and a hint of mustard, and you'll be enjoying potato salad. Or you can slice the boiled potato, add the onion and green pepper, and then drizzle it with olive oil for a Greek potato salad.

If the potato feels slightly soft, rehydrate it by peeling it, putting it in a pot of cool water for several hours, and then changing the water before cooking it. The soaking helps the potato firm up again.

An important note: If a potato has large lumps and a significant amount of sprouting and dark spots, throw it out. Really old potatoes can contain toxins.

Spinach

Even if you're faithful about checking the *use by* date on a bag of spinach, spinach doesn't hold more than about six days after you've opened the bag. If you still have half a bag in the vegetable bin and it's not quite fresh enough to make a salad, try one of the following suggestions:

✔ Sauté the spinach in a little oil, and add a hint of salt, pepper, and dried red pepper seeds for a side dish.

✔ Chop the spinach and sauté it with other veggies to serve over rice or toss with pasta.

✔ Stir the spinach into soup or a veggie stew.

✔ Spinach makes a great filling in an omelet when you add a white cheese or add it to a frittata. (You can chop up and use *so* many things in frittatas!)

✔ Chop the spinach and add it to rice as it cooks.

✔ Sauté the spinach with onions, pile it onto a slice of pita bread, and then top it with mozzarella cheese for a delicious sauceless pizza.

When you bring home some spinach from the grocery, separate the leaves, wash them, and then pat them dry with paper towels. Place several layers of folded paper towels in the bottom of a large plastic bag, add the spinach, and then seal the bag. The spinach will stay crisp for one week.

Tomatoes

Refrigerating tomatoes may prolong their life span by a few days, but it also robs them of flavor. For the best flavor, keep tomatoes stored on your kitchen counter. How long they stay fresh varies. If they're GMO (genetically modified organisms), they can last three weeks. If they're hybrids, they can last six days on the kitchen counter and perhaps eight or ten days in the fridge. Grape tomatoes last about a week in the fridge but only four or five days at room temperature.

You can recognize an over-ripe tomato by its wrinkled skin and the mushy feel when you press it lightly. If you see the top of the tomato (the stem end) starting to turn dark or black, throw it out.

Stumped about what to do with a couple of over-ripe tomatoes?

- ✔ Slice the tomatoes thin and make a margherita pizza on a tortilla with mozzarella cheese and fresh basil.

- ✔ Cut a tomato in half and sprinkle each half with Italian seasoning, a drizzle of oil, and a generous portion of grated Parmesan cheese. Then broil for about 3 minutes or until the top is lightly browned to eat as a side dish with dinner.

- ✔ Or scoop out each half, fill with an orzo (rice-shaped pasta) mixture, and bake at 350 degrees for 50 minutes or until the pasta is tender and the tomato is soft but still holds its form.

- ✔ Chop a tomato and add it to a salad, soup, chili, spaghetti sauce, or almost anything stewed.

- ✔ Chop a tomato and add chopped green pepper, onion, and dill to use as a salsa over a baked potato, or add some feta cheese to the tomato salsa to spoon on top of fried or broiled eggplant.

- ✔ And don't forget to make some gazpacho and bruschetta. (You can find a recipe for Greek Bruschetta in Chapter 13.)

Shriveling fruit

This probably won't come as a surprise to you, but if you buy fruit and don't eat it, it gets old. That's just a fact of life! If you discover fruit before it has started to mold, then it may still be salvageable; just follow the tips in the following sections for a few common fruits.

I know you don't want to bite into shriveled, starting-to-brown fruit, but you can peel it, pit it, or core it, and then you can use it in a recipe. Fruits that are beyond their prime can be chopped and added to pancakes and muffin batters, tossed into a blender with some milk or yogurt to make a smoothie, or mixed with a little sugar and hidden under a biscuit or pie crust to create a cobbler.

Apples

Even apples eventually start getting old; you can tell when the skin starts to shrivel and soft spots start appearing. Cut the apple in half; if the center is white, it's still okay to use the apple for cooking, even if you have to cut out a few small brown spots.

Try the following tips for using up apples before it's too late:

- ✔ Chop unpeeled apples, and then put them in a bowl with seedless grapes, chopped celery, walnuts, and either mayonnaise or softened cream cheese to create a Waldorf salad.

- ✔ Shred apples into pancake or muffin batter.

- ✔ Core an apple, stuff it with raisins and brown sugar, and microwave it for 6 minutes — this is always a nice treat!

- ✔ Thinly slice an apple into a custard cup, add seasonings, and top it off with a stretched refrigerator biscuit. Bake it at 375 degrees for 20–25 minutes or until the biscuit is golden to create your own mini apple pie.

- ✔ Make some applesauce or apple crisp with a granola topping.

- ✔ Toss apple slices into the blender the next time you make a smoothie.

- ✔ Chop and make caramelized apples to spoon on top of waffles or ice cream.

- ✔ Brown apple slices in a little butter in a skillet for a delicious side dish with dinner.

Bananas

Ah, if only bananas had the life span of apples and pears, but alas, they don't. You can tell that they're going bad when the skin is so loaded with brown spots that it's hard to see any yellow anymore. When they start to go, they go quickly (within a few days), so use them up as fast as you can with the help of the following tips:

- ✔ Mash bananas into oatmeal with a little maple syrup, or slice them over cold cereal.

- ✔ Mash bananas into yogurt or pancake batter.

✔ Make Bananas Foster (banana slices sautéed with a little butter, brown sugar, and cinnamon — this dish is yummy either plain or served over ice cream), banana walnut muffins, banana cookies, and banana smoothies.

✔ Cut a banana in half crosswise, brush it with honey or chocolate syrup, and then roll it in crushed cereal or granola. Wrap it in foil and freeze it to have for dessert.

✔ Slice bananas into a small baking dish and drizzle them with melted butter, agave nectar, and lemon juice. Bake at 375 degrees for 10 minutes, and then sprinkle them with flaked coconut and chopped pecans or walnuts for a great dessert.

Berries

Fresh berries are absolutely delicious, but they don't stay fresh for very long. If it's nearing a week since you bought them, you'd better use them up soon.

✔ Stir some into yogurt or make a yogurt parfait with berries and granola.

✔ Mash some raspberries with a fork and then whisk them into Italian dressing for a delicious raspberry vinaigrette salad dressing.

✔ Make a batch of blueberry muffins.

✔ Melt some chocolate as a fondue for dipping strawberries.

✔ Toss a handful of berries into the blender with some yogurt, milk, and vanilla for a smoothie.

✔ Add raspberries to the pan when you boil water for hot tea (or to refrigerate to make iced tea later); strain the water before pouring it into a cup (hot tea) or glass (iced tea).

✔ Simmer berries in a little water with cinnamon and sugar, smashing the berries with the back of a fork as they cook, to make a luscious syrup to spoon over pancakes, French toast, angel food cake, or ice cream; add a drop of almond flavoring after the syrup is cooked.

✔ And you can always just enjoy a bowl of berries topped with some whipped cream or milk.

Mangoes, melons, and pineapples

When dark spots start appearing on the side of a mango, it's starting to rot. A mango can rot from the pit, the skin, or from the non-stem end. Any black fibers also indicate that the fruit has started to rot, and at that point, you need to toss it into the trash.

What about cantaloupes and honeydew melons? Just touch the stem end. If it's too soft or has mold on it, toss the melon out. But if it's just a little soft, it's still good to use. If there are some really soft spots or shriveled areas on the skin, you can cut these areas out and then use the rest of the melon. Over-ripe watermelon may look and smell okay, but don't eat it when it starts to feel slimy.

Because pineapples don't continue to ripen after they're picked, they remain fresh for several weeks, especially if you keep them refrigerated. A pineapple should smell fresh and be fairly firm. If it's a whole pineapple, pull a leaf from the second to the last row; if the leaf pulls out easily, the fruit is ripe. After a pineapple starts to get old, the outside will shrivel and start to get brown spots.

Need to use up a mango, a melon, or a pineapple in a hurry? Try these suggestions:

- Chop a cantaloupe or a mango with some green onions to make a salsa to put over broiled zucchini.
- Put cantaloupe and mango slices on a dish with sliced avocados for a salad with dinner.
- Cut watermelon into salads.
- Make a watermelon mint salsa to spoon over rice.
- Skewer honeydew cubes and dip them into vanilla yogurt for a snack.
- Slice off a few rings of pineapple, drizzle them with dark corn syrup or pancake syrup, and broil for 2 minutes.
- Fold some finely chopped pineapple into a sweet potato casserole. Or if you're baking slices of sweet potatoes, tuck in some pineapple slices and then drizzle the top with maple syrup.
- Mince pineapple and add a little mint to make a salsa that you can serve over rice, couscous, or even ice cream.

Oranges

You're not the first person to discover an orange at the back of the fridge that's starting to get a wrinkled skin. If it's not too wrinkled, the orange is probably still good to eat. If, however, the orange has any dark spots, throw it out. Give the following ideas a shot when you need to use up oranges:

- Peel an orange, slice it on top of a salad, and add some walnuts and blue cheese.

- ✔ Cut an orange into thick slices, sprinkle them with a teeny bit of brown sugar, and then broil them for 2 minutes (this is great to have with breakfast).

- ✔ Chop up an orange and fry it in a little butter with walnuts and dried cranberries.

- ✔ Add the juice of an orange to a stir-fry.

- ✔ Use the juice of an orange as part of the liquid when you make muffins.

- ✔ You can always cut an unpeeled orange into sections and slowly simmer it in some water on the stove with some cloves and cinnamon sticks to make your apartment smell all warm and cozy.

Pears

Pears are great because they hold almost forever in the refrigerator . . . *almost* forever. When they start getting just a bit too soft, try one of the following ideas:

- ✔ Peel and chop some pears, and then make a batch of pear sauce (the same as applesauce but made with pears instead); don't forget to add a little cinnamon to it.

- ✔ Put a pear half on top of a salad, spread it with cream cheese, and then top it with crumbled blue cheese and chopped walnuts.

- ✔ Poach pear wedges in simple sugar water (1 cup water with 1 cup sugar), some cinnamon, and a dash of ground cloves for a nice, light dessert.

- ✔ Dice a pear and mix it with other cut-up fruits to make a fruit salad.

If you serve fruit salad with dinner, toss it with a lemon poppy seed dressing; if it's for dessert, toss it with apricot nectar.

Old cheeses

With cheese, the term *perishable* is associated with moisture content; the softer the cheese, the more moisture content there is and the sooner it will spoil.

In general, most cheeses have a natural, distinctive smell, so smelling a cheese won't necessarily indicate if the cheese is getting too old to use. Taste it — yes, just do it! Take a tiny bite, and if it tastes like spoiled milk, throw it out.

Soft cheese will mold. Cream cheese that's starting to go bad develops a fuzzy dark mold; cottage cheese that's too old to use smells bad and tastes sour. Even if there's mold only in one spot, throw it out because there is probably more mold that just can't be seen yet.

When hard cheese starts to go bad, it gets a white covering that almost looks like powdered sugar. You can cut these portions off and still eat what's left.

Old blue cheese may develop a dark ring around the edge. If you suspect that the cheese is old, take a very close look at the blue veining; if it looks fuzzy, the bad kind of mold has developed and you shouldn't eat it.

Cheeses like American, cheddar, Parmesan, provolone, and pepper jack are great for the following uses:

- ✔ Use each (or several in combination) for grilled cheese sandwiches; don't be afraid to add tomato, onion slices, and even a hint of brown mustard to your sandwich.

- ✔ Lay slices over baked potatoes or rice, over sautéed veggies, over veggie burgers, and inside wraps.

- ✔ Cut cheese cubes to toss into salads or to dip into mustard for a snack with crackers.

- ✔ Shred cheese over pizza, on tacos or taco salad, and into scrambled eggs and frittatas.

- ✔ Sprinkle shreds of cheddar cheese over hot slices of hardboiled eggs.

- ✔ Melt any kind of cheese to use as a fondue for dipping cubes of French bread.

- ✔ Stir shreds into polenta, veggie chili, and soups; over nachos; inside quesadillas; and on top of stuffed peppers.

- ✔ Don't forget to sprinkle grated Parmesan cheese on hot pasta, cold pasta salads, Caesar salads, tomato slices, and steamed asparagus.

Use up softer cheeses like cream cheese and cottage cheese in the following ways:

- ✔ Take that little bit of leftover cream cheese and spread it between slices of sweet bread or on top of a toasted bagel. In addition, you can mix it with shredded cheese and roll it in chopped nuts to make a cheese ball.

✔ If you have a partially used container of cottage cheese, mix it with some peanut butter and a dash of cinnamon to use as a dip for apple slices; you can also stir it into pasta along with an oil/garlic sauce.

Aging eggs

Egg cartons have a *sell by* date stamped on them. Legally, the *sell by* date is 21 days after the eggs are laid. A *best before* stamped date is 28 days after the eggs are laid. Usually, you can continue to use eggs safely for two weeks after the *sell by* date (that's one week after the *best before* date).

To check whether an egg is still fresh, put it in a pan of water. If it sinks, it's fine. If it floats, throw it out. Besides, bad eggs smell bad.

Eggs, like cheese, are pretty easy to use up at any meal:

✔ For breakfast, make scrambled eggs or scrambled egg wraps (adding a little salsa or hot pepper sauce and some shredded cheese makes the wrap even better). Omelets, quiches, and frittatas are options. If you have veggies left over from last night's dinner, chop them into your morning eggs. French toast involves dipping bread into an egg/milk/cinnamon mixture before frying or baking the bread; it's another good breakfast choice.

✔ Lunch can be a fried egg and cheese sandwich or an egg salad sandwich. Or spread refried beans on a tortilla, add slices of hardboiled egg, cheese, chopped lettuce, and salsa, and then roll it up. You can add some of last night's leftover rice to the wrap, too. Or serve the tortilla open-faced by substituting a fried egg for the hardboiled egg and then popping it into the microwave to melt the cheese.

✔ For a dinner side dish, make a batch of pickled eggs or whip up some deviled eggs. Other options include egg drop soup, fried rice (with a scrambled egg), and vegetarian egg foo yong (a scrambled egg mixture sautéed with fresh veggies and soy sauce). Eggs scrambled with fried potato cubes, sliced onions, green pepper, and mushrooms makes a great dinner.

✔ And don't overlook using up eggs for dessert. Make rice or tapioca pudding, custard, bread pudding, or a really great eggnog.

Bread and crackers that are drying out

Just because bread is too dry to eat for a sandwich doesn't mean it doesn't still have a lot of life left in it:

✔ Cut bread into cubes to make homemade croutons for salads or cubes for bread pudding or baked stuffing.

✔ Use slices or pieces to make milk toast for breakfast — it's delicious and simple to put together. Just spread butter on a slice of toast, sprinkle it with cinnamon sugar, tear the toast into small pieces, and set in a bowl; then pour a little warm milk over the toast.

✔ Cut bread into cubes and then dry bake them for 15 minutes at 350 degrees (don't let the cubes brown). Crumble them into a blender or food processor with some seasonings to make breadcrumbs for casseroles, to bread veggies (especially eggplant), to add to a potato pancake or latke mixture, or to mix into a vegetarian nut loaf.

✔ Make lasagna using slices of old bread instead of lasagna noodles.

✔ If the bread isn't too terribly stale, brush slices with olive oil and toast them in the oven for bruschetta, or make a scrumptious panzanella salad (tomatoes, onion slices, mozzarella cheese, homemade croutons or toast cubes, and basil leaves, with an olive oil and balsamic vinegar dressing).

✔ Assemble French toast from the night before so the dry bread has time to absorb the egg mixture.

Some hard-crust breads (like French bread) get very hard on the outside (we're talking teeth-cracking hard!). That means the bread is old but not bad; you can still use it to make breadcrumbs and croutons and to slice and float on top of onion soup.

Look bread over very carefully. If it has any mold anywhere, throw it all out. Even if you see mold on only one side, throw it out.

Crackers fall into the same boat with bread. Make cracker crumbs quickly by placing the crackers in a plastic bag and crushing them with a rolling pin or a meat mallet, and then try the following ideas:

✔ Fold the crumbs into cooked pasta with a butter or oil sauce.

✔ Sprinkle the crumbs on top of casseroles, vegetables, and chili or soups.

✔ Season the crumbs with cinnamon to sprinkle on yogurt.

✔ Season the crumbs with dill and roll a cheese ball in them.

✔ Add some melted butter and sugar to make a crumb crust for cheesecake or the bottom layer of layered cookies.

Leftover desserts

You don't have to reuse only savory ingredients; you can reinvent sweet stuff, too. Here are some signs that leftover sweets are on the verge of spoiling (or already spoiled):

✔ Whipped cream desserts can last anywhere from two to four days before the cream starts to crack and dry out and the liquid starts separating and collecting at the bottom of the pan. After this happens, it's beyond salvaging.

✔ The bottom of a filled pie crust stays crisp for a couple of days; by day three, though, it starts to get pretty soggy.

✔ Puddings, unfortunately, last only a couple of days before the contents start to separate and moisture accumulates on top.

If they're well covered, cakes (and brownies) usually hold for three days before they start to dry out. If you're stuck with leftover cake, try the following tips:

✔ Crumble it and use the crumbs in place of the flour called for in a cookie or muffin recipe.

✔ Sprinkle cake crumbs on top of ice cream, or dry them out and mix them with butter to make a pie crust.

✔ Put cake crumbs in a bowl and add a little *something* to help the crumbs stick together (chocolate or caramel syrup, canned frosting, whipping cream, and so on). Form cake balls and drizzle them with melted white or dark chocolate to create your own *petit fours*. (Freeze them for the next time you have company, or eat them yourself!)

✔ If you have yellow cake, put a square onto a dish, top it with canned peaches, and pop it into the microwave for a few seconds to warm. Now that's an easy dessert!

✔ Dip small cake squares into sweetened condensed milk, cover with coconut, and then toast under the broiler for 1 to 2 minutes or until the coconut is lightly toasted.

✔ Mix a carton of whipped topping with a carton of lemon yogurt, and then fold in cubes of cake to make a trifle. Or mix the whipped topping with blueberry (or any flavor) pie filling and then fold in the cake cubes.

Cookies usually dry out before they ever get a chance to get moldy. If a crisp cookie dries out, you can re-crisp it by placing it in a 300 degree oven for 3–4 minutes. If a soft cookie dries out, wrap it in a damp paper towel and microwave it for 20 seconds to refresh it. If you have leftover cookies, give the following ideas a shot:

- ✔ Crumble cookies for a pie crust, or spoon ice cream on one cookie and top with a second cookie for a quick ice cream sandwich.

- ✔ Crumble cookies over ice cream or puddings.

- ✔ Use cookie crumbs to make a yogurt parfait.

- ✔ If they're oatmeal or shortbread cookies, sprinkle them over hot oatmeal.

- ✔ Crumble cookies over canned fruit for a quick crisp (pear crisp, peach crisp, whatever crisp).

- ✔ Toss some into the blender the next time you make a milkshake or smoothie.

- ✔ Brush a frozen banana with honey and roll it in chocolate cookie crumbs. Eat it right away or freeze it for later.

Part IV
The Part of Tens

The 5th Wave   By Rich Tennant

"Don't worry, the marketing contains a lot of bull, but the product's purely vegetarian."

In this part . . .

No *For Dummies* book is complete without the Part of Tens, which consists of simple ten-item lists that stress important things you need to know. The first chapter in this part provides tips for those times when you want to prepare a meal that will impress guests. I cover everything from menu suggestions to setting an impressive table to garnishing the dish. The second chapter offers tricks for making any recipe vegetarian-friendly. By the time you finish reading this chapter, you'll be masterful at the art of substituting ingredients. You'll be able to make Grandma's famous beef stroganoff and have it be just as delicious as hers used to be . . . only yours won't have any beef or sour cream.

Chapter 16

Nearly Ten Tips for Creating a Vegetarian Feast for Guests

There will come a day when Mom and Dad or some other special people call to say they're visiting you at school. Don't panic! If you have a little notice, you can prepare a vegetarian feast that will definitely have the *wow* factor! Just follow the guidelines in this chapter to impress your guests.

Don't get all bent out of shape and stressed over entertaining. When was the last time you heard people talk about the great time they had at a frat party? I guarantee you they didn't mention the food that was there, let alone rate it! You want to impress guests with the food, but they're really coming to see *you*.

Devising a Delicious Menu

The best strategy for planning a vegetarian feast — whether it's for breakfast, brunch, lunch, or dinner — is to keep your menu simple but elegant. Make one or two dishes that take a little time to assemble, and keep the other dishes quick and easy. (You want to plan a few dishes that can be made ahead of time so you're not rushing around making everything at the last minute. And there's nothing wrong with using convenience foods to save you time.)

Here are some super-easy hints to help you decide what to serve:

✔ Think in threes. The perfect menu has three dishes featuring different colors, textures, and tastes. For example, you can include Blue Cheese Fettuccine from Chapter 12 (white), Pseudo Zucchini Parm from Chapter 12 (red), and Caesar Salad Deluxe from Chapter 11 (green).

✔ Use fruits and vegetables that are in season because that's when they're the least expensive and have the best flavor. You can check out an easy-to-read chart showing when specific fresh produce is in season at `www.scribd.com/ doc/301858/Fruits-and-Vegetables-in-Season`.

✔ The recipes in this book use low-fat milk, yogurt, cheeses, and the like because such foods are healthier for you. But when it comes to entertaining, it doesn't hurt to use whole milk (or even half-and-half) and all those good fat-containing ingredients to create delicious masterpieces.

When planning the menu, watch out for the following possible glitches:

✔ **The everything-won't-fit-in-the-refrigerator glitch:** Think about the sizes of all the dishes you want to serve and make appropriate plans for storage. For example, if you plan to assemble a large salad ahead of time, you may not have much refrigerator space left, especially if you share the fridge with other people. So instead of serving sandwiches (which also need refrigeration) with the salad, make a pot of homemade bean soup, and serve the soup and salad with some really good rolls.

✔ **The you-need-to-bake-two-different-things-at-the-same-time-at-two-different-oven-temperatures glitch:** Can you bake one item ahead of time and then reheat it later? If not, can you bake the dish requiring the higher temperature at a lower temperature for a longer period of time? If that answer is no, scratch one of the dishes from your menu and add something else.

Also, you should avoid having to bake one dish and broil another if you only have one oven. Ovens are great, but they can't do both jobs at the same time.

✔ **The you-may-not-have-enough-serving-platters glitch (when you're not going to be plating the food):** Decide on the platters you need for serving ahead of time. If there's one platter size that you don't have, you can visit a party store that sells decorative one-time-use platters and bowls for very little cost, or you can borrow what you need from a friend or neighbor. (FYI, *plating food* means that you spoon the foods onto individual dishes before serving.)

Setting a Beautiful Table

Decide on a color scheme for the meal, and include those colors in your choice of table covering, centerpiece, and even the garnishes on the dishes (I talk about garnishes in more detail later in this chapter). Having a color scheme adds *ambiance* (making everything look and taste better by setting the mood). For example, if you're planning a really fun party with lively music, use reds, yellows, oranges, purples, and pinks to jazz things up a bit. If, however, you have more of a laid-back setting in mind, set your table with creams accented with just one other color, keeping things simple.

If you have a tablecloth, now's the time to use it. (Iron it first — no one wants to see wrinkles.) A folded (and yes, ironed) sheet works, too. Matching place mats also look nice. If you don't have a cloth or mats, run two strips of a really wide ribbon down the length of your table.

One easy way to make your table look really special is with a centerpiece. Here are some inexpensive ideas:

- ✔ Group together any size and color candles you have and either set them in the middle of your table or place them strategically down the length of the table.

- ✔ If you're putting flowers in a vase, cut the stems short enough that the guests can see one another over the tops of the flowers. Even a single flower in a bud vase adds elegance to a setting. You can also float the heads of flowers in a bowl of water; lay a flower stem above, beside, or across each place setting; or scatter flower petals over the table.

- ✔ If you don't have a ready-made centerpiece, look in the fridge. You can pile some fruits or vegetables attractively in a bowl. Pick up some fresh leaves from outside, wash them off, and then tuck them in between the fruits or vegetables.

If your kitchen is table-deprived and all you have is a counter with stools, use the counter to serve your meal buffet-style. If you have a table runner, lay it down on the counter and then set your centerpiece at one end of the counter. Setting lit votive candles between the serving platters looks really impressive. Make sure you have enough seating in the living room for your guests — borrow some card table chairs if you have to. And while you're borrowing stuff, ask whether you can borrow some folding tray tables, too. The tables will save your guests from trying to balance dishes in their laps while holding drinks.

Party stores and some grocery stores carry pretty cut-out paper placemats in various colors; set one on each tray table and pick up a package of coordinating napkins. Get your tray tables set before your company arrives.

Do you have enough dishes, glasses, and silverware for everyone? If not, see whether you can borrow some. Unless you have a picnic theme, using plastic forks and knives just won't cut it (pardon the pun).

Do something fancy with each napkin — roll it, tie it with a ribbon in the center, and then lay it across the plate. Or gather it in folds and put it in the empty water glass so that most of it is above the rim of the glass.

Assembling Awesome Appetizers

Appetizers set the mood when you're out to impress people. Your guests can munch on some tasty snacks while you're busy in the kitchen getting the meal ready. Ideally, they're small (the munchies, not the people) and can be picked up with one hand without making too much of a mess. Here are some guidelines for putting together vegetarian appetizers (see Chapter 13 for recipe ideas):

- ✔ Big foods can become appetizers if you cut them into little pieces (for example, you can cut a vegetarian pizza into small pieces or slice a veggie wrap into thin circles).

- ✔ Anyone can plop something on top of a cracker and call it an appetizer, but that won't draw *aah*s from your guests. Take advantage of premade vegetarian appetizers from the freezer section of the grocery store. For example, you can serve stuffed jalapeños with a salsa dip, or veggie won tons or egg rolls with an apricot or hot mustard dip.

- ✔ Speaking of dips, never underestimate how much people like them — hot dips, cold dips, spicy dips, chunky dips, and beyond, surrounded by crackers, tortilla chips, pita bread wedges, bread cubes, or cut-up veggies. Whether it's a simple onion dip, your favorite hot spinach artichoke dip, or roasted red pepper hummus, dips are always a hit.

- ✔ Everyone loves spreads, too. A cheese spread, baba ghanoush (a spread made of eggplant, tahini, olive oil, lemon juice, and garlic), or a spicy bean and cheese spread will get raves.

✔ Traditionally, appetizers are served before dinner or perhaps before lunch but don't count out the idea of serving breakfast appetizers. If your friends or family are coming for breakfast or brunch, you can still set out a plate of appetizers to whet their appetite while you finish cooking. Good choices include small fruit kabobs, frozen miniature quiches (baked before serving), sautéed button mushrooms served with toothpicks, or an olive tapenade (a blend of minced olives, olive oil, and seasonings) served with wedges of pita bread.

Preparing Impressive Breakfasts and Brunches

You're probably not going to be doing much fancy entertaining early in the day, but if the occasion does arise, be ready with a few vegetarian foods that will awe your guests. The following are some suggestions of easy-to-prepare breakfasts and brunches that don't cost much and that you can make in a limited amount of space:

✔ Crustless spinach quiche topped with a drizzle of red salsa and served with an orange-grapefruit-kiwi salad and slices of pumpkin bread.

✔ Breakfast pizza is always fun. Use a store-bought crust and sprinkle the crust with minced onions, cooked meatless crumbles, chopped roasted red peppers — anything you like. Then pour on the eggs and top it off with shredded cheese. Bake it at 400 degrees for about 15 minutes. Top each slice with a sprig of fresh dill and serve with warm cinnamon apples and mint tea.

✔ A baked corn tortilla cup is an impressive holder for a scrambled egg mixture. Add chopped artichoke hearts and green onions to the eggs. Drizzle salsa on top before serving, and sprinkle with a little cheese to get *aahs* from your guests.

Fixing Scrumptious Lunches

Peanut butter and jelly sandwiches may not cut it for lunch with special guests, but other fabulous vegetarian sandwiches can. One idea is grilled eggplant and portobello mushroom slices topped with roasted red peppers and pepper cheese, set on a toasted kaiser roll. Serve this with a salad of spring mix greens, sliced strawberries, glazed walnuts, and a balsamic vinaigrette.

When making sandwiches, start with *artisan* bread (breads that are crusty outside and softer inside, like olive oil bread — you can find artisan breads at most grocery stores now). Use an exotic lettuce (arugula, red leaf lettuce, watercress, and so on) and top the filling with something special (pesto, hummus, salsa, hot pepper relish, mango slices, and so on).

Here are a couple of other fabulous vegetarian luncheon ideas:

- Make a salad of arugula, strips of zucchini, red peppers, white mushrooms, and onion. Add seasoned pecans and coarsely grated Romano cheese, and toss it all together with a vinaigrette dressing. Brush crescent rolls with olive oil and sprinkle them with Italian seasoning, shredded Parmesan cheese, and sesame seeds before baking them to serve along with the salad. Or put a pretty napkin in a basket and fill the basket with warmed, assorted mini muffins to serve with the salad.

- Serve tortilla soup with finger sandwiches (hummus and red pepper, guacamole with minced cucumber and onion, egg salad, and so on). For an impressive display, remove the bread crusts before making the sandwiches and then cut the sandwiches into small triangles.

Designing the Perfect Dinner

Serve a dinner that your guests will recognize but that they don't eat all the time, and serve it in a unique way to draw attention. You can't go wrong if you serve a really good pasta dinner, but why not think outside the box? Following are some suggestions for vegetarian entrées, side dishes, salads, and breads; mix and match them so you have different colors, textures, and tastes.

Entrée ideas include the following:

- Bean-and-cheese baked enchiladas over Spanish rice
- Broiled veggie kabobs over yellow or wild rice
- Eggplant parmigiana with pasta marinara
- Spaghetti pie
- Spinach and ricotta cheese–stuffed portobello mushrooms with pasta aglio olio (a sautéed, garlic-and-olive-oil sauce) or noodles Alfredo
- Stuffed peppers (stuffed with orzo, meatless crumbles, and spaghetti sauce) on a bed of sautéed spinach or shredded, sautéed, and buttered cabbage

✔ Vegetable lasagna

✔ Veggie stir-fry with cashews over refried rice

Some side dishes to consider include the following:

✔ Baked acorn squash rings

✔ Broiled fresh veggies in a balsamic-and-oil marinade

✔ Carrots with pecans and dried cranberries

✔ Cauliflower or broccoli with a cheese sauce

✔ Mashed potatoes made with caramelized onions

✔ Mushroom or onion pie

✔ Potato pancakes or latkes

✔ Sweet potato fries or baked sweet potatoes with a pecan caramel topping

✔ Twice-baked potatoes

✔ Zucchini casserole

Why not try one of the following salads with your dinner?

✔ Assorted melon ball salad with fresh mint

✔ Caesar salad (Use a dressing that doesn't feature anchovies or Worcestershire sauce.)

✔ Colorful bean salad topped with a sprig of dill

✔ Fruit and nut salad with a sprinkling of pomegranate seeds

✔ Greek peasant salad (made with green peppers, cucumbers, onions, tomatoes, and feta cheese)

✔ Hearts of palm salad with slices of avocado

✔ Watermelon and feta cheese salad

✔ Wild rice salad

Don't forget breads! Here are some serving suggestions:

✔ Artisan rolls

✔ Biscuits

✔ Breadsticks

✔ Cornbread with jalapeños

✔ Dill or zucchini muffins

✔ Garlic bread

Ending Your Meal with Decadent Desserts

Dessert is the final touch, the last opportunity to create the *wow* effect. You don't have to spend all day whipping up a fabulous vegetarian creation as long as what you serve tastes great and looks awesome. Try one of these creations:

✔ Something as simple as a butterscotch sundae can be impressive if you can borrow a few parfait glasses (or buy plastic ones at a party store). Create layers of ice cream, nuts, and sauce, and then top it off with whipped cream and chocolate curls.

✔ Make a bread pudding to satisfy your own special taste by adding chopped apples or peaches, sliced bananas, blueberries, raisins, and/or nuts before baking.

✔ You can make a store-bought apple pie look homemade-delicious by frosting it with a glaze. Stir together sifted powdered sugar, a little vanilla, a little cinnamon, and enough milk to form a pasty consistency. After baking the pie, let it sit for 20 minutes to cool slightly, then drizzle the glaze over the top.

✔ Small phyllo cups from the grocery's freezer can be thawed and filled for an easy dessert. Fill the cups with pudding topped with a dollop of whipped cream, with canned pie filling topped with a little crushed granola, or with any other dessert filling you like.

✔ Ice cream pie is simple to assemble. Just fill a crumb pie shell with softened ice cream. When you're ready to serve it, drizzle a caramel-nut topping over the top of each plated slice and sprinkle with chopped pecans.

✔ A slice of store-bought angel food cake is impressive when you top it with fresh strawberries and whipped cream, ice cream and topping, cinnamon peaches, or pudding that has fruit or crushed candy folded into it.

✔ You can make lots of desserts from refrigerated crescent rolls, whether you fill the rolls and bake them or spread them out in a pan to use as a base for a pudding dessert or bar cookies.

Check out the Pillsbury website at www.pillsbury.com for ideas.

✔ Everyone loves fresh, cut-up melon, especially if it's served out of a cantaloupe half shell. Tuck in a few fresh mint leaves for color.

Wash the melon's outside skin with a little dish soap and water before you slice it. The skin is often dirty and may even be contaminated with salmonella.

Adding Appealing Garnishes to Any Dish

Garnish is eye candy. It makes food on a plate look more tempting. If the garnish is pretty, somehow your mind thinks the food tastes better. (Don't look for logic on this one!)

A nice touch is to add a garnish to whatever drink you're serving, like

- A slice of lemon or lime with a glass of water
- An orange slice or a sprig of mint with a citrus juice
- A small, leafy stick of celery to be used as a stir stick with a vegetable juice
- A cut strawberry placed on the rim of a glass filled with fruit juice or punch
- A cinnamon stick to be used as a stir stick with hot cocoa

Turning a really simple breakfast into an impressive brunch presentation is easy if you add the right garnish. Here are some ideas:

- Top scrambled eggs with a drizzle of taco sauce or salsa.
- French toast, pancakes, and waffles will have even more eye appeal if you add chopped nuts to the syrup and set sliced and fanned-out strawberries on the side of the dish. (Chocolate-dipped strawberries look even more impressive!)
- Lay a fresh sprig of dill across the top of a slice of quiche before serving it.
- Sprinkle melon balls with dried mint flakes.
- Garnish cinnamon apples with cinnamon sticks.
- Lightly sift powdered sugar over an entire dish before plating the food.

At lunch, put something on the dish that's eye-catching but fairly simple. Alfalfa sprouts work — put a small clump on top of a salad or next to a sandwich and then top with a slice of avocado. Or you can chop parsley and sprinkle it over soups (hot or cold).

How you garnish a dinner dish depends on what foods you're serving. If your entrée has a lot of color, like lasagna, all you really need to do is sprinkle the dish with chopped parsley before plating. If the entrée is monochrome, though, add something green to the plate like parsley sprigs or a sprig of fresh rosemary. You can also sprinkle coarsely grated Parmesan or Romano cheese over pasta dishes.

Dessert garnishes can be simple or ornate, but you need some kind of frill to make any dessert look really impressive. Here are some great garnish suggestions:

- ✔ Use a small sieve to dust the plate with cocoa, cinnamon, or powdered sugar before setting down a dessert.

- ✔ Cut slices in a strawberry almost all the way through, and then fan out the berry. (Leave the green hull and leaves on.)

- ✔ Use a vegetable peeler to cut thin shavings from a chocolate bar to make chocolate curls. Use a rolling pin to crush chocolate to press into the frosting on the sides of a cake. Melt chocolate to drizzle over the top of a dessert.

- ✔ Roll damp blueberries or grapes in granulated sugar and set them on the side of the dish or on top of the dessert.

- ✔ Cut halfway through a thin slice of lemon, lime, or orange and twist each end in a different direction. Then set it on top of the dessert.

- ✔ Grate a lemon, lime, or orange and sprinkle the dish with the zest.

- ✔ Tuck a sprig of fresh mint into a dollop of thawed frozen whipped topping.

- ✔ Sprinkle crushed nuts, nut brittle, or spiced nuts over ice cream; on frosted brownies, cakes, and cookies; and on top of whipped cream and refrigerated desserts.

- ✔ When serving ice cream or a bowl of fruit, slide a thin gourmet cookie or a piece of chocolate-covered mint candy on the side.

Chapter 17

Nearly Ten Ways to Make Any Recipe Vegetarian-Friendly

In This Chapter

▶ Swapping meats for veggies

▶ Transitioning to tofu and tempeh

▶ Making the most of meat look-alikes

▶ Trying beans and broth

▶ Using safe noodles and butter substitutes

Admit it: Sometimes you get sentimental and think back to a special time in your life, remembering something that Grandma or Mom made that tasted absolutely delicious. You want to try to make the dish, but it contains meat (and maybe eggs or something else you don't eat anymore). Do the words *substitute ingredients* mean anything? That's the art of using *this* instead of *that*. In this chapter, I give you a number of delicious methods for turning any recipe into something safe for vegetarians.

Using Vegetables

I know, I know: The obvious trick for a vegetarian who wants to replace meat in a recipe is to use vegetables. But keep in mind that not all vegetables are alike; the key is to mimic the texture of the meat you're replacing. For example:

> ✔ If you're making a stew that traditionally features meat, add some bulky vegetables like chunks of potatoes to replace the meat. If you chop the veggies too small, you'll end up with soup instead of stew.

✔ You probably assume that beef stroganoff has chunks of beef in it. Okay, you're right about that . . . but it doesn't have to. You can substitute slices of baby portobello mushrooms for the beef. (Mushrooms are an all-around excellent substitute for beef in most recipes.)

✔ Shish kebab is a well-loved dish that's fun to assemble and doesn't take long to grill or broil. But if you leave the meat off, you're left with green pepper and onion slices, which isn't much of a dinner. Instead of the meat, fill the skewers with zucchini, yellow squash, cherry tomatoes, mushroom caps, and artichoke hearts; all of them are hearty enough to withstand grilling.

✔ If you want to replace a hamburger, grill or broil a vegetable that has a solid, meaty texture. Two really good options are a portobello mushroom cap or a thick slice of eggplant.

Here are some more ideas for move-out-the-meat-and-replace-with-veggies dishes:

✔ **Chicken pot pie:** Just add more chopped carrots, mushrooms, peas, broccoli, corn, and chopped roasted red peppers and leave out the chicken.

✔ **Stuffed peppers and stuffed cabbage:** Fill them with a mixture of chopped celery, carrots, onions, peas, and rice.

✔ **Crab cakes:** Use boiled shredded cabbage, shredded zucchini, or mashed okra in place of the crabmeat.

✔ **Meatloaf:** Use a shredded combination of onions, green peppers, chopped tomatoes, celery, shredded cabbage, and either rice or oats.

Adapting with Tofu

Tofu is made from soybeans, water, and a coagulant or curdling agent. It looks like a soft cheese-like food and has almost no taste, which is good because you can customize how it tastes with the marinades and sauces you add.

When cooking with tofu, use the right kind:

✔ Silken tofu (also labeled *soft silken* or *smooth* tofu) is good for blending because it doesn't get gritty. When a recipe calls for eggs to be whipped into a mixture, silken tofu often can be used in place of the eggs.

- ✔ Silken dessert tofu is usually flavored and sweetened; it's a good choice to use in place of eggs in dessert recipes.

- ✔ Soft tofu is good to use as a substitute for sour cream (adding some salt and lemon juice) to use in dips and spreads; you can also use it to stuff pasta shells and manicotti.

- ✔ Medium tofu is perfect when you want to mash it or make crumbles for use in lasagna or omelets.

- ✔ Firm and extra-firm tofu are good choices when you want to cube, dice, or grate the tofu. The firmer the tofu, the less it crumbles and the more it soaks up marinades. If you brown firm tofu cubes well in oil or butter, they're really good in almost anything, including stir-fries and stews.

Chicken has a milder taste than beef, so firm tofu works especially well at replacing chicken in recipes.

Despite the expiration date on a package of tofu, it can go bad really quickly if you're not careful. Follow these guidelines:

- ✔ Whether the package is opened or not, keep it refrigerated.

- ✔ If the tofu comes packed in water, transfer it to a plastic container with a lid and change the water daily.

- ✔ After you open the package, use the tofu within a day or two.

- ✔ If it has an odd smell (like old beans), throw it out, no matter how old it is.

- ✔ If you can't use all the tofu in a couple of days, drain it, wrap it well, and freeze it; it can be frozen for up to three months. Its texture will be a little spongy when you thaw it, but it's still fine to use in cooking.

Trying Tempeh

Tempeh, like tofu, is made from soy, but the soybeans are cooked and slightly fermented and then formed into a patty or cake. Tempeh has a distinct nutty flavor whereas tofu essentially has little or no flavor.

Tempeh, because of its fermentation, needs to be cooked before eating it; it usually comes frozen, so you need to thaw it just before cooking it. To avoid a slightly bitter taste, soak it first in boiling water for about ten minutes, then drain it and pat it dry before marinating it and cooking it. The soaking process softens it so it absorbs any marinade better.

Occasionally you can find tempeh in the refrigerated section of the grocery or health food store. You can buy it plain or pre-marinated, and there's even a bacon-style tempeh. You can also buy dehydrated tempeh online. Dehydrated tempeh stays fresh for months so it's great to take traveling.

Tempeh is better than tofu as a pork substitute because it has a firmer texture and a tangier flavor. You can coat it with barbecue sauce and grill or fry it. Pan-fry strips until they're crispy on the outside, and then use the strips in sandwiches, chop them into salads, or add them to soups or chili.

Picking Processed Meat Alternatives

Plenty of products out there look, cook, and taste almost like meat. I'm talking about veggie burgers, veggie crumbles, veggie sausages, veggie hot dogs, and veggie meatloaf, to name just a few. These products are made from tofu and tempeh (both of which I describe earlier in this chapter), as well as *TVP* (textured vegetable protein). You can buy TVP plain, seasoned, frozen, or dry (if you buy dry crumbles, you need to soak them in water before using). You can even find burgers made from cheeses, veggies, and nuts! If you can think of a meat entrée, you can probably find a vegetarian-friendly substitute.

Meat alternatives need much less cooking time than real meat. If you cook them too long, they can get tough. Be sure to follow the package's cooking directions to the letter.

Trading Meat for Beans

Beans are *so* healthy for you, and they fill you up. Don't be afraid to substitute beans for meat in recipes:

- ✔ Use black beans or refried beans (made without lard) instead of ground beef in tacos, enchiladas, and burritos.

- ✔ Mash chickpeas with a little mayo and chopped celery for a mock egg or tuna salad.

- ✔ In stews, casseroles, soups, and almost anything with a sauce, use a can of rinsed and drained beans instead of meat (garbanzo, navy, northern, pinto, or black beans work especially well).

✔ If you're making lasagna or spaghetti sauce, cook rinsed and drained canned beans (such as kidney, navy, or pinto) in a skillet with diced onion and garlic, and then simmer in the sauce a little bit before continuing with the recipe.

Considering Cheese

Just because a recipe uses meat doesn't mean that you have to use the meat (or a meat substitute). A lot of times you can substitute cheese for meat. Cheese not only helps hold ingredients like shredded vegetables together but also adds a bushel of flavor. (If you're a vegan or an ovo vegetarian, use a nondairy vegan cheese.)

A good example is quesadillas. If you have a recipe for a ham and cheese quesadillas, you can use two different kinds of cheese instead of the ham. Another example: When making baked ziti, skip the meat substitute in the sauce and instead lay a slice of mozzarella cheese over the top when you bake it — you'll never miss the meat.

Cooking with Vegetable Broth

In almost all recipes that list chicken broth or beef broth as an ingredient, you can substitute the veggie version. Choices include vegetable broth, veggie bouillon cubes, and veggie granulated bouillon. All add great flavor to foods. There's a little difference in taste between meat broth and veggie broth, but that's not a bad thing.

There's also a difference in taste between the different brands of veggie broth. Some are made with more onions and garlic, others with more spices, and still others with more mushrooms. As a result, some brands are stronger, lighter, sweeter, or denser than others. Try different kinds to see which you like best.

An opened and covered can of broth stays fresh in the fridge for only three days. If you're not going to use it up in that amount of time, pour it into a covered plastic container and freeze it for up to two months.

You have the option of making your own vegetable broth. Before you pooh-pooh the idea, think about it: You probably have aging veggies in the vegetable bin in the fridge. Instead of throwing them out in a day or two, wash them off and dump them into a big pot filled with water. You don't have to chop them first (unless they're too big to fit in the pot), and you don't even have to peel them (the skins add a lot of flavor). Cut an onion in half and smash one or two cloves of garlic to toss into the mix. Stir in some salt and pepper, and then let it all simmer for an hour or so. Strain the broth through a sieve into smaller plastic containers for freezing, mashing the veggies a bit so that some essence of vegetables seeps through into the broth. There, you just made homemade vegetable broth!

Incorporating Vegetarian-Friendly Pasta

You, my friend, are so in luck because most pasta is made from *durum semolina* (also known as wheat flour) and water. If you're planning on making an Asian dish, rice noodles are just rice and water, and Japanese soba noodles come from buckwheat flour. If you're vegan or lacto vegetarian, though, noodles are the big bugaboo because a lot of them are made with whole eggs, egg yolks, or egg whites. But even here, luck is on your side because you can use some quick-cooking vegan noodles like masala noodles. If you can't find vegan options, rigatoni and rice noodles are two excellent substitutions for egg noodles because of their shape.

Selecting the Right Substitute for Butter

If you're a vegan or an ovo vegetarian, butter is a big no-no. Substituting butter with margarine, though, isn't quite as easy as it sounds because a lot of margarines contain trace amounts of whey, casein, or lactose (all of which are dairy products). Butter-like products that are specifically marked as vegan nondairy spreads are on the market, but some mainstream brands of margarine also make vegan butter alternatives like Blue Bonnet Light Sticks, Shedd's Willow Run Soybean Margarine, Smart Balance Light Margarine, and Earth Balance spreads.

Some light vegan margarines have a lot of water content, so they're not good to use when baking cookies because the cookies will spread too much, and they can make sauces too thin and bland. Earth Balance not only tastes good on its own, but it also has a thicker consistency that doesn't dilute ingredients in a recipe.

Appendix

Metric Conversion Guide

• •

*N**ote:* The recipes in this book weren't developed or tested using metric measurements. Because some of the measurements in the following tables are rounded off, you may experience some variation in quality when using metric units to make the recipes.

Common Abbreviations

Abbreviation(s)	What It Stands For
cm	Centimeter
C., c.	Cup
G, g	Gram
kg	Kilogram
L, l	Liter
lb.	Pound
mL, ml	Milliliter
oz.	Ounce
pt.	Pint
t., tsp.	Teaspoon
T., Tb., Tbsp.	Tablespoon

Volume

U.S. Units	Canadian Metric	Australian Metric
¼ teaspoon	1 milliliter	1 milliliter
½ teaspoon	2 milliliters	2 milliliters

(continued)

Volume *(continued)*

U.S. Units	Canadian Metric	Australian Metric
1 teaspoon	5 milliliters	5 milliliters
1 tablespoon	15 milliliters	20 milliliters
¼ cup	50 milliliters	60 milliliters
⅓ cup	75 milliliters	80 milliliters
½ cup	125 milliliters	125 milliliters
⅔ cup	150 milliliters	170 milliliters
¾ cup	175 milliliters	190 milliliters
1 cup	250 milliliters	250 milliliters
1 quart	1 liter	1 liter
1½ quarts	1.5 liters	1.5 liters
2 quarts	2 liters	2 liters
2½ quarts	2.5 liters	2.5 liters
3 quarts	3 liters	3 liters
4 quarts (1 gallon)	4 liters	4 liters

Weight

U.S. Units	Canadian Metric	Australian Metric
1 ounce	30 grams	30 grams
2 ounces	55 grams	60 grams
3 ounces	85 grams	90 grams
4 ounces (¼ pound)	115 grams	125 grams
8 ounces (½ pound)	225 grams	225 grams
16 ounces (1 pound)	455 grams	500 grams (½ kilogram)

Length

Inches	Centimeters
0.5	1.5
1	2.5
2	5.0
3	7.5
4	10.0
5	12.5
6	15.0
7	17.5
8	20.5
9	23.0
10	25.5
11	28.0
12	30.5

Temperature (Degrees)

Fahrenheit	Celsius
32	0
212	100
250	120
275	140
300	150
325	160

(continued)

Temperature (Degrees) *(continued)*

Fahrenheit	Celsius
350	180
375	190
400	200
425	220
450	230
475	240
500	260

Index

• C •

• E •

• F •

Notes

Notes

Notes